DEAL
WITH THE
DEVIL

Grace Tobin is a journalist originally from Brisbane, now based in Sydney. She started her career in 2009 as a crime and court reporter in regional Queensland. Grace is currently a producer with the Nine Network's flagship current affairs program *60 Minutes*. In 2017, she won a Walkley Award for the *60 Minutes* story on Matthew Leveson's death.

GRACE TOBIN

DEAL
WITH THE
DEVIL

EBURY
PRESS

An Ebury Press book
Published by Penguin Random House Australia Pty Ltd
Level 3, 100 Pacific Highway, North Sydney NSW 2060
penguin.com.au

Penguin
Random House
Australia

First published by Ebury Press in 2018

Addresses for the Penguin Random House group of companies can be found at
global.penguinrandomhouse.com/offices.

A catalogue record for this
book is available from the
NATIONAL
LIBRARY
OF AUSTRALIA
National Library of Australia

ISBN 978 0 14379 021 1

Front cover images: photo of Matthew Leveson courtesy Mark and Faye
Leveson; ripped paper © ESB Professional/Shutterstock, © Cafe Racer/
Shutterstock
Back cover: photo courtesy Mark and Faye Leveson
Cover design by Ella Egidy © Penguin Random House Australia Pty Ltd
Map by Ice Cold Publishing
Typeset in 11.5/15pt Sabon by Midland Typesetters, Australia
Printed in Australia by Griffin Press, an accredited ISO AS/NZS 14001:2004
Environmental Management System printer

MIX
Paper from
responsible sources
FSC
www.fsc.org
FSC® C009448

To Matty's parents, Mark and Faye.
And to my own, Peter and Narelle.

CONTENTS

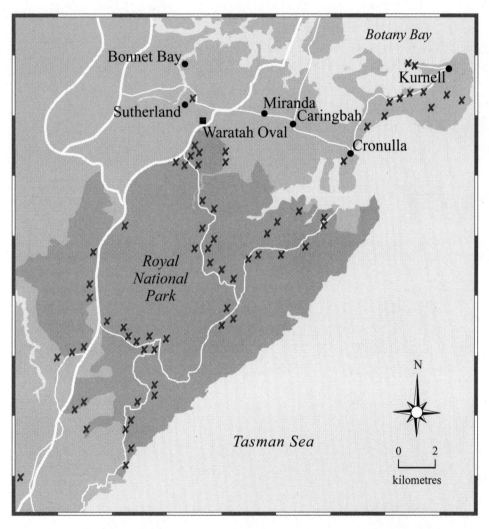

Areas searched by Mark and Faye Leveson, 2007–2017

PROLOGUE

The sound of cicadas is deafening. A mournful chorus pervades the still night air.

It's cool for late September, yet the sweat pours down his face as he struggles to carry his heavy, motionless bundle.

He places one foot in front of the other across an uneven forest floor, and stumbles as his foot catches on a prickly shrub. *Keep going, you're almost there.* He's disorientated. Unnerved.

Guided only by the moonlight, he nears the edge of a freshly dug hole, two metres long and a metre down. He releases his grip on the load and it crashes to the ground. Straddling the pit, he catches his breath before heaving the bundle deep into its bush grave.

Grubby hands clutch the handle of a mattock that sends chunks of dirt and torn roots over the earthy opening.

Suddenly he freezes.

The hum of an engine whirrs in the distance. Fearful of piercing headlights, he drops to his stomach, heart racing, sweat dripping, blood pounding in his ears.

Get up, finish this. The nightmare is almost over.

PART I
THE DISAPPEARANCE

1.

ONE LAST DAY

Saturday 22 September 2007

9.15 am

It was just another Saturday morning for Matt Leveson.

The 20-year-old started his day like so many others that year. He stood in front of the bathroom mirror, fresh from the shower, and gazed at his reflection, turning his head from side to side. Most days he liked what he saw looking back at him: almond-shaped blue-green eyes framed by manicured brows, high cheekbones and a straight nose. Full lips that concealed startlingly white teeth. When he smiled his whole face lit up, top gums flashing and deep-set dimples puckering his cheeks. It was one of his most alluring features; the kind of smile you couldn't help but smile back at.

Matt was also starting to be known for his great physique. As a tubbier teen, he'd always been conscious of his weight and body shape, but lately he was looking fitter than ever. He'd been hitting the gym hard, lifting weights, and exchanging meals for protein shakes. As his muscles bulked up, so too did his self-confidence.

But contemplating himself in the mirror that morning, his focus was fully on his hair, which he was pedantic about. Today, he decided, was a bad-hair day. The dingy bathroom he shared with his older boyfriend, Michael Atkins, was lit harshly by a fluorescent tube above the mirror that made his peroxide-bleached hair look more yellow than blond, reason enough to put his mood out of kilter. Smacking an expensive straightener down on the counter, he sent products skidding into the sink. The straightener beeped, signalling it was time to begin a well-practised routine. He ran fingers through his thick mane, catching tufts of hair between the two hot plates, then he worked a carefully portioned blob of gel through the front. His eyes searched the bench for a light-blue-and-yellow bottle of cologne: Calvin Klein's One Summer, a subtle citrus scent with hints of watermelon, flashy and playful.

Matt pulled on a pair of jeans and a neatly ironed shirt. Even though his employer, NRMA Insurance, didn't require him to wear a uniform, he still made an effort to dress well for every shift. After one last look in the mirror, he emerged from the bathroom into a dark hallway. There was no need for him to tiptoe around the small apartment that morning. His boyfriend had already left home even though it was Saturday. Mike, as an electrician, had needed to be at the job site by 7 am for a training course. He'd be home by the afternoon.

Scooping up his most prized possessions, a matching Louis Vuitton wallet and key ring, Matt checked the time on his red Samsung mobile and headed for the door, mindful of being punctual for his 10 am shift.

1 pm

In the air-conditioned offices of the NRMA call centre, Kerrieann Waud looked at her watch; it was well and truly time for lunch. She looked over the top of her computer screen to her young colleague Matt, who had a black headset on and was agreeing enthusiastically with a customer on the line. She made eye contact and mouthed the word 'lunch'. He nodded in acknowledgement of their Saturday-lunch tradition.

Kerrieann reached for her handbag under the desk and pulled out some lipstick. At 47, the divorced mother took great pride in her appearance. Her lips were never without lippy – usually the bright pink variety – and her wispy blonde hair was always piled immaculately on top of her head, fastened with a butterfly clip or sparkly barrette.

Kerrieann and Matt had hit it off right from the moment they met, five months earlier at the company's new-employee training program. She found him playful, intelligent and well mannered, especially for a young man of only 20. He found her boisterous, funny and a bit of a mother hen. Their colleagues noticed the strong bond between the pair and, at first, many thought they may have actually been related. Kerrieann made a running joke of it, often referring to Matt as 'my son'.

When Matt removed his headset, he leaned back against his chair in a dramatic stretch, arching his back and reaching his arms out over his head. He looked through the text messages on his phone. There was an SMS from his boyfriend Mike: *im freezing the cold wind blowing through here! An no jumper! Finish hour an half! Cant wait! Not boss he came into work! Miss ya x x x*

After flicking a quick text back Matt was ready to go, and Kerrieann leaped to her feet. But as they walked downstairs, she sensed that Matt was on edge. He wasn't at all talkative.

Kerrieann would later say that Matt wasn't himself in the weeks leading up to that day. He'd turned up to work a number of times visibly upset, and had confided in Kerrieann that he was having difficulties with Mike. In her opinion, these issues were mainly due to Mike's controlling nature and the couple's age gap. Matt was 20, about to turn 21, and Mike claimed to be 34.

Kerrieann had first met Mike at her apartment. She'd promised to hem some pants for Matt and the couple had turned up together. The Eagles were blaring from her stereo in the lounge room, and as Kerrieann went to turn down the music she made a comment about how much she loved the band, a hit act in the 1970s. Mike told her he was also a big fan, and it dawned on Kerrieann that he was probably a lot older than he was making out. It was obvious to her that his hair was thinning, plus Matt had once told Kerrieann, as they read a *Cleo* magazine together in the lunchroom, that Mike had got botox in his forehead and around his eyes.

Kerrieann's first impression of Mike hadn't been a good one. No sooner had she asked if they'd like a drink than Mike had tapped Matt on the shoulder and told him that they had to leave. The couple had exchanged a look, unspoken words strung between them like a tense trapeze cable, before Mike followed up with a stern warning: 'Matthew, we have people waiting.' Mike had made a beeline for the door as Matt threw Kerrieann an apologetic look and kissed her goodbye.

Kerrieann and Matt emerged from their office block into a busy street in Hurstville, a large multiethnic suburb in Sydney's south a half-hour drive from the flat Matt shared with Mike in beachside Cronulla. Matt whipped out a pair of Christian Dior sunglasses that crowded his face and which his mum called his 'Louie the Fly' sunglasses. Matt would always shrug and explain how on-trend they were.

Kerrieann got straight to the point. 'So, what's going on with you and Mike?'

Matt sighed and decided not to mince his words, not that he ever really did with Kerrieann. 'I don't know what I'm doing. I'm thinking of getting my bonuses together and going to London.' He paused. 'I've had enough of Mike's bullshit. He's too jealous.'

'What do you mean, jealous?'

'He thinks he's God's gift to man and he can do whatever *he* wants, but if another guy shows any interest in me, he gets the shits.'

Kerrieann was taken aback by Matt's sudden fury. 'Don't let Mike push you around,' she counselled.

'No. I'm going to stand my ground.'

It was the first time Kerrieann had ever heard Matt talk about standing up for himself. For weeks now he'd been confiding in her about Mike's jealousy on the one hand, but on the other Mike's burning desire to have threesomes. Mike had tasked Matt with picking up 'young boys' at ARQ, a gay nightclub where the couple partied on weekends. In recent weeks he'd become quite aggressive about the idea. It was weighing Matt down.

Worse than that, Matt also suspected Mike was cheating on him. He told Kerrieann that he'd come home from work one day to find two glasses in the sink and in their bedroom, and remnants of a cheese platter with a used condom lying next to it. Mike claimed he'd used the condom to masturbate; neither Matt nor Kerrieann bought the story.

'I don't know if I really want to be there,' Matt admitted. In her mother-hen way, Kerrieann told Matt he didn't have to put up with that kind of treatment. They spoke about what his options would be if he ever left Mike, and where he might live. Of course he could move into Kerrieann's apartment if he needed somewhere to stay. Matt joked that they'd probably end up fighting over hair products.

When they returned to their desks after lunch, Matt's mood lifted. He gossiped with Kerrieann and they discussed his outfit ideas for the night ahead. Whatever he wore, it had to be something cute, he told her.

At the end of their shift, Matt walked Kerrieann to her car in the underground car park – something he did after every shift to make sure she was safe. They hugged each other and turned towards their separate vehicles.

Matt's car was a green Toyota Seca, a 1999 model. As he turned on the ignition, he rolled down his window and a heavy, thumping bass echoed through the car park. Matt loved music played at eardrum-bursting volume. The whole car rattled as he bobbed his head in time. Second only to his Louis Vuitton accessories, his other baby was a subwoofer installed by Pete, his older brother. Pete had originally built the boom box for himself with chipboard and Soundstream speakers, but when he'd bought a new car a few months ago it wouldn't fit. After

Pete helped wire up a new amplifier, the subwoofer took pride of place in Matt's car, filling the entire boot.

As Kerrieann unlocked her car door, she realised she'd forgotten to tell Matt about some plans she had for that night. She yelled across to him. Techno music shot off the car park's concrete walls. Kerrieann stomped across to Matt's car in frustration, her left ear throbbing as she bent down to his window.

'Turn that thing down, Matty! You're going to be deaf by the time you're twenty-five!'

He turned the volume dial to the left and laughed. 'It drives Mike mad too.'

5 pm

Michael Atkins stood at the kitchen sink of his poky two-bedroom apartment. He'd called the tired waterfront block, within walking distance of Cronulla's beaches and cafés, home for the past two years.

His muscular physique loomed over the stainless-steel basin, where he focused on something in his hands. At 44, Atkins was an unusual-looking bloke; he was buff and defined, and stood at five foot ten inches, around 1.78 m, but his broad shoulders and large arms made him appear out of proportion. He didn't pay much attention to his legs at the gym, and it showed. Two skinny pins holding up a top-heavy torso, which was coated in a layer of fake tan.

Atkins concentrated on the task at hand. Clasped between his index finger and thumb was a tiny plastic fish, the type found in sushi shops filled with soy sauce. But this one had been emptied, and freshly washed and dried, so there was no trace of the condiment. Atkins was very particular about this cleaning process. Every week he emptied out a new batch of soy-sauce fish, then washed and air-dried them on his kitchen bench. It was harder than it looked to get the soy sauce out from every crevice. But he'd learned from experience that if he wasn't pedantic about the process, the leftover soy would darken the clear liquid he was about to squeeze inside.

GHB, formally known as gamma hydroxybutyrate, is an illicit recreational drug especially popular on the gay party scene. As a central nervous system depressant, it slows down the rate at which the brain sends out chemical messages to the rest of the body. GHB is usually mixed with alcohol, or taken as a shot and chased with something sweet. It has a foul taste, astringent and salty. But the drug absorbs itself rapidly, meaning peak effects are felt about 30 minutes after swallowing. Most users experience a state of euphoria, of tranquillity and trust, which lowers inhibitions and increases sex drive. For many, it's simply a much better version of alcohol, and a liquid version of ecstasy.

But combine it with other depressants, such as alcohol, or take too much – which is very easy to do – and the consequences are dangerous: sweating, dizziness, nausea, hallucinations, amnesia, aggression, confusion and anxiety, and even loss of consciousness. Even though consciousness can be regained relatively quickly, given GHB is absorbed and eliminated so rapidly within the body, the drug can be lethal in excessive doses. It works like a general anaesthetic, and, during a drug-induced sleep, unconsciousness can stop a person's breathing altogether.

Atkins could only recall having one bad experience with the drug, when he felt 'manky', a term used on the party scene meaning 'drug-affected'. He had been forced to sit down, and he remembered feeling disassociated with the room, hearing people around him but not being able to interact with them. But it was a one-off. Atkins took GHB and ecstasy most Saturday nights because the drugs made him want to dance, and he loved the euphoric feeling of the high.

The doses Atkins was preparing over the sink that afternoon weren't for personal use. It was strictly business, and he treated it as such. Both Atkins and Matt sold drugs at ARQ every weekend, and they did a roaring trade. They'd started by dealing to friends or acquaintances, but recently word had spread that if you were looking for drugs, they were your men. It had all begun some months prior as a way to make money and cut back on the cost of their own weekend drug use. They wanted to buy wholesale. Atkins spoke with a friend of a friend, who knew someone who could provide GHB in bulk quantity. Another guy became their main supplier of ecstasy pills. At first they invested a small sum, several hundred dollars, but their business grew quickly from there. By now they kept a decent amount of stock at home: a thermos filled with at least half a litre of GHB and around 100 ecstasy pills. The pills, worth about $900 wholesale, were sold for about $30 each in the club, so Atkins and Matt would make a profit of $2100 in cold hard cash from the ecstasy alone. Tax-free too.

In the lead-up to a night out at ARQ, Atkins and Matt would prepare the product for anticipated sales. Packaging the GHB in the plastic fish was the most finicky part. It sounded like a chore, but strangely enough Atkins quite liked the little routine. He didn't know why, but he thought it was a fun thing to do. Once they were cleaned, Atkins set the fish aside and poured GHB from the thermos into a glass. Taking a fish in his hand, he pinched tightly, squeezing out the air. He poked the opening – the fish's mouth – down into the colourless liquid and released his grip, creating a vacuum so the container sucked up the GHB. He secured the dose with a red screw-top lid.

Atkins checked the time. Matt would be home from work soon to help him organise that night's ecstasy sales. Usually they each took about 20 pills into ARQ and left a larger quantity locked safely in the glove box of Matt's car, parked nearby. Atkins felt a rush of anticipation for the night ahead.

8 pm
The TV was blaring, its lights flickering across the dark room. An old two-seater couch against the lounge-room wall was the centrepiece of the otherwise bare apartment. Pete Leveson picked up the remote to channel-surf once again. He was

slumped on the couch and, for once, was home alone in the unit he shared with two housemates in Caringbah, a ten-minute drive from where his brother Matt lived in Cronulla. Pete was waiting for Matt and Atkins to give him a lift into the city to ARQ. Pete and his little brother had a close bond, and though they had separate lives, they shared a love of clubs and partying.

Matt had been partying perhaps a bit too hard lately. Atkins had told Pete of at least two times this year when Matt had overdone it at ARQ and Atkins had taken him home to look after him. Pete wasn't exactly an angel either, but he didn't go out nearly as much as he used to. The truth was that Pete was relatively shy; he didn't possess the outgoing genes that Matt had plucked from somewhere.

Pete was keen to get going. He decided to text Atkins to find out how far away they were. Better than trying his brother, who always took so long to get ready. Matt tended to be moody and a bit of a princess if he wasn't treated right. Pete typed: *Any idea what time? I'm getting bored Lol.*

His phone beeped with Atkins' reply: *Lol no! About 9:30?*

Pete sighed. Not exactly the answer he'd been hoping for. He peeled himself off the couch and walked to the bathroom. Picking up a tin of hair wax from the counter, he scooped out a sticky chunk. Compared to Matt, Pete wasn't that fussy about his appearance, and the brothers looked nothing alike, either. Matt had always had chubby cheeks and straight blond hair, whereas Pete had curls, these days closely cropped, and fine facial features.

Pete worked the wax through his hair with a quick, clumsy motion. He wore a navy-blue Abercrombie & Fitch T-shirt and denim jeans. Now that he was ready, he decided to skip the lift with his brother and texted another friend instead. He'd head in early and see Matt and Atkins in the club.

10.20 pm
Horns blasted and tail-lights were flashed angrily as traffic crawled along Flinders Street. The busy main drag into Darlinghurst, an

inner-Sydney suburb, intersected with Oxford Street – a one-kilometre strip best known for its gay bars and clubs.

Jack Smith stood hunched over his phone outside the entry of ARQ. Skinny arms and bony elbows poked out from the side of his body as he scrolled through his latest text messages. The phone screen lit up his long oval face and a head full of short dark-brown curls. Stray chest hairs nudged out the top of his V-neck. The foot traffic was scarce along Flinders Street at that time. There wouldn't be much action at all around those parts until almost midnight, when the clubs started pumping and the main-event DJs played. Until then you'd find the patrons of ARQ, and Darlinghurst's other well-known clubs, hanging out in tiny city apartments, chatting and gossiping over pre-drinks and takeaway food.

Smith checked the time on his phone. He was sick of waiting. It had been ten minutes already. Surely his mates Mike Atkins and Matt Leveson weren't far off now. Smith had invited them to hang out at the apartment he shared with his fiancée, Sally White. But first, they'd arranged to meet outside ARQ to pay the cover charge, which was $10 cheaper if you entered before 11 pm, something all the regulars knew. Smith and Sally lived in Alexandria, close enough to the Darlinghurst clubs to cheat the system. They always came in early on a Saturday night to get stamped before heading back to their place for pre-drinks. Lately Matt and Mike had been doing the same.

'Jack!' A gleeful voice pierced the air as Matt bounded across the street towards ARQ. He was wearing white shoes, cargo shorts and a tight black singlet with the boxing and fitness brand Morgan printed in white across his chest.

Smith smiled at Matt. Mike was trailing behind. As he levelled with Smith, Mike shot him a suggestive look. Mike was a little too familiar with Smith at times; even his cheek kisses tended to linger that bit too long. It was obvious to Smith that Mike wanted to have sex with him. There'd been times on the dancefloor at ARQ that Mike had come up close, touching and feeling him; one time he'd started grinding his leg.

It didn't usually happen when Matt was around; Mike was too careful for that. Smith had known Mike for a while now – he'd met him during a night out at ARQ six months before Mike had started dating Matt in August 2006. In some ways it was surprising their relationship had lasted as long as it had. Mike had always been a real player, with a new fling every week.

After paying their cover charge, Matt and Mike followed Smith to his car. Matt's car was parked around the corner in his usual spot, a laneway tucked behind the Shell service station. It was only three minutes' walk from ARQ, a convenient position to store extra supplies of drugs in the glove box. If business was good Mike would pop out to the car during a long night of partying to pick up more vials or pills for potential customers. Smith was pretty familiar with those trips. Sometimes, if they'd been dancing or chatting inside together, he'd even accompany Mike. It wasn't like they were super close mates, but they appeared to trust each other. They'd shared some secrets since they'd met, and Mike had even started opening up about his elusive past – unusual for a man of such few words.

11 pm

Pete Leveson scanned through his phone contacts for his little brother's number. 'I'll just find out where he is,' he told his friend. The pair was driving aimlessly around Darlinghurst, looking for something to do. They'd already been to ARQ to check out the vibe and pay their cover charge. The place had been completely dead and there was no sign of Matt or Atkins, nor anyone else from their group of friends.

The call connected, and Matt told Pete to head over to Jack Smith's place in Alexandria. By the time Pete arrived, his brother, Atkins and Smith were all sitting in the lounge room together, laughing and sipping drinks. Pete plonked down next to Matt. He was curious to find out how his younger brother's savings situation was coming along; for months now he'd been talking about buying a Mazda RX-8 sports car in bright red. Cars were another of their common interests.

A heavy beat thumped from the house's speakers. They were all in high spirits. It was Saturday night; time to let loose after a long week of work. Atkins pulled out a bag of ecstasy pills and took one for himself. He would begin to feel the effects of the drug within 20 to 40 minutes, and by the time he hit ARQ he'd be 'peaking', enjoying the drug's sensation of energy and warmth.

As Pete and Matt chatted in the corner, Smith pulled out his digital camera. 'Hey, you two, say cheese,' Smith called out as he raised the camera to his eye.

Pete leaned in, and Matt did the same. Shoulders touching lightly, their smiles carefree and candid.

1 am

Green lasers flashed around the dancefloor as hundreds of bodies bounced in time to the beat. It was peak hour at ARQ, and a steady stream of excitable men, and women, was surging through the venue's revolving doors to the main dance areas, one upstairs and the other downstairs.

John Burns moved through the crowd with his new boyfriend Kevin at his side. Heads spun towards them and eyes locked onto John in particular. Tall and slim, with white-blond hair, he was a sight to behold: cute and handsome.

'Come on!' he said to Kevin, looping an arm through his. 'Let's go find Mikey and Matty.' John couldn't wait to get to ARQ that night. They were celebrating Kevin's 19th birthday and had spent the day in Newcastle with Kevin's family. John was 22, in no way a cradle-snatcher, but at that age every year felt a leap in maturity. Three years was nothing compared to Mikey and Matty's age gap. John was led to believe there was something like 13 years between them; he thought Mikey looked way older but, then again, he was a smoker.

Merging with a fresh wave of club-goers, John and Kevin slowly made their way towards the bar. It was so packed that John's body was crushed behind some random guy. When they finally made it to the front of the queue, John ordered two vodka Red Bulls before getting his phone out of his jeans pocket. He shot off a text to Mikey: *Where are you?*

Almost immediately he got a response. Mikey was on the balcony, on the top level of the club, above the upstairs dancefloor.

'Let's go,' John shouted to Kevin over the music. They grabbed their drinks and headed towards the stairs.

As John and Kevin reached the balcony, they saw Matty and Mikey standing side by side, shirtless, their chests glistening with sweat. John ran excitedly towards his friends and Matty squealed with delight, opening his arms for a hug. The pair hadn't seen as much of each other over the past few weeks. Truth be told, it had been a bit tense between them lately.

A month prior, before John had a boyfriend, Mikey had tried to initiate a threesome with him and Matty. It wasn't a threesome in the usual sense of the word because it was basically all for Mikey's own pleasure. There ended up being two separate occasions: once at the couple's unit after a Saturday night out at ARQ, and then a few days later when Mikey insisted that John come over for dinner and drinks. As soon as he'd arrived, Mikey offered him free GHB from a thermos stored in a kitchen cupboard. The drug made John feel more energetic, sexual and trusting. Mikey had tried to have sex with both boys, but separately, while the other watched on. While John had no real attraction to Mikey, he thought Matty was beautiful, but the one time he managed to kiss Matty it was quickly shut down by Mikey.

Things had been awkward ever since. Mikey had started paying John a lot of unwanted attention. Just two weeks ago on the dancefloor, he'd told John, 'If I wasn't with Matt, I'd be with you.' The comment was unsettling. John had become quite stand-offish with Mikey after that.

It was a pity, because Matty and John had started becoming close friends. Matty seemed to trust John enough to tell him that Mikey was possessive and controlling, and wouldn't let him do anything on his own. Recently, John had picked up Matty to go to ARQ with some friends on a Sunday night; Mikey wasn't invited and, besides, he had work the next day. But Mikey had decided to follow them in his car and tagged along at ARQ. Matty was furious, and punished Mikey by refusing to talk to him all night. Mikey only left when it was time to drive to work in the early hours of the morning. During the day, he called John several times to find out where Matty was and what he was doing. Mikey could be a total control freak at times.

Tonight, at least, things didn't appear to be anywhere near as awkward. John pulled out his digital camera and told the couple to strike a pose. Mikey draped his big arms around Matty's hairless body: one hand clutched his waist and the other the back of Matty's neck. Mikey grinned widely for the camera; his jeans were slung low and fastened with a Mustang belt buckle.

'That's hot!' John yelled over the music. As he leaned in close to show Matty, he also asked his friend for an ecstasy pill and vial of GHB, which Matty gave him. Matty was energetic and happy. He wanted to dance. Without so much as a backward glance at Mikey, they grabbed each other's hands and ran off towards the dancefloor, Kevin bobbing behind.

1.30 am
Pete Leveson finally arrived at ARQ after having ventured over to Sydney's north shore to visit friends at a party. Walking into the club, he fired off a text to his little brother: *Hey where you at?*

Matt replied quickly: *Just sittin down, wot u doin?*

Pete looked up to the club's overhanging balcony and sent a separate text to Atkins: *Hey are you upstairs?*

Atkins was always either hanging around up there or in

smokers' alley, the passage at the side of the club where smokers and their friends gathered for some fresh air and a chat. As Pete climbed the stairs to the balcony, his phone vibrated with Atkins' incoming text: *there in a min x*

Pete found an empty spot in the corner of the balcony, and within seconds Atkins was beside him. He couldn't help but notice Atkins' sullen face. Something was up. 'How's it going?'

'Not good,' Atkins grunted.

'Is Matt in one of his moods?'

Atkins shot him a look. 'Yes.'

It was clear to Pete that Atkins was on something, and judging by his dilated pupils he figured it was probably ecstasy. But given the downcast look on his face, the drugs seemed to be having little impact on Atkins' downer mood. He must have already peaked, that stage at the beginning of the high that felt like reaching the top of a roller-coaster before the intensity levelled out and eventually dropped off.

Pete ducked downstairs to the bar to buy some bottles of water. It wasn't unusual that Atkins wasn't drinking alcohol at this stage in the night. Ecstasy caused severe thirst, and the mega-clubs tended to use that fact against their patrons. With drugs such a big part of the gay party scene, bottles of water were charged at a premium: at least $5 each, and that was for a small bottle. And, as Atkins had mentioned, there was no way to cheat the system by filling empty containers from the bathroom taps; the plumbing had even been tweaked so that only hot running water was available.

As Atkins waited for Pete to return, he whipped out his phone. It was 1.46 am. He texted Matt: *Where are you? I'm on balcony with Pete x*

Leaning against the balustrade drinking their water, Atkins and Pete attempted to talk over the deafening music. Before long, Matt ran past them on the balcony. Pete could see his younger brother was bouncing around all over the shop, and he could tell Matt had taken something. He tried to talk to Matt but his brother dodged him, flat out ignoring both him and Atkins. Instead Matt jetted off again downstairs, and without another word Atkins trailed after him.

2 am

Waiting near the exit to ARQ, Mike Atkins was fed up. It was reasonably early for a night out. Usually he and Matt would keep dancing until around 6 am before driving home to bed. Just minutes before Atkins had sent his boyfriend yet another text: *Where are you?*

Seconds felt like hours. Still no reply. Atkins was becoming agitated. He fired off another message: *I said sorry 3 times! I need more lollies I sold out and owe pat 2 im near cloak room x*

'Lollies' was his code word for ecstasy pills. Atkins had a sale on the cards, and he needed to return to Matt's car to dig out some extra pills.

Within ten minutes Matt joined him. In the doorway of the exit, they both pulled on their shirts and walked out. They crossed Flinders Street, with Matt striding off in front.

3 am

Sweat dripped from John Burns' brow. He and Kevin had been dancing up a storm near the DJ booth. He desperately needed a drink of water and some fresh air. He grabbed Kevin and they headed out to smokers' alley. Leaning against the brick wall and catching his breath, John dug out his phone once more while Kevin went to the bar to get a couple of bottles of water. It was late now, or early on Sunday morning, depending on which way you saw it.

John hadn't spotted Mikey or Matty in ages, and he was keen for some more dancing before he and Kevin called it a night. He texted Mikey first: *Where the hell you keep moving on me*

Kevin returned from the bar and after a few big gulps John checked his phone again. There was no reply. He texted Matty too: *Hey babe where are you?*

John and Kevin finished their water and headed back inside. Maybe the boys were on the balcony again. As he scoured the faces in the crowd, John's phone vibrated in his pocket. Matty's reply. It was 3.19 am: *Mike's having a fucken cry. He is taking me home and won't let me stay! Fucken cunt!*

John showed Kevin. 'They've had a fight and left,' John yelled over the roaring music. 'Let's find the others instead.'

He quickly shot a text back to Matty: *Oh shit that's not too good*

Minutes later Matt responded again: *He needs to fucken get over himself!*

Kevin pulled on John's arm. 'Come on, let's just go dance!' It was his birthday and he was sick of waiting around while his boyfriend texted.

At 3.31 am, John pinged off one last message before they rejoined the dancefloor: *Oh well im sure you'll be right*

But Matt Leveson wasn't. As his Toyota Seca took off into the night, with Mike Atkins behind the wheel, he was driven to his death. There was only one man who knew the truth of what happened from that point forward. But, for the next ten years, he wouldn't tell a soul.

2.

MEET THE LEVESONS

In the waterside suburb of Bonnet Bay, 40 minutes south of Sydney's CBD, Mark and Faye Leveson were sleeping soundly in their beds. They'd had what could only be described as an uneventful night, so much so that neither of them has any clear memory of what they did the evening their 20-year-old son spent his last hours on earth.

There now remains only one certainty: the night of Saturday 22 September 2007 was one of the last times Faye Leveson ever enjoyed a full night's sleep. More than a decade on, she is constantly tormented in her dreams. She often wakes up with a start at 3.20 am, the exact time of the final series of text messages Matt sent before he disappeared. Mostly she can't get back to sleep, so she lies awake staring at the roof, tossing and turning, while her husband Mark is deep in slumber beside her.

Every morning she forces herself to get out of bed. Her thoughts orbit only around her Matty. She wonders what he'd be doing now. How he'd look. What adventures he'd have enjoyed. But all she and Mark can do is imagine. For them, Matt will forever be 20 years old. Forever frozen in time, and forever young.

Matthew John Leveson was born on 12 December 1986. 'He was in a hurry to come into this world,' Faye reflects. Then, face crumbling, she says, 'But he left early as well.'

Matt, the second child of Faye and Mark, was born at the Sydney Adventist Hospital in Wahroonga following a dramatic pregnancy. Before he was due, Faye fell ill and suffered from severe nausea which was so bad that it brought on an early labour. The young mother was less than seven months along. Mark called the hospital in a panic, and the nurses directed him to bring her straight there. No time for an ambulance. The trip to the hospital took half as long as it usually would have as Mark sped down the main drag at 120 kilometres an hour. When they arrived, Faye bent over with pain, the nurses were at the door waiting, one with a syringe in hand. The injection, and several others afterwards, stopped the labour in its tracks, and Matt remained safely cocooned inside. He may have been ready to make his entrance, but he'd have to wait a couple more months yet.

When they finally allowed him out, Faye needed to be induced. It was 11 December, the birthday of her eldest son Peter, who had just turned two. That wouldn't do at all. Her boys each needed their own special day. She told the nurses to back off as they'd need to wait until at least midnight. As soon as the clock struck 12, it was on. Matt had waited long enough. The chubby, blond-haired bub would later become big brother to Jason Paul, who was three years Matt's junior. The three boys were Mark and Faye Leveson's world.

The couple were practically babies themselves when they first became parents. Both were in their early 20s, but by that stage they'd been together seven years. Mark Leveson had met Faye Corkill in 1977, when he was 19 and she was 17. They locked eyes at Faye's cousin's wedding; the bride was Mark's childhood neighbour. Mark and Faye suspect they probably first met as ten-year-olds playing cricket in the street. In their late teens, seated side by side at the reception dinner, they hit it off. *Really* hit it off. Kissing all night on the balcony. The official wedding photographs show them canoodling closer than the actual newly-weds. The whole wedding saw them, much to the disapproval of

Faye's strict parents. But Faye was on cloud nine. She'd met her man and nothing could bring her back down to earth.

Mark and Faye were unofficially engaged two months later. It took another five before Mark plucked up the courage to ask Faye's dad for her hand. It didn't go well. He picked his timing badly; Mr Corkill, a recreational fisherman, was in the backyard with that day's catch, a huge filleting knife in hand. Mark was all bulging eyes and clenched teeth. Faye's dad made them wait until Faye turned 18.

They married on 9 September 1978, and they describe the after-party as the 'reception from hell'. Their photographer was drunk and hardly took any photos, and the servers spilled creamy dessert all over Faye's apricot satin going-away outfit. The honeymoon was better: a long drive to the Gold Coast followed by a few days relaxing at a hotel.

Then it was back to work: Mark as an accounts clerk at the *National Trotguide* newspaper and Faye in accounts receivable at a marine company. Years later, when Faye was three months pregnant with Jason, Mark said he wanted to start his own business. Faye was nervous, but they took a deep breath and started up their own accountancy practice, working out of a downstairs bedroom in their home. The team consisted of Mark, Faye and one other employee, and there was a crèche in the room next door for the three tearaway boys.

The brothers used to fight like crazy. They were boisterous boys, full of beans. Matt and Jason were constantly at loggerheads; each had fiery, short-fused tempers, and they were more stubborn than Mark and Faye combined. But Matt was always the one Faye had to watch. He loved playing pranks and experimenting. At one stage he became obsessed with power points. One day when Matt was five, Faye found him sitting quietly in the lounge room, an extension cord plugged into the wall, a jar of soapy liquid in one hand and a toothbrush in the other. He was daintily brushing the liquid onto the electrical prongs and watching with sheer amazement as a pretty arc jumped up and over the cord. The plastic plug was charred black. The incident forced Faye to tape plastic cockroaches over all the unused power points in the house, as Matt hated cockroaches. It worked a treat.

Matt loved animals. In a colourful school project in 1998, a 12-year-old Matt declared that his ambition was to become a vet. He also loved tennis, piano, Celine Dion and chocolate, and his favourite TV show was *Better Homes and Gardens*.

Mark and Faye had always known Matt was different from other boys his age. For years, they both had a fairly strong inkling he might be gay. Matt's femininity, though not overt, had started manifesting in his mannerisms by the age of four. At preschool Matt was far more popular with girls than boys, and he found himself drawn towards games of dollies, mummies and daddies, and playing house and home. These interests were by no means proof of him being gay, but they hadn't gone unnoticed by his parents.

Mark loves to laugh at a memory of Matt running as a little boy, with stiff arms, his hands straight out by his side, fingers spread into 'jazz hands'. Mark would try to show him more 'manly' ways of running, with clenched fists. Matt would look at him earnestly and say he'd give it a try, but it was no use.

Neither parent minded that Matt was probably gay; they loved him unconditionally, and nothing could ever change that. If anything, it caused Faye to love him even harder. As mother and son, Faye and Matt were always close. They shared a temper, and had the potential to butt heads, lose their cool and fire up at lightning speed. It was the same with Matt and Jason.

As Matt matured into a teenager he maintained his hot temper; he was quick to react in any situation, especially as his confidence grew. He held his ground defiantly. But his vigour and self-assuredness was a blessing, as it served him well in the most vulnerable moment of his young life. Coming out.

3.

'PLEASE DON'T HATE ME'

November 2004

Matthew Leveson was 17 years old when he came out as gay. It was the Sunday before his Year 12 exams began. He'd left home that morning to go to the house of his friend Daniel, a boy from school he'd introduced to his parents a few months earlier.

It was delightfully quiet in the Leveson household, where they live to this day. Their two-storey brick home is perched on a hill, and their verandah overlooks the roofs of homes peppering the shoreline of Bonnet Bay. A 20-minute drive from the tourist-packed beaches of Cronulla, the suburb is refreshingly laidback. The family's property, on a corner block, is accessed by a long paved driveway. To the back of their home is bushland that separates them from the neighbours further up the hill. It's a peaceful spot, with only sounds of the odd car passing by or birds chirping in the surrounding trees. The family has half a dozen resident kookaburras that swoop in for a feed on the back verandah most afternoons. When Faye sees them hanging around outside the kitchen window she quickly races to the fridge to grab a handful of mince – the kookas' favourite delicacy – and handfeeds them from the wooden rails.

On this typical Sunday afternoon, Mark was working away in his study downstairs. Faye was busying herself in the large open-plan kitchen when her phone sang out. A text message from her Matty. He told his mum he'd left her and his dad a letter in his room. Faye's heart sank. She thought the pressure of exams might have got to him; that he might have run away, or worse still.

Faye raced to Matty's room and found a typed letter laying on his bed. As she scanned the first paragraph, her heart was in her mouth. But by the time she'd finished reading, she let out a long sigh of relief. He was gay – that was all.

Now to tell Mark. Faye took the letter down to her husband, and his reaction was much the same: a knowing smile. They hugged, and that was that. There was little to discuss with each other; the most pressing thing was to speak with Matt.

Faye sent him a text: *Matty, we love you so much. It doesn't change anything. Now get your butt back home!*

Matt's coming-out story is one of Mark and Faye's favourite memories to reminisce over. It's a moment they cherish: the time their brave 17-year-old boy stood tall and told the world exactly who he was, with no apologies. They've never publicly shared Matty's coming-out letter, which presents Matt in his rawest form: vulnerable and at times self-doubting, unsure how his parents will take the news. Mark and Faye have decided the time is right to share this piece of Matt with the world, to help others understand the boy he was, and the man he would go on to become.

To Dear Mum and Dad,

I know this is not the most appropriate way of telling you what I'm about to say, but I can not think of another way to do it, and I want to clear it up before the HSC so it doesn't worry me. I do not no what the outcome of this letter will be, but I hope you will love me and accept me for who I am.

The rumours that you have probably been hearing and vibes you have picked up about me are true. I am gay. Please don't hate me as this is just who I am and it is the decision I have made, nothing can change it as this is who I am. I love you so much and I will forever love you. I am writing to you in hope that you can understand my life's choices and so I can try to be more open to you and not live me life as a lie. I wan to be honest with you about me and my life. As you are reading this please take into mind that this is very difficult for me to say and that's why I found it easy writing to you.

As you probably guessed by now, Daniel is my boyfriend and I do deeply love him. And he is my partner to the formal. Please do not worry about what my friends will say, as they do know about me and Daniel and they have been so supportive over the last couple of months. I do have such great friends and I thank you for this because I would not have them without you letting me go to Inaburra [School].

I am so grateful for what you have given me in my life and my life yet to come. I will forever love you as my parents and I hope you will love me back.

Love Always,
Matthew John
xoxoxo

A few days later, when the family came together, the topic of Matt's newly declared homosexuality came up around the dining table. Matt explained how his friend Daniel was actually his boyfriend. Mark and Faye had thought as much when they'd first met him. Faye also strongly suspects Daniel helped a little with the grammar and sentence structure in the letter, even though a few spelling mistakes still slipped through. Matt was never really any good at English at school.

Matt's brothers were just as understanding. Faye thinks Pete and Jason probably knew long before she and Mark were ever told. At the family meeting of sorts, the ice was broken by Jason, who was only 15 at the time, and had blond hair, a round face and chubby cheeks. Jason looked up to his big brother; they'd grown closer recently and, as they did when they were kids, would often tease each other for fun. When the serious talk was coming to an end, Jason directed a sly smile at Matt. 'So, does this mean we can't have any more poofter jokes?' he said.

There was a beat of silence before the whole table erupted in laughter, Matt especially. He knew it was Jason's way of telling him that nothing would ever change between them. They'd still have the same playful relationship they'd always had.

But Faye was worried about Matt facing the world as a young gay man. She shed some private tears thinking of all the hate he could potentially encounter from ignorant, nasty or homophobic people. She warned Matt over and over that he had to be careful.

There was the school issue too. Matt had come out while still attending a Christian college. For Matt's Year 12 formal dance he opted to go alone, and Daniel went with a girlfriend of theirs. But once the event was underway the boys sat together and had couple photos taken by their friends. Some of the parents shot disapproving looks across the room at Mark and Faye, but they held their heads high. They couldn't have been prouder of how comfortable Matt was in his own skin.

At school, Matt had preferred the creative subjects. Media studies was his favourite class. He loved learning about cameras, audio and editing, and putting together short films with his classmates. It's where he bonded with Rachel Sanki, his first and only proper girlfriend before he came out.

Rach and Matt had started out as friends in their first year of high school in 1999. As 12-year-olds, they were both a little shy and unsure of themselves, and were drawn to each other's similar sense of humour. At first they only hung out within a circle of friends, but as they started taking more classes together they realised how much they had in common. Rach remembers the simple fun they'd have together.

But when they finally became a couple in Year 10, three years into their friendship, they found themselves the centre of schoolyard teasing. It didn't go unnoticed by the other kids that Matt and Rach refused to kiss or be affectionate like so many other teenage couples. The comments and nasty sniggers were hurtful and upsetting for them both, but at the time they tried to brush away the negativity. Eventually, though, peer pressure got the better of Matt and he ended things with Rach quite unexpectedly over email. The bitter memory of Matt's rejection remains all the more unforgettable for Rach because Matt was her first love, and their break-up was played out in the most public way possible, in front of dozens of kids in IT class.

Rach remembers looking over at Matt sitting with a group of their classmates, who were all giggling and seemed to be egging him on about something. Later in the day, she overheard one of their friends telling Matt to hack into Rach's emails and delete something. Rach had no idea what it could be and so, naturally, she logged in to her inbox and there it was, the break-up email. Rach felt embarrassed but also confused. She had no idea it was coming. When she confronted Matt, he wouldn't stop apologising. He told Rach that he hadn't wanted to break up like that, and had got caught up in the peer pressure. He instantly regretted it once the email sent. But the damage was done.

The week that followed was by far the toughest of their relationship. They refused to talk, a decision all the more difficult given they went to school together, took the same classes, worked together on the weekends and were also completing a traineeship alongside each other. The inseparability they'd revelled in just a week earlier became pure torture, but it was what ultimately saved their friendship. After a week or two, it became too hard and, quite frankly, too boring not being together. A new phase of their relationship began, this time as best friends. Rach and Matt remained a large part of each other's lives until the day Matt died.

Rachel Sanki today is much like Rachel back then: tall and striking with long brown hair and enviable curves. One of the first things you notice about Rach is her flawless make-up, complete with a set of eyelash extensions and light pink lipstick. She's bronzed from her weekly spray tan, a ritual that's been going since high school days. Her love for all things glamorous rubbed off on Matt too. Faye Leveson says her son would use more make-up, moisturisers and tanning products in a month than she'd owned in her entire life.

He started by pinching a few products here or there from Faye's modest collection. Matt came across Faye's Elizabeth Arden perfume Green Tea, and he loved its fresh, light scent. If Faye was missing her bottle she'd go straight into Matt's room, and there it would be on the shelf. Its scent is still so familiar and evokes a memory so powerful that when Faye catches a whiff in shopping centres or cafés, it makes her think of Matt and smile.

Mark and Faye gained a daughter in Rach. By the time she and Matt transitioned to best friends, following their short-lived love affair, Rach was already considered part of the Leveson family. The pair would spend hour upon hour hanging out in Matt's family home watching movies, gossiping or experimenting with recipes.

Of Matt's chef moments, Faye remembers best his 'sushi phase', when he became hell-bent on creating homemade sushi rolls. He and Rach boiled up a huge saucepan of sushi rice in the kitchen before rolling out stiff pieces of seaweed on the bench. Their laughter carried through the house as they teased each other over the many failed attempts to create something which even slightly resembled an avocado-and-chicken hand roll. Hours later, their handiwork was ready to serve. Carefully laid out on large serving platters were dozens of sushi pieces next to overflowing saucers of soy sauce and pickled ginger. The whole Leveson family tucked in. Perhaps even more memorable for Faye was the almighty mess she discovered afterwards on her once sparkling, spotless marble benchtop. She laughs now, but at the time she had to spend an entire afternoon scraping and scrubbing starch off all the kitchen surfaces.

By the time their final year of high school rolled around, in 2004, Rach and Matt were closer than ever. With their friendship well and truly cemented, they told each other everything:

their wildest dreams and hopes for the future as well as their deepest, darkest secrets. The most difficult one for Matt to tell was also by far the most important for a best friend to know. Rach had suspected Matt might be gay long before he ever told her. She started noticing little things about him about six months after they broke up in Year 11, but she didn't dare bring it up with him. If Matt *was* gay, then Rach wanted him to tell her in his own time. To make matters even more confusing, Matt had started dating another girl at school, much to Rach's surprise. But after a short while, Matt broke it off. Perhaps that final straight relationship was a last-ditch confirmation in his own mind that, yes, he was most certainly gay.

Not long after, Matt and Rach were hanging out in his bedroom, chatting casually about school and friends, when quite suddenly the mood shifted. Rach remembers how nervous Matt seemed as he took in a deep breath. He looked her straight in the eye as he confessed his biggest secret. 'I'm gay,' he said quietly.

Before Rach even had a chance to respond, he quickly divulged a second secret: that he'd already been chatting with some gay guys online.

Matt trusted Rach implicitly, so much so that she was the first person he ever shared this raw truth with – months before he told his parents and brothers. Even at the tender age of 17, Rach was wise enough to know how important this declaration, and her own reaction, would be. This moment could shape the way Matt felt about coming out to others, including his parents. Yet Rach's response came naturally; she let Matt know she had nothing but love and respect for him. Rach pulled Matt into the tightest bear hug she could muster. She told him nothing would change between them. 'You're still the same Matt,' she said.

But it was her next words that were aimed to dispel any judgement of him. Rach's eyes lit up as she excitedly demanded that Matt show her 'all the hotties' he'd been talking to online. Matt's shoulders relaxed, and he flashed Rach a smile from ear to ear. It was the start of yet another beautiful phase of their friendship.

4.

THE BEGINNING

Monday 24 September 2007

7.48 am

The shiny factory floor of Coca-Cola Amatil was pulsing with activity. Machines groaned, conveyor belts screeched, forklifts let out ear-piercing sirens. It was an all-too-familiar white noise to the dozens of workers manning their stations. With every minute that passed, watchful eyes scanned the hundreds upon thousands of colourful soft drink cans being packaged.

At the construction site next door, tradesmen dressed in hi-vis shirts and vests were armed with power tools and welders. They came in droves every day, a fluoro army tasked with building a massive extension to Coca-Cola's original warehouse. The new facility was one of the biggest constructions of its kind in the southern hemisphere. The concrete slab had been laid and the clad rack installed, but there was still much more to do. Part of the building was without a roof, and the electrical fit-out was already beginning in a covered section of the warehouse.

Lying on his back under a brand-new machine, an experienced electrician was hard at work. But Michael Atkins' mind wasn't really on the job. Less than hour after signing in at work that morning, he had decided to send his boyfriend Matt a text: *Good morning, baby. How are you? I woke up and you not in bed! Did you go out to ARQ with Luke and Paul? Just let me know where you are plz! Miss you xxx*

Atkins' alarm had sounded at five that morning. There was nothing standard about this Monday, given Matt had by now been gone for over 24 hours, but he treated it as such and headed off for work. As an employee of a labour hire company called OMNI, he was contracted out to a number of food factories around Sydney to install new machinery. For about a month now, he'd been working at the Coca-Cola factory in Northmead, more than an hour's drive from his unit in Cronulla. His job was physically taxing. It entailed crawling around on his hands and knees, and manual work that required strong arms and nimble fingers to connect wires, test voltage and shift heavy machinery into place.

The content of Atkins' cute text to Matt might seem rather mundane, but it marks the moment that he started spinning what would become a web of lies and deceit.

11.41 am

As the lunchtime break approached, Atkins sent yet another text. It was simple, laidback, without the slightest hint that anything was amiss: *Hey baby, how you going? What you up to? If you asleep, give me a call as soon as you wake up! xxx'*

Quick messages like this between Atkins and Matt were common. The communication between the couple throughout their working days, at their respective full-time jobs, was fairly regular. They'd check in on each other, talk about what time they expected to finish work, whether they'd be heading to the gym or not, and what they might have for dinner. At least in its digital record, their relationship seemed like any couple's.

Matt first came across Atkins in 2004 when he was 17 and Atkins was 41. It was the same year Matt came out as gay and told his best friend Rachel that he'd started talking to some 'hotties' online. Atkins was one of them. Their relationship started slowly, with a shallow encounter over a website called

Gay Matchmaker that was essentially the 2004 equivalent of dating or hook-up apps like Tinder and Grindr. Users uploaded profile pictures and included details about themselves to attract the attention of other men searching for company or sex.

Over many months, Matt and Atkins' relationship escalated to the next level. They swapped numbers and started speaking with each other over the phone. They constantly spoke about meeting up in person, but it wasn't until mid-2006 that they did.

It was a Saturday evening and Matt was out with some girl-friends, dancing up a storm at a nightclub in Kings Cross. Later in the night he left his friends to meet up with Atkins in the city. Matt was newly single, and Atkins was uncommitted. Things progressed rather quickly from there as they began, in Atkins' words, 'sort of dating', and before long Matt moved in to the unit Atkins rented at Cronulla.

The two-bedroom apartment was in a blond-brick complex known as 'Bayside Court'. Sandwiched between the railway line on one side and the water on the other, the residence was situated on a cul-de-sac and backed onto a local sports oval. Not exactly a private spot, but the first-floor unit was largely protected from the hordes of beachgoers visiting Cronulla.

Atkins had lived there for two years by the time Matt joined him, and by September 2007 they'd lived together for more than a year. Each week they split the rent – $300 between them – and halved their utility and grocery bills.

As a couple they were 'very happy together', Atkins would later say. They didn't fight much. And they were close. 'Really close.'

1.14 pm
Luke Kiernan was sprawled across the couch watching tele-vision. As his phone lit up with a new text message, the 23-year-old flicked his lavish fringe out of his big brown eyes. Even in his lazy state, he was a sight to behold. With his surfer

looks and high cheekbones, he received a lot of attention from gay men of any age.

Luke saw the incoming message was from his mate Mike Atkins. That was unexpected in itself, as Luke was much closer friends with Mike's boyfriend Matt. They'd met a year earlier at ARQ, and along with Luke's boyfriend Paul the trio had become instant 'besties'. Matt, Luke and Paul jokingly called themselves the Power of Three, a term from the fantasy television series *Charmed* referring to a bond formed by 'three magical beings'.

Luke's mind ticked over. Mike wanted to know if Luke and Paul had gone out the night before with Matt. They rarely went out on a Sunday night, and if Matt had even considered going to ARQ he would have definitely texted him and Paul as they lived in an apartment right across the road from the club.

Luke clicked back to his messages and created a new text to Matt: *Hey mikey messaged me and asked if u went out with me last night did u say u did or?*

Perhaps Matt needed Luke to cover for him. Lately he'd confided that he wasn't happy in his relationship with Mike. They'd been fighting a lot, and Matt was confused about whether he wanted to stay. He told Luke that Mike was a very jealous person and, in Luke's opinion, that jealousy was pushing Matt further and further away. He thought it was only a matter of time before they broke up.

4.40 pm

Vehicles in merge lanes stalled and brakelights flashed as an endless queue of motorists commuted home. Traffic had been banked up for kilometres during Mike Atkins' hour-long journey from western Sydney to the Sutherland Shire. His blood pressure was through the roof. White knuckles gripped the steering wheel and his shoulders rounded as he hunched forward in his Mazda Eunos. The 1990s model was a two-seater sports car, sleek and impractical. Not a typical tradie's car. It was all bonnet and no boot, low to the ground, and had little space inside.

With the peak-hour battle almost behind him, Atkins charged through the southern Sydney suburb of Miranda. He was a man on a mission. He had shopping to do. A couple of sharp turns later and he lurched into a car spot outside his destination, Paul's Warehouse. The outlet store was hard to miss: painted bright blue, it advertised discounted sporting goods along the length of its exterior. But within seconds of stepping inside, it was clear to any shopper that the store's specialty item was shoes, which was exactly what Atkins had come for. Making a beeline for a wall of runners, he searched the shelves and snatched up a pair of size 10½ red Brooks running shoes. He turned on his heel and went directly to the cash register.

It was a quiet afternoon in the store. As Atkins approached the counter, a young blonde woman dressed in short shorts and ugg boots greeted him. 'Just these ones?' she chirped, reaching for his selection.

Atkins grunted the affirmative. As she carefully scanned the shoes, he grabbed his wallet and pulled a credit card free. Thinking better of it, he pushed the card back in and pulled out cash instead. He tried to look casual as he waited, gazing around the room. His eyes found a CCTV camera perched on the wall above the counter. Looking down the barrel momentarily, he twitched and rubbed his nose.

When the sales assistant finally passed him his goods, Atkins reached for the plastic bag and headed straight out the door.

Tucked away in his car, his mind turned to his young boyfriend once more. Grabbing his phone from his pocket, he punched out yet another text message: *Baby will you please call me! whats up! x x x*

6.20 pm

In the brightly lit, shiny aisles of Woolworths, Pete Leveson and his girlfriend Meredith perused their food choices. As usual, they were completely undecided on what they each felt like for dinner. They'd spent almost ten minutes wandering around the shop when a familiar face emerged out of the crowd. There, standing by the glass cabinets of the seafood section, was Mike Atkins. The boyfriend of Pete's brother was dressed in a pair of camouflage cargo pants with a mauve polo shirt stretched across his muscular chest.

As he approached Atkins and his half-full trolley, Pete smiled and said, 'Hey, how's it going?'

Atkins looked up, surprised. 'Hey, all right thanks.'

The three of them stood in awkward silence for a beat. 'Sorry, this is Meredith.' Pete gestured towards his girlfriend. 'Meredith, this is Mike. Matt's boyfriend.' Both smiled politely and nodded their heads.

'Where's Matt?' Pete asked. This wasn't the first time he'd run into Atkins at Caringbah Woolworths. But every other time Pete's brother had always been there too. He got the impression the couple liked to do the grocery shopping together.

Atkins responded, 'Oh, I haven't seen him.' He seemed kind of down in the dumps.

'What's up?' Pete quizzed.

'We had a fight yesterday and I haven't seen him since then. I went to sleep, and I woke up and he was gone.' Atkins paused before adding, 'He was supposed to go out with Luke and Paul last night but I haven't seen him since.' He shrugged. 'I don't know where he is.'

Pete's forehead crinkled. It all sounded a bit odd. Then again, Matt and Atkins fought a lot. He'd seen them in a stand-off at ARQ on the Saturday night just gone. 'Oh . . . have you tried calling him?'

'Yeah, he's not picking up his phone.'

'He will turn up,' Pete said, before changing the subject altogether and asking Atkins how work had been treating him. After a few more minutes of general chitchat, they went their separate ways and got on with their shopping.

Pete thought his younger brother was probably over at Luke and Paul's, just as Atkins had said. Maybe Matt was in one of his moods; he did have the tendency to sulk at times. He'd probably turn up later that night.

6.33 pm
The sound was muffled. A faint trill, whirring away. Tucked inside a secret cavity, a mobile phone vibrated. The call droned on and went unanswered. Matt Leveson couldn't pick up.

7.43 pm
Alone at his Cronulla unit as bedtime crept closer, Mike Atkins sent one last text for the day: *Baby where are you? you got to work tomoz! call me when you turn you phone on! x x x*

Electronically, Atkins' concern for his boyfriend's absence was escalating. This was his third unanswered message in 12 hours. And come morning, he'd up the ante.

5.
'WHERE'S MATTY?'

Tuesday 25 September 2007

10.30 am

Bonnet Bay was quiet. It was mid-morning on a school day and the suburb was drained of its usual inhabitants. A lone lawn-mower hummed monotonously in the distance. A thicket of gum trees creaked in the breeze.

Inside the Leveson family home, the only sound to be heard emanated from the downstairs bedroom of Mark and Faye's youngest son, Jason. In a groggy slumber, his breaths were deep and ragged. The 17-year-old was home alone; sick in bed with glandular fever. He was too ill to do anything but sleep, and with his parents' accounting practice only two minutes down the road, Faye planned to check in on him around lunchtime. When she'd left home a few hours ago, Jason had already fallen back asleep after enduring a restless, feverish night. Having ensured he had plenty of painkillers and water within arm's reach, Faye had gently shut his bedroom door behind her. She was hopeful he'd snooze for most of the day.

Suddenly, the home phone blared, splintering the still-ness. With a handset on both floors of the house, the piercing sound filtered through Jason's door. He stirred and impulsively touched his hand to his throat. It was throbbing with pain.

He reached for a glass of water by the bed, chugged it down and rolled back onto his stomach. Sleep took hold again.

Half an hour passed before the landline again sprung to life. Jason pulled himself up and fumbled for the door through half-opened eyes. Out in the hallway he snapped up the receiver and grunted hello.

Inside the NRMA call centre, Kerrieann was almost beside herself. The initial shock that hit her after learning Matt hadn't turned up for work that day – neither of them worked on Mondays – had now morphed into determination. She needed to find out if he was okay. For the past hour she'd been making phone call after phone call to his mobile and family home number. Matt was never, ever late for work and had always let her know if he was sick. Even if Matt was running a bit behind, he called ahead to let their manager know. Even more concerning was that their manager had taken a call from Matt's boyfriend earlier that morning to say Matt hadn't come home last night, and that he was wondering if Matt had turned up for work.

For Kerrieann, something didn't add up. She pressed the phone receiver to her ear and waited for someone to pick up. It was the second or third time she'd tried the Leveson household with no answer.

'Hello?' The barely audible mumble was music to her ears.

'Yes, hello! It's Kerrieann here from NRMA – I work with Matt. He hasn't turned up for work, and it's just really not like him, and we are all wondering if you know where he is?'

There was so much to ask, so much to know and so little time to find out. When Kerrieann finally came up for air, her next sentence to Matt's little brother was cut short. His words were grumbled and curt.

'Look, I'm sorry but I'm not well. I haven't seen Matt but maybe you should try his mobile.'

The line went dead. Kerrieann let out an exasperated cry. Launching herself out of her chair, she marched over to the manager, Lee, who'd taken Mike Atkins' earlier call. Kerrieann asked if he'd left a mobile number. Lee told her she'd just got off the phone with Atkins, who'd called back a second time. Lee said she had suggested Atkins contact a few of the local hospitals and, failing that, he should report Matt missing to police. Atkins' response was strange; he'd said he would report him missing when he got home from work, and didn't seem too worried.

Kerrieann frowned and agreed the whole thing was strange. She jotted down Atkins' mobile number on a sticky note and returned to her desk. She punched in the digits and waited. He picked up after a couple of rings. This is how Kerrieann recalls their conversation:

Mike, it's Kerrieann. How are you?

Good.

Look, I'm ringing up about Matt. Have you heard anything?

No, have you?

No! That's why I'm ringing you. Mike, just tell me what happened. Did you have an argument? Was there a tiff?

No, well we were out, he had a bit to drink and he didn't want to come home. But he was okay, we came home. It was fine.

And then what?

I told him that I had to go to bed 'cause I had work the next day. And when I got up, he was gone.

So where did he go, Mike? Was he meeting anyone?

I don't know. When I got up, he was gone.

Okay, so do you think he has gone out and maybe met up with people? Do you think he has had too much to drink or maybe someone spiked his drink?

Well, anything's possible.

Has he taken anything? Clothes?

He's got so much stuff, I don't know if he has until I have a really good look.

Is there a bag missing?

Not that I can tell.

Mike, I'm calling his mobile phone . . .

Oh yeah, I've been trying also and he's not answering.

Mike, everyone is really worried. Please keep me informed.
I'm going to keep trying to contact him.

Yeah, I'll give you a call straightaway, as soon as I hear anything.

The dial tone sounded, and Kerrieann sat frozen in her chair. A tear rolled down her cheek. It was no time to lose it, she told herself. Leaning across to her colleague, she asked for her help, and together they called Matt's mobile over and over again, into the afternoon.

12.44 pm

By the time Mark and Faye Leveson had any inkling of trouble, it was far too late; Matt had already been dead for two days. On that nauseating afternoon when their whole world was shattered forever, they were working in their accounting practice.

Seated at her desk, with a sandwich unwrapped before her, Faye Leveson picked up her office handset. She'd been thinking of Jason all morning and hoped he'd managed to get some rest. The receiver on the other end clicked as the call connected and Jason's voice mumbled down the line. After telling his mum he still wasn't feeling well, Jason remembered his phone conversation with Matt's work colleague. He told Faye that NRMA had now rung twice looking for Matt as he hadn't turned up for work.

A lump instantly formed in Faye's throat. Trying her best not to give away her concern, she told Jason to go back to bed and not to worry. She'd find out where Matt was.

Faye walked into Mark's office to relay the information. Mark calmly advised his wife to check in with Mike Atkins. They didn't have his mobile number, but Pete did.

After calling Pete and scribbling down the number he gave her, Faye disconnected and punched in the digits. Atkins' phone rang and rang, until an automatic voicemail cut in.

'Hi Mike, it's Faye . . . um, Matt's mum. Matt hasn't turned up for work and I was wondering if you knew where he was? Can you please give me a call as soon as possible? Thanks. Bye.'

Faye dialled the office number for NRMA and asked to speak with Matt's supervisor. She was shocked to hear that Atkins had already called there earlier that morning to see if Matt had turned up at work.

About 45 minutes after she first called Atkins, he rang back. His voice sounded muffled on the other end.

'Where's Matty?' she asked.

His answer baffled her: 'I don't know where he is. I woke up late Sunday morning and Matt was gone.'

Faye couldn't believe her ears. Her son had been missing since Sunday morning. It was now Tuesday, and this was the first she'd heard of it.

'Why didn't you call us?'

Atkins spoke painfully slowly, and in very little detail. He told Faye that he and Matt had had a tiff on Saturday night. Matt had been falling asleep at the club, so Atkins bundled him into the car and took him home. Matt had the shits about it; he wanted to stay out. When they got home, Atkins went to sleep and by the time he woke up the next morning Matt was gone. He figured Matt must have left to hang out with his friends Luke and Paul.

'He's done this before,' Atkins said. 'I didn't think anything of it at first, but when he didn't turn up for work I got worried.'

His words filled Faye with dread. Not again. As much as she hated to admit it, this wasn't the first time Matt had gone missing.

6.
NOT AGAIN

August 2006

It was early on a Saturday morning when Faye received an agitated phone call from Matt's manager. As a 19-year-old in his second year out of school, Matt was working casually at the Big W store at Menai, a suburb away from his family home. He was a reliable employee, the one his bosses would always call if they were short-staffed. In his three years working there, Matt had worked his way up to a supervising role. He was a responsible and hardworking member of the team, and so it came as a shock to Faye when his manager told her Matt hadn't turned up for work.

Matt had been rather withdrawn in the lead-up to this disappearance. He and Daniel had just broken up and Matt, who was still living at home with his parents, seemed upset. There was no denying that Daniel was his first true love. Mark and Faye had both tried to ask Matt what had happened between him and Daniel, but he was a closed book.

The phone call from Big W sent Faye into a spin. She called all of Matt's friends, including Rachel, but no one had heard from him. Finally, she got in touch with a mate who told her Matt had been at ARQ the night before. He'd gone there to meet a guy called Mike, but no one seemed to know who this Mike guy was. By lunchtime Faye and Mark were beside themselves with worry and decided to call the police at Sutherland station. When two officers arrived at their home, the parents reported Matt as a missing person, informing the police that their son had been very upset and introverted because of his relationship break-up. The officers made their own enquiries with Matt's friends, eventually ascertaining that 'Mike' was Michael Atkins, who worked as a security guard at the Sutherland United Services Club.

As the police worked to obtain Atkins' contact details, Faye received a call from one of Matt's mates. He'd spotted Matt's car parked on Allison Crescent at Menai, right near the small shopping centre where Matt worked. The Levesons called the police station and arranged to meet the two officers at the car's location. The green Toyota Seca was locked but Faye had the spare key. The police inspected it and told the Levesons they could take it home.

As the hours ticked by, Mark and Faye became increasingly sick with worry. By late that night, they decided they should probably get some rest. But sleep was impossible. Matt was technically an adult now, but in their eyes he was still their little boy. It made no sense at all that he would have disappeared like this; his phone was perhaps off or flat, but why hadn't he contacted them?

Finally, at 1 am, the phone call they'd been longing for came. When Faye heard Matt's voice on the other end, her relief was overwhelming but so too was her anger, sparked by the intense worry Matt had put her and his father through. But she never got a chance to be mad; Matt claimed that emotion right away. The 19-year-old was furious at his parents, and demanded to know why on earth they'd called the police. He was *fine*. He'd just needed some time to clear his head. His phone had gone flat and he was staying at a friend's house that was undergoing renovations. The power was out.

Faye didn't believe him for a second. She told him sternly that he had to go to the police station and let them know he was okay. Matt pushed back, but Faye wasn't having a bar of it. The argument carried on until Matt hang up.

It happens to all parents: that moment they realise their child is slipping away, growing up and leaving the nest. But as far as these moments go, this was a particularly harsh one for Mark and Faye to come to terms with. Matt never returned home after that day, at least not to sleep. He stayed living wherever he'd disappeared to for the night – his friend Emma's place, he told them. But, as Mark and Faye would soon learn, that was a lie.

7.
HOW OLD IS HE?

November 2006

It's difficult to describe a bad feeling, but there's never any doubt when it's there. Mark and Faye Leveson felt it the first time they met Michael Atkins. The feeling could have been a premonition, but they shrugged it off. Their priority was their middle son's happiness, so they each shook the hand of Matt's new boyfriend, smiles plastered on their faces.

The much-anticipated introduction took place at a café a few streets back from the beach in Cronulla. Faye was still struggling to get over the shock of what her son had revealed to her only weeks earlier: the friend he'd been living with all this time; well, he wasn't exactly a friend. His name was Mike, and they were dating. Matt had warned Faye he was a bit older, '30-something'. Matt wanted to introduce his new man to Mum and Dad, and though it took Faye everything to disguise her anger at her son lying to her for months, at his many secrets of late, she agreed. Her Matty wasn't her little boy anymore.

Faye and Mark had barely seen their son in the flesh since he'd gone AWOL in August. Matt had held a grudge with them for calling the police, and perhaps because he was embarrassed. For weeks now, he'd only returned to the family home during the day, when he knew his parents were at work. He'd sneak in, pick up fresh clothes and pick at leftovers in the fridge, then continue with his new-found freedom. Faye missed her son terribly, and wanted him to involve her in his life again. Meeting Mike was her chance.

The café meeting coincided with a family birthday. The details are sketchy after all these years. It was a weekend; lunch was the plan. Matt should bring Mike. It'd be a lovely afternoon together. In reality, it was beyond awkward.

When Faye was finally seated across the table from Mike Atkins, her mind was paralysed by only one thought: 'How old is he?' Mark was also shocked; Atkins looked like he was their age. As parents, they didn't approve but they refused to let on to Matt that anything was amiss. Faye knew Matt was the sort of kid who'd have dug his heels in and perhaps even ceased contact with his parents if they'd said too much about the age gap.

Instead, in the following weeks, Faye took every chance to reiterate to Matt that he was welcome to move back home anytime. Their door was always open, a room ready for him at a moment's notice. He would say he was keeping his options open. Faye wasn't surprised. She knew Matt loved living by the beach, the hustle and bustle of Cronulla, the mall, the coffee shops. But that knowledge didn't deter Faye from keeping Matt close. She and Mark opened their hearts and their home to his new boyfriend, constantly inviting Matt and Atkins over for a home-cooked meal. But no matter how much time they spent together, the Levesons never felt like they got to know Atkins any better. He was a closed book. Cold and uninterested.

At another family birthday, at the Levesons' favourite restaurant, they felt more bad vibes from Atkins. The rest of the family was already seated and waiting when Matt bounded through the door, Atkins trailing behind. Faye leaped to her feet and embraced her son, kissing him square on the cheek. She attempted the same with Atkins, but he was a cold fish.

Occasions like that were always a cause for celebration for Mark and Faye: their three boys all together for once. A few drinks, and maybe a schnapps or two. But Atkins wasn't having a bar of it. He was distracted by his phone, which repeatedly vibrated on the table, interrupting the family's conversation. Calls and texts came through thick and fast. He'd hop up from the table or rudely pick up the call in front of them.

Mark relentlessly tried to break the ice with him. He was his son's boyfriend, after all, so he had to have some redeeming qualities. He asked him about work, his favourite music, what was happening in the news, but Atkins wasn't up for small talk, and certainly nothing deeper than that. He was short with his answers, and wouldn't look the Levesons in the eye; it was as though there was a force field between them. And then he'd be gone. Every time Atkins dined with them, he'd have an excuse ready to roll out within minutes of the meal finishing: an early start for work the next day, meeting up with friends, Matt's tired. Mark and Faye heard it all. They wouldn't have cared so much if it was only Atkins leaving early but he'd always take Matt with him too, and they desperately wanted to spend as much time as possible with their son.

One of the few places Matt had visited them alone was their Bonnet Bay accounting firm. He'd turn up at their office randomly by himself, simply for a chat. Faye loved those visits; just her and her son. It was like old times. She'd fix him a coffee in the kitchenette out back. They'd gossip and laugh together, munching on biscuits from the office jar. Giggling and lowering their voices if they heard Mark on a business call in the next room.

By September 2007, Faye was finding it increasingly difficult to secure a single moment alone with her son. Even the office visits became tainted. Atkins had never shown any interest in visiting Mark and Faye during the working week before, but suddenly there he was.

Faye remembers one occasion when Matt and Atkins turned up unexpectedly at the office. She was happy to see her son but, to her great concern, Matt seemed down in the dumps. He wasn't his usual chirpy self. She wanted to ask him what was wrong. In an attempt to separate Matt from Atkins, she got the receptionist to engage Atkins in conversation. She got Matt in the kitchen for a split second before Atkins appeared, and her son clammed up. She still wonders what he would have told her that day.

Then there was the very last time she and Mark saw Matt, at the birthday of a family friend. When they said goodbye, Matt gave her the biggest bear hug. 'It was like he never wanted to let me go,' she recalls. 'He just said, "I love you", and that was the last time I saw him alive.'

8.

THE MISSING PERSON REPORT

Tuesday 25 September 2007

It was almost midnight on the worst day of Mark and Faye Leveson's lives. They felt helpless, agitated and exasperated. Only hours ago they'd learned their middle son had already been missing for two days and they were completely in the dark as to where he could be.

Fluorescent lights beamed down on the pavement outside Sutherland Police Station, where they were waiting for Mike Atkins. Mark couldn't believe Atkins hadn't told them sooner about Matt's disappearance. And Atkins had been acting strangely all afternoon. He was supposed to meet Pete in the city earlier that day to search for any sign of Matt or his car, but he'd pulled the pin at the last minute, leaving Pete to go alone. After some hours trawling the streets of Kings Cross and Darlinghurst, Pete had called it a night and drove directly to Atkins' unit to speak in person. Atkins once again relayed what he knew, only this time he revealed that he'd taken Matt home from ARQ on Saturday night because Matt had taken too much GHB. Atkins said they'd woken up the next day. He hadn't really said what time, but Pete was under the impression it was late morning. In relaying this information to his parents, Pete omitted the part about Matt's drug taking. He didn't want to upset them unnecessarily. Besides, Atkins didn't seem overly worried about where Matt might be.

Behind the scenes, Atkins was telling a very different story through his text messages. Earlier that evening he'd tried several times to call Jack Smith and Sally White. When neither picked up, he'd texted Sally to ask if Matt was with her. Sally responded at 6.17 pm: *No he's not. Why? Pete asked me the same thing earlier.*

Atkins replied: *He not been home for 2 nights! an he didnt show up for work an he not answered his phone for 3 days i so worried been crying all day x-*

Mark and Faye had spent the entire afternoon and all evening ringing around Matt's friends. They thought Atkins was out searching, and when they discovered he'd made zero effort they hit the roof. They were beside themselves with worry and wanted to make a missing person report. But Atkins hadn't seemed fazed, and even appeared reluctant to do so. In the end, over a heated phone call, Mark had ordered Atkins to meet them at the police station.

As he approached the Levesons, Atkins had his hands in his pockets and his eyes cast down. He stumbled over his words as the two parents fired question after question at him. He told Mark that when he'd woken up late on *Sunday afternoon*, Matt was gone. Faye's eyebrows shot up. That wasn't what he'd told her on the phone earlier. He'd said *Sunday morning*. Immediately she was full of suspicion about the man who stood before her. The same man who, if she was perfectly honest, she'd never really liked or trusted in the first place.

Inside the police station, they approached the counter and Mark took the lead. He introduced himself, Faye and Atkins, before explaining their situation to the officer behind the desk, Senior Constable Stuart Ferguson, who nodded his head as Mark described the circumstances which had brought them there. Faye noticed that Atkins was pacing around the room, scratching himself and wiping at his sweaty forehead.

Tapping away on the keyboard, Ferguson opened a new event entry in the Computer-Operated Policing System, a database known as COPS. The program, used by NSW Police, included information on all reported criminal incidents, data on police actions and other events attended by or reported to police. It was essentially a running chronology of events during an ongoing investigation.

As Ferguson asked for their full names, addresses and birth dates, Atkins grabbed a bit of scrap paper and scribbled away. When the Senior Constable requested his details, Atkins slid across his prepared paper. Faye's eyesight wasn't strong enough to make out the digits but Mark zeroed in on his date of birth: 6 *April 1963*. Just as suspected. Atkins was in his 40s, not his 30s as he'd told Matt.

Ferguson reached for a notepad and fired a string of questions at the trio. 'Who was the last person to see Matthew?'

Mark and Faye diverted their full attention to Atkins. He paused before responding, 'I did.'

'Can you tell me what happened up until you last saw him?' Senior Constable Ferguson asked.

Atkins responded, 'Matthew and I went out on Saturday night. I wanted to leave early, which we did. But I don't think Matthew was happy with leaving.' He paused again. 'We got home but didn't say much to each other. We woke up the next morning and everything seemed fine.' He shrugged. 'I was talking to Matthew and he was talking to me.'

Ferguson nodded, prompting Atkins to continue: 'Between 8 pm and 9 pm that night was the last time that I saw Matthew.'

'That night being Sunday the twenty-third of September?' The officer made a note.

'Yeah, Matthew said he was going out with friends in the city. He had Mondays off from work.'

Faye's head was spinning. This was yet another version of events. She started questioning her own memory of what Atkins had said outside, and earlier that day.

'Can you tell me what happened next?' the officer asked.

'I also think that he went out again because I made him leave early the night before.'

Ferguson enquired as to what Matt was last seen wearing.

'A pair of light brown cargo shorts, a black singlet and some white leather shoes.'

'Michael, other than the issue on Saturday night, had Matthew and yourself ever had any major fights or disputes between yourselves?'

'No,' Atkins responded bluntly. 'Our relationship had been going fine. We have never fought or had any problems.'

The policeman made a short entry in his notebook. 'How did it come about that you thought that Matthew was missing?'

'When Matthew didn't come home yesterday, I thought he may have been staying with some friends. But it wasn't until his manager at work called and said that he hadn't turned up at work today that I became concerned.' Atkins breathed out heavily before continuing, 'I then got in contact with Matthew's parents to check if they had seen him.'

Faye's eyes darted up to the officer's face. 'We told Michael that we hadn't seen Matthew. That was when we decided to come to the police station.' She wiped at a tear that was forming. 'Matthew may not have always told us or Michael where he was, but he would always notify his work if he would not be attending.'

As Senior Constable Ferguson wrapped up his questioning, he told the trio that he'd need to make further enquiries with the local hospitals and a full list of Matt's friends. Then one last question occurred to him. 'Were there any drugs involved?'

For Mark and Faye, the answer was a bombshell. 'Matt had taken some eccies,' Atkins told the officer.

'Right, so there were party drugs involved,' Ferguson said, making another note. It was the last thing Faye remembers about the police interview.

Faye recalls now that she was 'a bit of a mess that night'. Finding out her 20-year-old son was into party drugs was the final straw in Faye's futile attempts to hold herself together.

As soon as she and Mark left the police station, Faye unleashed on Atkins. She asked him what on earth he had meant when he said Matt was a 'recreational drug-taker'. Atkins' voice was low and sulky; he told the Levesons that Matt would usually take ecstasy and GHB at the nightclubs. Every weekend.

Faye's anger levels erupted, boiled over. She simply could not believe what she was hearing. 'You are the adult in the relationship!' she yelled. 'Why did he do it?'

Atkins, cornered, struggled to respond. 'I dunno, I tried to tell him drugs were bad, but he wouldn't listen to me.' He shrugged his shoulders and studied a spot on the pavement. An unbridgeable silence formed between the three, and they parted without saying goodbye.

9.

A GOOD CATHOLIC BOY

1963–1987

Michael Peter Atkins has always been a mysterious character, a tightly closed book who even friends and ex-lovers describe as fiercely private and protective, a keeper of secrets. But scratch the surface of his upbringing and it isn't difficult to decipher why he formed a propensity to conceal the truth.

Born in 1963 at the Glenelg Community Hospital in South Australia, Michael Atkins was the first son and second child of Peter Atkins and his wife Pamela. The couple had an older daughter, Bernadette, and went on to have a second daughter, Lisa, when Michael was a toddler. The fair-haired sisters took after their mother in complexion, but it was Michael who claimed her eyes and mouth.

The Atkins family maintained a quiet life in Adelaide. But behind closed doors, theirs was a home that in no way resembled a sanctuary of happy childhood memories. Michael's father was an alcoholic, and a violent one at that. He was physically abusive towards Pamela. His dark personality wrought havoc when he drank, to the point that Peter Atkins is described by his only son as a Jekyll-and-Hyde character.

As a child, Michael lived in a constant state of fear. The violence shown towards his mother was bad enough, but he too was a target. From a young age, Michael was sexually abused by his father over many years, and as an adult, Michael was haunted by vivid flashbacks. He severed ties with his father and refused to see him for about 20 years at one stage. When he reached his 40s, Michael reluctantly got in touch once or twice when Peter Atkins fell ill. Michael's father was in and out of hospital for some time before he eventually passed away in August 2008 at the age of 76, at Tweed Heads in northern New South Wales. He and Michael's mother were long divorced by that stage.

Atkins has always pandered to his mum. Pamela, a petite blonde, is a lifelong devout Catholic who spoke to her son about 'hating gays'. Catholicism, and its disapproval of homosexuality, were major features of Michael's upbringing. He was taught early in life that it was wrong to be gay.

Michael and his sisters were enrolled at the local Catholic schools from age 13. For their senior education, boys and girls were split into single-sex schools, and by the time Michael reached high school the family had relocated to Sydney after Peter Atkins received a job transfer. They settled in the Sutherland Shire, and Michael attended the all-boys De La Salle College at Caringbah, which was run by the Brothers. Michael and his classmates were frightened of their teachers. The strap was brought out regularly and used for the most minor offences on the boys, who refused to look sideways out of fear of being beaten.

Outside the classroom, Atkins was also targeted by bullies. His group of friends were a bit dorky, but decent people. A friend from those years says Michael was best known as 'Smike'. He wasn't a sporting person but did have some involvement in the local Venturers group, a version of the Boy Scouts for an older age group. Weekends meant excursions to the great outdoors, where Scout leaders would take the boys abseiling, rock climbing and kayaking.

In 1979, at the age of 16, Michael Atkins dropped out of high school after completing Year 10. He worked as an electrical apprentice while he studied at TAFE. He stayed in contact with his school friends, celebrating 18th birthdays by playing pool and drinking beer. Photographs of a young Atkins reveal a scrawny kid with big glasses and a flop of curly brown hair styled into an attempt at a mullet. His smile is wide and geeky. In another picture he's photobombed a friend and wears pegs clipped onto his glasses. The look of sheer delight on his face tells a story of a life less complicated.

After completing his four-year apprenticeship, Atkins worked as an electrician on major commercial industrial projects before becoming a foreman on building sites. He supervised electrical installations in new buildings throughout Sydney, including a high-rise at a TAFE college.

But work wasn't his only interest as a man in his early 20s.

10.
SENSEI ATKINS

1992–2000

Pedalling past the Engadine train station on his way home from school, Keira Tanko slammed on the brakes. 'Check it out!' he called back to his friend Jason, who was trailing behind.

A black-and-white poster was taped to a telegraph pole by the roadside. In big, bold letters it proclaimed: *Ninjutsu, complete self-protection*. Underneath, a drawing depicted two men dressed in black, fighting. One was striking the other in the neck, in what looked like a classic 'karate chop' to the untrained eye.

For Keira, the poster was a beacon of hope. At five feet (1.52 m) tall, he was a whole lot shorter than his 17-year-old peers, and skinny. His mate Jason was only two inches (5 cm) taller, and just as scrawny. The pair stuck together like glue in the schoolyard, but it didn't seem to help much against the taunts of the other boys. But maybe this would. *Ninjutsu*. They'd be real-life ninjas and kick arse like Bruce Lee and Jackie Chan. No one would dare mess with them anymore.

The advert gave the class location as the Anzac Youth Centre, just down the road, and nominated a time of 6.30 pm on Wednesday evenings. The instructor was listed as *Sensei Atkins*.

After running the idea past their parents, both boys turned up to the next class for a free introduction session. They were excited, full of beans, but had absolutely no idea what to expect aside from what they'd seen at the movies. Hopefully it'd be just as action-packed.

Keira vividly remembers entering the youth centre that evening. About a dozen people dressed in black uniforms milled around the middle of the hall, a big open space used for indoor sport and local dances. Colourful, soft mats covered hardwood floors. As Keira took in their surroundings, there was a sudden movement from across the room. In what seemed like only three bounding steps, the instructor made his way over to their side. He introduced himself as Sensei Michael Atkins. With thick dark hair, sideburns, a goatee and moustache, the 29-year-old was confident, friendly and enthusiastic. He welcomed the boys to his dojo, or classroom, and explained that ninjutsu was essentially the 'art of the ninja', one that anyone could and should learn. No degree of physical fitness, strength or previous martial arts experience was required, and the sport wasn't about brute force but self-defence, strategy and outsmarting your opponent. It all appealed strongly to Keira.

There were rules, of course – plenty of them – and they were strict. Instructors at all times were to be called sensei, meaning teacher, and in return they would respectfully address each student as Mr or Ms. Respect also needed to be shown to anyone higher in rank than yourself.

Sensei Atkins explained the grading system. There were only three coloured belts: white, green and brown. Each represented a person's general level of experience, and a specific grade was indicated by white or yellow stars above the school badge. If Keira wanted to do well, he had a long road ahead. It would take well over two years of regular training before a student could even hope to become a black belt. Even then, there were another ten degrees at the highest level. Sensei Atkins was a third-degree black belt, and had been practising ninjutsu for five years now.

Keira and Jason gave Sensei Atkins their full attention in that first class. The two 17-year-olds thought he was beyond impressive. Sensei Atkins was *ripped*. And ninjutsu was *wicked*, in their humble opinions.

More than 25 years later, I met with Keira Tanko at a pub in Sydney's CBD. Now in his 40s, married and working in a senior marketing role, his ninjutsu days are well behind him. But his memories of Michael Atkins haven't faded.

Perhaps the most lasting impression Atkins left on him occurred on that first night, after class ended. Keira chuckled to himself as he recalled the scene that sent him and Jason racing home to their parents begging for money to enrol. 'Everyone was changing out of their uniforms, and I remember Sensei Atkins took off his shirt. My eyes nearly fell out my head,' Keira told me. He quickly elbowed his friend Jason in the ribs and pointed to Atkins, whose biceps and forearms were huge. 'His lat muscles in his back were so big that they stood out even from the front.' This was their own chance to get ripped.

Keira and Jason had never seen muscles like that outside of their favourite Jean-Claude Van Damme action movies. They joked together all the way home that Sensei Atkins was a real-life Van Damme. Their secret nickname stuck.

I'd asked Keira a few days before meeting up with him if he had any old photographs of Michael Atkins that he could bring along. He didn't disappoint, as he had kept everything stored in a blue folder with plastic sleeves. The folder contained multiple photographs of a young, fit, bearded Atkins along with Keira's original induction letters. Perhaps the most intriguing inclusions were the quarterly newsletters written by a Sensei Wayne Roy.

Sensei Roy was apparently a big deal, not just in Australian martial arts circles but around the world. He'd travelled to Japan in the 1980s to live and study ninjutsu, and had returned to Australia after earning the rank of *Shidoshi*, meaning True Teacher of the Warrior Way. Keira had learned quickly that Sensei Roy was highly respected throughout the martial arts community for his innovative teaching methods. He owned nine schools across Sydney, and Michael Atkins managed and taught at one of them.

Atkins had started ninjutsu training in 1987, when he was 24 years old. At the age of 18 he'd started practising tai chi, a Chinese martial art known for its slow, graceful movements and popular with senior citizens for its health benefits, but later he decided to switch to the more intense ninjutsu. He trained at Sensei Roy's Hurstville dojo before becoming an instructor himself in 1991. In a 'Special Double Issue' of *Ninjutsu Today* that Keira showed me, Atkins is profiled alongside Sensei Roy's 16 other teachers. Under his photograph, Atkins comments, 'Since I started my training, I have achieved goals and skills that I had not even dreamed of. I have heard many top speakers and motivators, but none can match the personal development offered by Sensei Roy.'

As a teacher, Atkins was confident, structured and serious. Keira says he was very switched on: 'not book smart but definitely street smart'. Back then, Atkins would command the room. At the beginning of each class, he'd stand front and centre in a circle of more than a dozen students. After politely welcoming them, he'd launch into that night's lesson. Atkins would conduct the class in a loud, assertive voice. He was controlled and professional.

Each week, he'd demonstrate the technique to be practised in front of the class. Keira was often called out from the group to help. Afterwards, the class would break into pairs and Atkins would circulate, watching, passing on encouragement and correcting styles. Keira trusted his teacher, and Atkins took Keira under his wing.

After some months of training, Keira became the assistant to his sensei, a position he was proud to hold. Keira got to class early and helped set up the equipment. Atkins was an electrician at the time and would turn up to the youth centre in his work vehicle, a closed-in ute with tools in the back. He'd still be in his uniform when Keira greeted him at the door. But despite years of one-on-one time before class, Atkins gave little away about his personal life.

'He was cagey. He wouldn't go into any depth about his life, never spoke about family or friends.' Keira learned more about Atkins by living in the same area and coming across him outside of class. He'd sometimes see his sensei strolling through Cronulla. When Keira turned 18, Atkins was working as a bouncer at a nightclub in Cronulla mall. He'd let him and his friends in without cover charge.

Even at times like this, away from the formal classroom setting, Atkins remained reserved towards Keira. The friendliest Keira ever saw him was in the mid-1990s, after Atkins had left his job as an electrician to own and operate a Pizza Haven franchise at Caringbah. Atkins managed the hole-in-the-wall shop himself and would often be there until late on a Friday or Saturday night, when Keira would wander in from the pub after one too many beers. He remembers Atkins' grin, a pat on the back and a free pizza shoved into his arms.

Keira took ninjutsu seriously for the time he practised, and Atkins was part of his life for at least eight years before they finally lost touch. After relocating to London in the early 2000s, Keira gave up ninjutsu and moved on with his life. From time to time he'd wonder what his old sensei was up to. But it wasn't until 2016 that Keira finally punched Michael Atkins' name into Google. Page after page of articles appeared. He pored over them all. At first he couldn't be sure it was the same man. Not only had Atkins' appearance completely changed, but the words 'gay' and 'boyfriend' stuck out. The man he'd known all those years ago was most definitely straight, or he claimed to be. One of the few things Michael Atkins revealed about himself during his pre-class chitchats with Keira was the existence of a long-term girlfriend.

Her name was Jane.

11.
YOUNG LOVE

1990–2000

It wasn't love at first sight. Not even close. It was more of a slow burn; two work colleagues who grew to like each other over a long period of time. She was all blonde hair, blue eyes and a cute button nose. He was burly, dark and mysterious. But Jane Brown would find out much too late in life that Michael Atkins wasn't the one.

They met through mutual friends in 1990. Atkins' guitar teacher was married to a girlfriend of Jane's. The four of them signed up as part-time salespeople for a cleaning product company called Amway. The job meant weekends away together on sales trips. Long drives and late nights. The spark might not have been fireworks but Jane and Atkins started dating anyway a couple of years later, when he was 29 and she was 26.

During their first year together, Atkins lived with his mother and younger sister Lisa in the family home at Woolooware, near Cronulla. The single-storey brick house was quaint, with a well-kept front lawn and garden. Set back from the tree-lined street, the cosy three-bedroom home became his own when Atkins purchased it off his mum in 1993. His older sister Bernadette and her husband John had children of their own by then and Pamela wanted to move closer to her grandchildren, south of Wollongong.

But even after the purchase, Atkins and Jane didn't move in together. Instead, he found tenants to help pay the mortgage.

Jane remained living in what she called her 'fishing shack' at Caringbah, and would stay with him a couple of times a week.

Jane wasn't Atkins' first girlfriend. He'd had other relationships with women since finishing high school, but this time was different. The couple were together for seven and a half years. But looking back now, Jane reflects that their relationship was going nowhere fast.

Jane found her boyfriend to be absent-minded. He wasn't the type to have deep and meaningful conversations about his feelings. Atkins hated confrontation and rarely lost his cool. He was never aggressive towards her; if anything, she was the more dominant partner in the relationship, and he only ever raised his voice three times.

At one stage, after dating for two years, Jane broke things off with Atkins. She felt empty, and like she hardly knew him at all. The entire time they'd been together, he'd only ever said 'I love you' once. Yet somehow they managed to get things back on track. They travelled together to Tasmania and Brampton Island. Year after year, they coasted along.

Family seemed important to Atkins. They would visit his sisters and mother about once a month. He was close with his younger sister Lisa, and he got on well with his brother-in-law John. He doted on his mother, often travelling to her small townhouse to help with gardening and household chores. But there was a disconnect between them: as Pamela was a strict Catholic, Atkins tended to hide a lot of his life from her.

During their time together, Jane completed a university degree while Atkins chopped and changed between several jobs. Aside from his full-time gig as an electrician, he also worked as a mobile DJ on weekends. At one stage, he bought a basketball gaming arcade machine that he positioned at the Sutherland Basketball Stadium, next to an area called Waratah Park that had a sporting field, Waratah Oval. He'd go there regularly to collect the money and check the machine. His fingers were in many pies; he enjoyed making money and was strict with his spending.

As Atkins aged, Jane started noticing a strange quirk. He never wanted people to know his real age. He also surrounded himself with young friends: men mostly, ten years his junior. Atkins never took drugs and rarely drank alcohol, something Jane suspected stemmed from his experience of his father's own alcohol abuse. They enjoyed a quiet life together, going to dinner at Cronulla and taking strolls along the seaside path of the Esplanade.

But the meals and long walks by the beach were filled with long silences too. By 1999, Jane was struggling to stay afloat. Her boyfriend was still refusing to open up. At 33, she wanted marriage and a family of her own. But it was becoming crystal clear that Atkins was never going to give her either of those things. They attended a relationship counsellor to help repair the growing void between them. But session after session passed and Jane felt as though she was the only one trying.

Finally, they called it quits. At no stage did Jane ever suspect that the real reason her boyfriend couldn't commit to her was because he actually liked men. Looking back with the benefit of hindsight, there was only one occasion where he may have shown his true colours. They were out to dinner and Atkins was overly friendly with the waiter. Jane had a chuckle because it looked as though her boyfriend was flirting with the young man. But when she made a joke about it, the look on Atkins' face wiped the smile from her own. End of discussion.

By that point in life it's likely Atkins knew he was gay, but he'd never acknowledged it openly. Nor is there evidence to suggest he acted on his desires during his relationship with Jane, or even allowed himself to have contact with other gay men.

After the break-up, Jane rarely saw Atkins. She needed space and time to move on. Eventually she found new love and, before long, she started a family with her husband. But she thought of Atkins as a friend, and made an effort to check in on him every now and again. From what he told her, it appeared he was still spending a lot of time with male friends a lot younger than him. He once revealed that he'd recently had the best night of his life. He'd been out on the town with a bunch of 18- and 19-year-olds.

By the early 2000s, Michael Atkins was pushing 40. His hair was receding and his face was crinkling, but none of that really mattered because by now the real Michael Atkins was being unearthed. The discovery was taking place in clubs along Oxford Street, in the heart of what Atkins himself described as Sydney's 'gay mecca'. And it was happening with boys less than half his age.

One of those teenagers was Andrew Danvers. The quiet, sweet schoolboy was only 17 when he first started chatting with Atkins online in 2003. Andrew was still coming out at the time and hadn't yet told all his friends that he was gay. He saved Atkins' number in his phone under 'Michelle' just in case anyone saw one of his many text messages come through.

For Andrew's 18th birthday, Atkins offered to take him out to a club in the city called Stonewall, just around the corner from ARQ. They started meeting up after school too, Andrew in his school uniform and Atkins in his tradie gear. They'd have looked an odd pair at their restaurant dinners, beach days and running errands.

Andrew's mum Leanne, with whom he was very close, wasn't particularly impressed when she found out there was an age difference between him and Atkins. They weren't lovers but they were spending a lot of time together. Leanne was keen to meet this 'Mike'. She'd thought *older* meant by a few years, and she wasn't prepared for the shock of realising just how much older Atkins was.

He'd come over one day to pick up Andrew from home. Standing on her front step, he was immaculately dressed and clean shaven. Despite her surprise, she politely invited him inside and made small talk as they waited for Andrew to appear.

Staring at his deep frown lines and the crow's-feet around his eyes, it struck her that he was probably around the same age as she was. Much like the Levesons' later experience, Leanne wasn't at all comfortable with her boy spending so much time with this older man, but what could she do? Andrew was technically an adult; he promised they were only friends; and, as his mother, she wanted him to feel like he could trust her and tell her anything. Revealing that she disapproved would have only pushed him away. She bit her tongue.

Despite Atkins being the older one, it was Andrew who offered him guidance and words of wisdom. Having successfully navigated his own coming-out period, Andrew advised Atkins on how to do the same. Even though Atkins and Jane had been broken up for four years, he still hadn't told his family he was gay.

'He was really worried about what they'd think or say to him,' Andrew revealed to me many years later. Atkins told his younger sister Lisa first. She was kind and considerate, and it was a relief to come out to her. Andrew remembers Atkins calling him immediately after he told his older sister Bernadette. It had gone well. 'He said that I would have been so proud of him,' Andrew recalls. 'He said, "I told them and they were so happy."'

Atkins chose never to tell his mother Pamela directly, given her strict Catholic beliefs. It wouldn't be until he started dating Matt Leveson three years later that she'd finally discover the truth. Atkins introduced Matt to Pamela as his friend, but she could tell the younger man was gay. She was shocked and annoyed about the way her son had chosen to reveal his true sexuality.

It seems the hardest person Atkins ever came out to was himself. Atkins grew closer to Andrew as he'd helped him to feel more comfortable about the person he truly was, and an attraction gradually formed. But Atkins was new to the gay scene, and he was sleeping around with a variety of toy boys. He'd have a different fling every weekend, and despite mutual friends encouraging them to become an item, Atkins resisted.

It took a major scare before he finally admitted his true feelings to Andrew. It was early 2005, and Andrew hadn't heard from Atkins in three days. The radio silence was highly unusual as they spoke every day. Andrew knew Atkins had been under a huge amount of stress recently as he was in the process of losing his house after filing for bankruptcy. He'd told Andrew that he and a friend had made some investments, but one of them turned out to be a dodgy deal, and Atkins had remortgaged his house to purchase an expensive apartment. He was in over his head. Atkins had nowhere to go and was forced to store his possessions in a family member's garage while he attempted to sort his life out. He sank into a deep depression. There were days when he couldn't get out of bed to go to work. Atkins had sought professional help for depression in the past.

One day Andrew received a phone call out of the blue from a distressed Atkins, who was breathing heavily down the line. He was highly emotional, and he could barely speak as he forced out a shocking confession: he had tried to kill himself.

Andrew was speechless. He listened intently as Atkins bared his soul. He'd come so close to death, he told Andrew. But something stopped him.

'I couldn't leave you like that,' Atkins said through sobs. 'I realised I couldn't do that to you. I couldn't end my life like that.'

So began the romantic phase of their relationship. It took some time for Andrew to recover from the shock of Atkins attempting suicide. 'I told him not to be so stupid, but I was grateful he didn't go through with it.'

Eventually, Atkins moved on from the bankruptcy hysteria and found a two-bedroom unit in Cronulla to rent for himself. The address was 1 Tonkin Street. The cul-de-sac became his sanctuary and home to his new life as an openly gay man.

But once he'd developed that taste for men, it became apparent that he couldn't commit to just one. His eyes constantly roamed the streets and restaurants, beaches and nightclubs, scouring the potential flings available to him. But, in a habit that would continue for many years to come, most of his tail-chasing was done online. Dating websites like Gay Match Maker and Gaydar were among his favourite hunting grounds.

To this day, Andrew still isn't sure how many times Atkins cheated on him during their nine months as a couple. Andrew was still living at home with his mum in the Blue Mountains, west of Sydney. The distance between them provided the perfect cover for Atkins, who was often juggling two or three, if not more, sexual partners at the same time.

As the months went by, his true colours emerged. 'Things weren't adding up,' Andrew reflects. 'He'd say he was going to the gym, and then when we'd speak later in the day he'd tell me yet again that he was about to go to the gym. He'd forget what he'd told me earlier because he was lying . . . I'd question him and say, "But you've already been", but he'd just deny it or make something up.' Andrew describes Atkins as a sweet-talker. 'He could get anything he wanted. He was a salesman, and could make you believe different things.'

But Andrew was no fool, and he had no interest in putting up with a philandering partner. The final straw came on a day when Andrew had an argument with Leanne at home. He was upset and he needed some comforting words, a cuddle from his boyfriend. He called Atkins' mobile. It connected, but before he could even explain what had happened, Atkins brushed him off, said he'd call back in a minute. But half an hour later, he still hadn't picked up. Andrew was furious. He decided to call Atkins on a private number. 'A random guy picked up the phone.' The memory even all these years later is still a painful one for Andrew. 'They were . . . in the middle of it.' He pauses. 'I heard them doing whatever it was they were doing.' Atkins was at home, having sex with another guy.

'That was it,' Andrew says. 'I snapped. I called him back from my phone and when he finally picked up, I just lost it at him.'

Atkins told him he was being crazy, a 'psycho', but Andrew held his ground. They broke up, and for a whole week they didn't speak. It was the longest period of time they'd gone without seeing each other in the two years since they'd met. The romantic phase of their relationship was over, but Andrew remains perhaps the closest friend Atkins has ever had. Atkins wanted to keep him in his life. Following their week of silence, he drove out to the Blue Mountains and made things right.

For the next 12 months, Atkins would tell Andrew all about the highs and lows in his life, including talking up his latest toy boys and flings. But it seemed to Andrew that no one came even close to the kind of relationship they'd shared. That was, until mid-2006.

'He told me that he was going to meet up with this guy called Matt. The next time I heard from him, he said they'd met up for a date as planned, but then the very next day Matt turned up at his unit to stay the night.' Atkins complained to Andrew that he wanted Matt to leave. He said he'd run away from home and his parents had called the police. Atkins said he'd pushed for Matt to go home but as the days went on, Matt seemed to be under the impression that they were now an item.

'They weren't,' Andrew says firmly. 'At least not at first.' But it turned out Atkins didn't tell Andrew everything, because the way he eventually found out – to his surprise – that his ex had a new boyfriend was through social media. Atkins had declared on his Myspace page that he was in a relationship with Matt Leveson.

When Andrew called, Atkins told him that Matt had grown on him. Needless to say, Andrew's first impression of Matt, from afar, was not a good one, filtered as it was through Atkins' words. When Andrew and Matt eventually met in ARQ one night, they were stand-offish at first. But they eventually became fonder of each other, and in the end Andrew thought Matt to be a nice guy. He invited Matt to come along with Atkins to his 21st birthday party.

But their friendship ended three months before Matt disappeared. In June 2007, Andrew Danvers moved overseas to Canada to start a new life on his own terms. His parting impression of Michael Atkins and Matt Leveson as a couple was not a positive one. 'If Matt didn't get what he wanted from Mike, he'd have a fit.' But, he also concedes, 'Mike was controlling of Matt, and possessive.'

12.

SEX IN NEWCASTLE

Wednesday 26 September 2007

Another night had passed and there was still no word from Matt. The silence was deafening. But word had spread quickly that the popular 20-year-old was missing and, much like Matt's parents, his friends from school and ARQ were shocked to hear he'd been gone for days.

After the official missing person report was lodged, Senior Constable Ferguson had attempted to call Matt's mobile a number of times, only to find it switched off. He'd then contacted Sutherland, St George and St Vincent's hospitals, with no result.

But somewhere, cradled in a dark, cosy spot, Matt's phone was filling up with messages. In the early hours of Wednesday morning, at 12.58 am, a girlfriend had desperately texted: *Matt if you turn your phone on and see this message please call me. Or message. If something is up and you need somewhere to stay call me anything to let me know you are ok. I love you baby x*

Another friend wrote: *Matty im so woried wer da hel r u?*

Most tragic of all was the pleading message that came from Faye: *Pls ring me need 2 hear your voice 2 know u ok u can always come home luv u no matter what xxoo*

Then there was Atkins. For him, this was day four of no reply from his boyfriend. He implored Matt over text message: *Baby no matter what happened just give me a call! plz baby!*

we all worried sick x x x By that stage he'd dutifully sent six text messages, in increasing order of concern. He was a worried partner – *worried sick* – begging his lover – *baby* – to get in touch. But he hadn't yet tried calling Matt once. He also had other matters to attend to; Matt may have been missing, but Atkins' life rolled on. Through text messages he made arrangements to buy ecstasy pills in bulk at $13.50 a pop.

8 am
In Bonnet Bay, Mark and Faye Leveson were experiencing stomach-punching, knock-the-wind-out-of-you apprehension. They went into their office that morning. They had clients to attend to, commitments to fulfil. But Faye found herself sitting at her desk shifting between work and worry. She called Matt's employer, but he hadn't turned up for the second day in a row. She rang more of Matt's friends, or the same ones all over again, to check if they'd heard any news. Her mind was blank. Where on earth could her boy be? Matt wouldn't have run away. There was no chance. He loved his family and his friends; he had dreams and ambitions he was actively working towards. He was saving for a new car and planning his upcoming 21st birthday party.

Faye picked up the phone once more and called Atkins, who told her, 'I've been crying under a machine at work.' Those words stuck in her brain. He had no news to report about her boy.

10 am
At the NRMA call centre, Kerrieann Waud strode straight to her desk, plonked down her handbag and collapsed into her chair. Matt's desk was empty again. How she'd wished and hoped his smiling face would be there this morning. He'd say it was a big misunderstanding, and then it'd be back to normal again, reading gossip magazines in the kitchenette, eating chicken rolls at the public pool and shopping for bargains on their days off. But the bubbling in Kerrieann's stomach told her otherwise. Something really wasn't right. She picked up

her headset and carefully positioned it over her fluffed-up hair. She knew Atkins' mobile number off by heart by now and quickly dialled it.

'Mike, have you heard anything?' She was breathless. 'Do you know where he is yet?'

'No. The police were informed last night.'

The news came as a relief to Kerrieann. He'd at least done that. After her shift the day before she'd called Atkins from home and hounded him to contact the police.

'Are you ringing around?'

'Yeah, the parents are ringing, and I'm ringing everyone I know.'

It was a barefaced lie.

2 pm

Rachel Sanki had just hopped off the phone to Faye Leveson. There was still no news. Tears rolled down her face, leaving tiny tracks through her makeup. It had been this way since the day before, these random outbursts of weeping. She'd been at a friend's house when Faye called to check if she'd heard from Matt. Rach hadn't spoken to her best friend since the weekend, and she instantly freaked out when she heard he hadn't turned up for work. Something was seriously wrong. Matt had sworn to her after the last time he went MIA that he'd never scare her or his family like that ever again. He'd really meant it too. He'd been deeply embarrassed and ashamed.

Rach had been calling Matt over and over again for almost 24 hours now. Every third phone call was to Mark or Faye Leveson, checking in for an update. The more time that passed, the sicker Rach felt. She knew that Matt would have contacted her by now. They spoke almost every day; long-winded phone calls, cute little text messages or quick-witted exchanges over Myspace and MSN Messenger.

Rach's stomach churned with worry. Every time the phone rang she hoped it would be Matty's name on the display. But she knew deep down that this wasn't like last time. Not even Matt's boyfriend knew where he was.

6.30 pm

It had been yet another long day for Michael Atkins. He was tired, hungry and dirty. His fluoro yellow shirt was covered in grime, his boots coated in dust. A construction site was no place for a clean freak.

Back home at last, he had so much to do that evening. Matt's mum Faye had called, again, to say that Miranda Police Station had taken over the missing person enquiry. The station had a larger team of detectives, and Matt's case would mostly be handled by them now. She'd asked Atkins if he knew where the station was, but he knew the Sutherland Shire like the back of his hand. She'd said the police needed a few more details from them; photographs and Matt's bank account details were a priority. Atkins told Faye he'd drop them at the station.

There was an awkward silence, then Faye's voice softened a little as she asked, 'Would you like to come over to our house?'

Atkins stumbled his way through a polite decline.

'Oh, okay,' she'd said, downcast, before adding, 'You'd probably prefer to remain at home in case Matt called?'

He'd agreed and hung up. His mind turned to the visitor arriving shortly. Then, at last, he'd be on his way to a much-anticipated appointment.

6.45 pm

Brendan Arnold was cruising through Cronulla in his car. The 21-year-old hairdresser had finished work for the day and was in the mood for a chat with friends. He'd been texting with his mate Mikey Atkins earlier and, given he was near his place, decided to give him a quick buzz. Brendan would often drop by unannounced. It was nice to see Mikey and Matt outside of a deafening club every now and again. The call had connected, and Mikey's soft, husky voice came through the phone's speaker.

Brendan raised the idea of a quick visit; Mikey hesitated before inviting him over. Brendan was now pulling into the cul-de-sac.

Brendan had known Mikey Atkins for a while. They'd met in 2005, when Brendan was 19. They got chatting on Gaydar and enjoyed each other's banter. Mikey's profile, with the name Nulla_Boy, said he was 36. It'd taken a few months of online chatting and flirting before the pair decided to meet up in person. Mikey offered to pick up Brendan from his home. He arrived in his small black sports car and drove him back to the Tonkin Street unit. They sat on the couch and made small talk, which seemed like a procedural requirement before they got down to the real reason they were both there. It was the first of many times they had sex. They established a relationship as 'friends with benefits'. Sex with no strings attached. Brendan had thought their dynamic would have changed dramatically when Matt entered the picture, but having a boyfriend didn't seem to worry Mikey or change his extracurricular activities too much.

Brendan had first seen the couple together at ARQ one night and had thought, 'Mikey's boy of the week'. When he asked Mikey about Matt, he said Matt had stayed over once and just hadn't left. Not a great way to describe the beginnings of a relationship with your so-called boyfriend. But Brendan knew that Mikey didn't treat his relationship with Matt as monogamous; he'd made out with Mikey at ARQ one night after Matt had walked off in another direction. They'd also continued having secret sex until only a few months ago. Mikey was always saying to him, 'I had great sex with you. We had the perfect relationship. I liked the freedom I had with you.' His words were flattering, and in Brendan's opinion Mikey and Matt's relationship was toxic. Mikey had told him of their fights; he'd claimed Matt was bringing other men home and it was making Mikey upset. Mikey also told Brendan that Matt was the real jealous type, and that he needed to grow up.

Brendan buzzed Mikey and Matt's security door that Wednesday night and pushed it open when he heard the familiar click.

Inside they sat on an old blue lounge. Mikey must have just got home; he was still in his work clothes. They talked about general stuff, two friends catching up, until Brendan noticed that Mikey was holding a digital camera in his hands. 'What's that for?'

'I need to find the cable to Matt's camera to upload a photo,' Mikey said. There was an edge to his voice.

'Why?'

'Ah, Matt's missing.'

The words hit Brendan like slap to the face. 'What!' They'd been sitting here all this time, casually chatting, and Mikey was only now bringing this up.

Mikey fidgeted, looked at his feet. 'Well, we went out on Saturday night, we went to ARQ. Matt had too much G and started to get manky, started falling asleep. I took him home but Matt woke up in the car and was shitty and wanted to go back.' He paused, collecting his thoughts. 'Matt had his manky sleep and wanted to go back out, and I said no.' He breathed in. 'We got home and went to sleep. Woke up on Sunday and everything seemed to be okay, but Matt still seemed to be shitty. He started saying to me, "I want to go out tonight", and I said, "You can't go out tonight".'

Brendan sat in silence, his mind absorbing every word. Mikey continued without prompt. He was babbling. He explained that he'd fallen asleep on the couch about 9 pm and woke up at 1 am, when he found Matt was gone, as was his car, his wallet, his phone and his key card. Mikey said he'd looked everywhere for Matt's stuff. But he watered down Brendan's concern by letting him know that this wasn't the first time Matt had got the shits on Sunday night and gone out.

To Brendan, Mikey looked lost and disconnected, a shell of himself. He didn't respond to Brendan's attempts to comfort him.

Brendan badly wanted to help. He jumped up off the couch and went searching for Matt's camera cord in the kitchen, a small, dingy space with junk stacked in the corners of the bench.

He looked through paperwork, bits and pieces stacked on shelves, until he found the cord. But something else caught his eye. In plain sight were Matt's Louis Vuitton coin purse, some cash and a set of keys. His brain crunched. Mikey had said these items were missing. But as he walked back to the computer, Brendan didn't bring it up. Instead, he showed Mikey how to upload photos from the camera.

As the thumbnails loaded, Mikey peered closer. He clicked on a few and gave a little laugh. 'Check this out,' he said as he pulled up photos of random men from a recent party. 'This bloke tried to pick me up once . . . Oh, and this one too!'

Brendan's brow furrowed. What an odd thing to say at a time like this. He leaned over the keyboard and took control of the mouse, showing Mikey how to attach a photo to an email. Afterwards, he said goodbye.

A short while after Brendan left, Atkins grabbed his car keys and headed for the door.

8 pm

All Mark Leveson wanted to know was: where was Matt? After the debacle of the previous year, he didn't believe his middle son would have disappeared. At the very least, he'd have contacted Pete or Rach by now. The matter was in the hands of police but, still, Mark couldn't just sit there doing nothing. It'd been a hellish day at work. September was a busy time for accountants. Most of his clients were only now getting around to doing last financial year's tax and, as always, they wanted it done quickly. Mark would conduct numerous house calls, especially for his older clients who lived too far away from Bonnet Bay to come in person.

That night, driving home from Sydney's north shore, he took a detour through the city's nightlife hotspots. Calling Faye on his hands-free device, he asked her to find out from Atkins where Matt usually parked his car in Darlinghurst.

As he waited on the response, he trawled the grubby streets

of Kings Cross. The iconic Coca-Cola billboard flashed red and white, lighting up the main intersection of the red-light district. The gateway to the Cross. The seedy strip-club-lined area was humming with its usual crowd: young backpackers, cashed-up locals, trendy restaurant-goers, the homeless, and crusty old men who sucked on durries between nicotine-stained fingers or gulped down schooners of heavy beer in the pubs.

Faye's return call blasted over the car speaker. 'He said behind the Shell service station off Flinders Street,' she reported. Mark hung up and pulled the steering wheel around 180 degrees; a U-turn towards Darlinghurst, the next suburb over.

9.30 pm
The doorbell chimed through Jake McCloy's tidy two-bedroom apartment. His visitor had arrived. Butterflies whipped around his stomach. The 23-year-old university student was about to meet the man he'd been chatting to online for the past three months. They had a sexual connection, and tonight they were going to do something about it.

Jake lived in Newcastle, two hours' drive north of Sydney, quite a hike for a one-off date. The distance was the reason it'd taken this long for him and his mystery man to meet up. They'd constantly talked about hooking up during their endless late-night online chats. They'd also had phone sex multiple times, and often used webcam. But the promise of following through in person had only ever lingered as a distant possibility. Nulla_Boy, as he was called online, had a boyfriend. According to him, they had an open relationship. Jake wasn't entirely sure what that meant, and he'd quizzed him about how that worked practically. But Nulla_Boy had always managed to bat the interrogations away; all he'd said was that his boyfriend didn't mind if he had sex with other men. Once or twice, Jake had spotted Nulla_Boy's boyfriend in the background of the webcam, walking to the kitchen and seemingly oblivious that the camera was even in operation. He looked a lot younger than Nulla_Boy, even younger than Jake. They must have had a fair age gap between them. But none of this was really Jake's business.

Jake felt excited to experience being with an older man. When Nulla_Boy had contacted him late last night to see if he would be free for a home visit, Jake jumped at the chance. His flatmate was away, so it was perfect timing; they'd have the place to themselves. It'd be a late-night meet-up because Nulla_Boy had to come from work. He'd reiterated this point by calling multiple times on his drive up the highway and telling Jake that he was still wearing his dirty work clothes. He'd said he would need a shower as soon as he arrived. Jake said it was no problem.

Jake heard a knock at the front door and danced up the hallway. Blond and slim with baby-blue eyes, he was more pretty than masculine; he was what other gay men often referred to as a 'twink'. To give a general image, Urban Dictionary defines a 'twink' as 'the gay answer to a blonde bimbo cheerleader'.

Jake flung open the door. There stood Nulla_Boy, or Mikey as he'd disclosed was his real name over the phone earlier. Jake's eyes widened. Bulging muscle filled the space of the doorway.

'Hey!' Jake was nervous.

'Hi, mate . . . The shower, thanks?' Mikey, dressed in a hi-vis shirt and work shorts, made his way through the door with an overnight bag in hand.

Jake gestured to the doorway on the left. Mikey entered and slammed the door behind him. Jake closed the front door and proceeded back down the hallway to the kitchen. He was an open, friendly person but nervous at times, and he tended to over-compensate with friendliness in awkward situations. He settled himself and reached for a bottle of red wine sitting on the bench. He'd walked down to the bottle shop earlier and picked it out specially, spending a lot more than usual. Mikey was older so probably had good taste in wine, and Jake was keen to impress.

As he busied himself carting out the wine, two glasses and an extensive cheese platter to the dining table, Jake heard the bathroom door open. He looked up just as Mikey appeared in the room, butt naked. Jake was relieved that his guest wasn't so uptight after all.

They had sex right then and there in the living room. It was quick, strictly business, nothing to write home about. Afterwards, they cuddled on the couch together, sipping on wine. It was a good drop. Jake launched into interrogation mode.

'So, why tonight? Why have you come up, you know, all of a sudden?' Mikey murmured something about the timing being right, and tried to brush the question away. But Jake's curiosity was running wild.

'Where's the boyfriend tonight?'

Mikey avoided his eyes and said, 'He's gone away.' Then he moved to new topics. He talked about his work and asked Jake about himself. He came across as a passionate person, sexually charged but softly spoken.

They had sex a number of times that night; Mikey wanted it over and over again. It was clear he'd come up just for that. After a while the sex-cuddle-sex-cuddle routine started wearing thin. Jake was bored, and Mikey had a very different sense of humour, the type Jake didn't find at all funny. He didn't want to endure a whole night with him.

Jake was saved by the bell when a friend called, begging for him to come out to Fanny's, one of Newcastle's main clubs. Wednesday night was student night, and it absolutely went off in there. Cheap drinks and good times. It was just the excuse Jake needed to get this old man out of his house.

They got ready and walked out onto the street together. Mikey stopped by his car, which was parked under a leafy tree, and chucked in his overnight bag. He had the staunchest walk Jake had ever seen: chest out, arms flexed like an ape, and legs marching.

Inside Fanny's, hundreds of 18- to 25-year-olds split themselves between an RnB bar area and hard-house room. Jake chose the latter, which was extremely loud and dark. It allowed him to not talk to Mikey. After meeting up with his friend, they all got on the gear; he says Mikey took an ecstasy pill and a cap of MDMA. The drugs were a big mistake. If Jake had thought him irritating earlier, the pill-and-MDMA cocktail made Mikey really chatty. Over the top of ear-pounding beats, he kept leaning in to talk to Jake. His dancing was also bad: stiff, flexed arms soldiering back and forth. Jake needed to ditch him.

When a smoke machine went off in the corner, momentarily clouding the crowd in mist, Jake made a run for it. He ducked down the hallway and out the front door. He stumbled home and once inside took the security buzzer phone off the hook. He didn't want Mikey coming back there. As he undressed for bed, he switched his mobile phone off too. That was the end of that liaison.

13.

STRIKE FORCE BOWDITCH

Thursday 27 September 2007

2.30 am

It had been a slow night shift for the officers rostered on at Sutherland Police Station. Constable Richard Hill was on patrol duty in his marked police vehicle, with zero action coming through on the radio. Truth be told, the beat was a fairly monotonous one. The Sutherland Shire was statistically a low-crime area. There were few murders, rapes and vicious attacks, especially on a school night. The biggest issue raised by local residents and business owners was 'malicious damage', though that made it sound too exciting. Simply put, the Sutherland Shire had a problem with graffiti and vandalism. Mostly the culprits were bored teenagers.

As Constable Hill patrolled the streets that night, he was accompanied by two colleagues. Starting at 6 pm and due to knock off at 6 am, they had just over four hours to go before heading home to bed. Making their way down Rawson Avenue on the southern edges of their beat, they pulled into a driveway leading to Waratah Oval. The sports grounds were normally dead quiet at this time of night, but from time to time they'd had problems with the toilet blocks being used for sex by blokes, usually the closeted and married variety. Among a certain crowd, Waratah Oval was well known as a gay beat.

Dense bushland surrounded the football and cricket fields, and they were only a stone's throw from the outskirts of the Royal National Park. Within the vicinity there were also tennis courts, a basketball stadium and a leisure centre.

Looping around the park's internal roadway, the police officers found little of interest until arriving at a car park adjacent to the sports oval. A lone vehicle was parked in a bay facing the fields. With their headlights pointed towards the rear of the vehicle, Constable Hill managed to read the NSW numberplate: VRM 961. He radioed it in and within seconds the police operator returned the details. The vehicle was registered to a Faye Leveson. Something pinged in Constable Hill's brain: the missing person report. He and his colleagues had all been made aware of the report during an earlier briefing, and he remembered the Leveson name.

Each of the car's doors was locked. Flashing his torch inside, Constable Hill noted that nothing appeared out of place. He observed that debris from surrounding trees and bushland had built up around the car, perhaps an indication it'd been parked there for some days.

The officers returned to their own vehicle and drove around, hoping to locate the missing person. But Matt Leveson was nowhere to be found.

7.30 am

Sergeant Melissa Cooper strolled towards to her desk. Her shift as a plainclothes detective at Miranda Police Station was just getting started. But as she passed through the office, she could already sense tension in the air.

At 32, the officer had done well for herself. She'd been a detective for five years and had recently been promoted to the position of sergeant following a gruelling examination process. Blonde, with a friendly, rounded face, she looked much younger than her years. But as a newly appointed sergeant in the Miranda criminal investigation branch, she was starting to take charge of some bigger jobs. Only yesterday she was assigned as officer in charge of a local missing person case. According to the file she'd read on COPS, the circumstances relating to the young man's disappearance were highly questionable.

As Cooper logged on to her computer, two of her colleagues made their way over. They informed her that a car belonging to her missing person had been discovered, abandoned at an oval in nearby Sutherland. Police had been dispatched to the location and, after finding no signs of damage to the vehicle, they'd organised for NRMA Roadside Assistance to unlock the car. The NRMA workers had conducted an initial cursory search inside. Nothing jumped out at first but when the officers opened the boot they found something suspicious. They'd rung it in, and now a crime scene was being established. Sergeant Cooper wasted no time getting over there.

It was all systems go in the car park. A row of police vehicles, marked and unmarked, cordoned off a hive of activity focused on a Toyota hatchback. The car was parked nose in, facing the oval.

Cooper hopped out of her vehicle and surveyed the scene. On the outskirts of the oval, officers in dark navy jumpsuits searched the perimeter with a German shepherd off the leash. Cooper walked over to a huddle of fellow detectives standing near the car. The doors were all open.

The mood was subdued, the detectives' attention keenly focused on a woman dressed head to toe in white scrubs kneeling next to the car. Crime Scene Officer Ellen Konza was already processing the scene. She was used to working under pressure, and the piercing stares of the detectives did little to distract her from the task at hand. Cooper took her position in the semicircle of spectators, and watched as Konza bent down to the floor of the front passenger seat and picked up an empty plastic container of Coles chicken caesar salad. Konza bagged it, along with a Kit Kat wrapper and water bottle, for further examination.

Konza rounded the car to the driver's door and leaned in, hanging her body over the seat. She gently took wet and dry trace swabs of all the usual places a driver would touch: the steering wheel, handbrake and internal door handles. She signalled to the detectives standing close by, handing them the items one by one. They'd need to be processed immediately.

Cooper edged closer as Konza made her way around to the back of the car. So far there'd been nothing of note in the car's interior. But the boot was yet to be examined. Lifting up the door, Konza stood back and took in the space. It was a decently sized boot for a small car and could be made even larger if the two back seats were laid flat.

At first glance the boot appeared empty aside from a few stray electrical cables in a tangled mess. Konza lifted her camera to her eye and it flashed as she photographed the space. She leaned in for a closer look and her body stiffened. There, resting on the dark grey carpet was a small piece of paper. Konza flipped it over in her gloved hand. She read for a moment, then spun on her heel to face the group of detectives standing behind her. 'We've got something,' she said.

Cooper retrieved the freshly bagged evidence. Shielding her eyes from the sun's glare, she pinched the paper between her fingers. Her brow furrowed. It was a retail receipt. As she scanned the fine print, her pulse quickened. It was one from Bunnings Warehouse in Caringbah and dated the Sunday just gone, 23 September. Cooper's head spun. Listed on the tax invoice were two separate items costing a total of $34.25 and paid for in cash.

Cooper's eyes widened. There it was, in black and white. The purchase of *Tape – Cloth Norton*, and *Mattock – Gardenmaster with handle*. Duct tape and a piece of digging equipment. She needed to get to work. And fast.

Racing towards the police station, Cooper directed a colleague to start working on Matt Leveson's bank records. If there was any chance he was still alive, or that his credit cards were still being used, they needed to know right away. Back at the station, Cooper googled the Bunnings Caringbah phone number. She called and asked if the store had kept CCTV footage from the previous Sunday. The voice at the end of the line said they had.

It was the answer Cooper was banking on. She asked for the footage to be located immediately and put aside. She'd be there in person shortly.

Cooper hung up. She knew, was trained to know, that the earliest stages of an investigation were the most important of an entire case, especially when investigating a missing person case or a suspected homicide. This was potentially the latter. The discovery of Matt Leveson's abandoned car had pivoted a missing person report into something far more sinister. Add to that the mysterious purchase of heavy-duty digging equipment and industrial duct tape, and they were now confronted with some ominous signs.

10.30 am

Cooper whisked through the sliding doors of Bunnings and familiarised herself with the gigantic store. Her heeled boots clicked against the shiny concrete floor as she hurried towards the office of the manager, George. Inside the air-conditioned room, George hovered over a computer.

The security footage from Sunday was already loaded up. George pressed play and faint pictures jolted across the screen. The first footage they viewed was from a camera near the entrance of the store. Sunlight flared through the sliding doors she'd walked through only moments before. The time on the display read 11.45 am but George explained that the clocks were slightly out; the actual time was 12.10 pm.

Hordes of customers flowed in through the entry gates, grabbing trolleys on their way through. Cooper could make out that dozens more were milling around outside, gorging on freshly cooked sausages in bread. To the left of frame, a mother

DEAL WITH THE DEVIL

plonked her daughter in the front seat of a trolley while her son waited at her side.

Suddenly the shape of a lone white male appeared in the doorway to the right. Cooper leaned in even closer to the screen, as George explained that this was the guy who bought the mattock and tape at the till. Sunglasses shielding his eyes, the man moved uneasily through the doors. His head was quite clearly tilted down towards the floor. Cooper squinted. The footage wasn't fantastic quality, but she could still make out the man's physique: he was of a muscular build and didn't look particularly young. He wore a light pink polo shirt, white joggers and cargo pants with a camouflage pattern. He looked familiar. But within seconds he vanished from view.

Cooper asked where the man had gone next, and George explained that the only other footage he could find was at the counter and the exit. He'd located the first by using the time recorded on the receipt: 12.21 pm. This camera, perched high above a row of cash registers, picked up the customer in question waiting in a queue. Sunglasses now rested on top of his head, he seemed to fidget uncomfortably and constantly swung his head around to look at other customers. When his turn came at the register, he pulled out his wallet and handed over the cash. But as he picked up his purchases from the counter, the angle of the camera blocked the view of him leaving.

Cooper was yet to lay eyes on the mattock and tape. It was imperative that they link the items to this person. But there was one last bit of footage to come.

The mouse clicked as George loaded it up on the screen. The entrance camera popped up once more. The man in the cargo pants walked around the corner and out the door. Just as his figure was fading into the glare of sunlight outside, his left arm moved from the front of his body to his side and there, swinging in his hand, was a metre-long mattock, its heavy head hanging just above the ground.

It was a chilling sight. The mystery shopper was perhaps not quite as anonymous as she'd initially thought. Cooper couldn't be 100 per cent sure at that exact moment, but based on the photograph she'd viewed of the missing person's partner, Michael Atkins, she was fairly confident it was the same man.

Cooper's recognition of him directly connected him to the Bunnings receipt and his boyfriend's abandoned car. It was enough to set off alarm bells.

12 pm

Cooper returned to the station and called a briefing in the training room. Nine officers attended, including the super-intendent of the region and the acting inspector. They formally established Strike Force Bowditch, the operational name for the now ramped-up investigation into the disappearance of Matt Leveson.

Standing front and centre, Cooper talked her colleagues through the series of events that had played out so far: the discovery of Matt Leveson's green Toyota Seca at a known gay beat, the receipt from Bunnings in the boot, and the CCTV footage that seemed to depict the partner of the missing person, Michael Atkins. As the detectives in the room took notes, Cooper explained how Atkins had provided a series of conflicting versions of events to the missing person's mother, Faye Leveson. Another strike against his name.

Cooper designated duties within the team and identified their main priorities: to organise surveillance of Atkins' movements that afternoon, to make a request for the triangulation of Matt Leveson's phone in case there was a chance it was still active, and to make an application for a search warrant for the unit Atkins shared with Leveson. This would need to be executed as soon as possible, and before Atkins arrived home from work. The troops moved out and knuckled down to work.

Alone at last, Cooper heard a knock on the door. An officer, who told her the homicide squad had now been informed of the case. As was the protocol in 2007, the homicide squad provided assistance to local area commands through its on-call team in cases that looked, felt and smelled like a suspicious death. But the leadership of the case would remain with Cooper and her detectives unless it was decided otherwise, based on the complexity of a matter and the level of experience of the local team. Things were really starting to heat up, and the involvement of Homicide was proof of that.

14.

ON HIS TAIL

Thursday 27 September 2007

3.20 pm

Oblivious to the shadows now looming over their son's case, Mark and Faye Leveson sat anxiously in an interview room at Miranda Police Station. It'd been 40 hours since they reported Matt missing and they'd barely heard a thing from the police. Mark had spoken with a detective senior constable the day before to ask if they could go to the media about Matt's disappearance, but the idea was shut down by the male cop. It was apparently far too early for that.

The same officer, an old-school cop in his late 40s, now sat across from them in a cramped, windowless room. He'd chatted with them the whole way down the corridor about how he was 'counting down the days' to his retirement. His idea of small talk was just as off-putting. On the topic of their gay son, he let them know that he wasn't homophobic but there was also no way he'd ever volunteer for duty on Mardi Gras night. He was the first police officer that the Levesons had dealt with on more than a superficial level, and Mark remembers thinking in the interview that he was nothing like what he'd pictured a detective to be. He was carefree, and not particularly probing in his questioning. He told the couple that he only needed to interview Faye, as he believed a mother to be more observant. Mark had shrugged and accepted the point. He figured the police knew what they were doing. Mark was at least allowed to stay in the room as the detective went over Faye's account.

An hour in, the door swung open. A blonde detective walked in and introduced herself as the officer in charge of their son's case. Cooper went through Michael Atkins' differing versions. Faye made it clear that the first time she spoke with him he'd definitely said he'd woken up late Sunday morning, and that Matt was gone, but outside the police station he'd said it was late Sunday afternoon when he'd woken up. Cooper scribbled down the details, thanked the Levesons and breezed back through the door.

At her desk, Cooper called the detective in charge of securing the search warrant for Atkins' premises and asked him to include Faye Leveson's latest information. The discrepancies in Atkins' account would increase her chances of obtaining the warrant.

Cooper made another call, to the Duty Operations Inspector who was processing her triangulation request for Matthew Leveson's phone. The technique allowed police to track a mobile phone's movements by analysing signal data. Concealed inside a mobile device is an operating system that sends pings to local phone towers searching for the strongest or closest signal. The phone towers keep track of the pings and, by obtaining this data, police can narrow down the phone's last known location, and the more towers, the more accurate the location. But the inspector was the bearer of bad news: the triangulation request couldn't be approved because, under section 5287, the matter wasn't 'life or death'.

Cooper baulked. This may well be a life-or-death situation. She sternly explained as much to the inspector, and asked him to try again.

Her phone shrilled with yet another incoming call. The search warrant had been approved. Cooper sighed with relief, and there was more positive news to come: detectives from Parramatta

Police Station had conducted surveillance of Atkins' job site and located his vehicle. They were under strict instructions to tail his every move from that point forward. The moment Cooper had been waiting for had finally arrived. It was time to phone their man.

'Michael Atkins? It's Detective Sergeant Cooper here, from Miranda Police Station.' Silence down the line. 'I need to talk to you about the disappearance of your partner Matthew Leveson.'

Atkins cleared his throat. 'I'm just finishing work at Girraween.'

'Right, where's that?' Cooper asked, racking her brain and making a note of the suburb on her notepad.

'Ah, Penrith . . .'

That didn't sound right to Cooper. 'Okay, what time can you be here?' She listened as he breathed in.

'I'll come straight from work but it may take a while, depends on traffic. Probably over an hour.'

Cooper told Atkins she would expect to see him shortly, and hung up. She called the two detectives who had him under surveillance. They relayed to her that he'd just left Parramatta, and they were tailing him. So Atkins was in Parramatta after all, not exactly close to Penrith, where he'd claimed to be. Why would he lie about something like that? To give himself extra time? Cooper dialled the Duty Operations Inspector once more about their triangulation request. It had gone through, and they had something.

The inspector explained that Matt Leveson's phone was currently switched off, but they were able to trace the last cell tower that it passed through. The ping had occurred at 5.48 pm the day before, Wednesday, near a cell tower on King Georges Road in Beverly Hills, a suburb in Sydney's south-west. Significantly, Cooper thought, it was smack bang in the middle of Atkins' daily commute between his Cronulla home and Parramatta worksite.

5 pm

The door to the interview room burst open once more. Faye Leveson gave a little start in her seat. She'd been midway through wiping her eyes with a tissue, taking a momentary breather from the monotonous questions of the detective senior constable, when the nice female detective once again whisked through the door and took a seat across from her. The expression on Cooper's face was deadly serious. Goosebumps erupted all over Faye's skin, and she felt frozen. Rubbing her arms for warmth, she pleaded with the detective to provide some answers. Anything at all. Had they found her Matty?

Cooper clasped her hands on the table and leaned forward. 'We can tell you this now,' she said sympathetically. 'We didn't want to say anything earlier and potentially taint what you said in your interview.' She paused. The clock on the wall ticked loudly. 'We've located Matt's car.'

Faye gasped, and a cold sweat broke out across her body. 'And what about Matty?'

'His car appears to have been abandoned,' Cooper explained. 'It was found parked and locked at Waratah Oval in Sutherland.'

Mark and Faye turned to face each other, bewildered. Mark was shocked. 'Why on earth would Matt's car be parked at a sporting oval in Sutherland? Were there signs of a struggle? Was there any blood? Any sign of Matt?'

But the police officers refused to give much more detail away. Instead Cooper asked a few more questions of them. 'Do either of you know if Michael Atkins owns a pale pink shirt and cargo pants?'

Mark strained to remember. He wasn't really one to pay attention to another man's fashion choice. But Faye was quick to jump in. 'Yes, I've seen him wear something like that before.'

Cooper nodded and paused before her final question. 'What's your gut feeling, Faye, on what's happened to Matthew?'

Tears welled in Faye's eyes. 'I think Atkins has done something to him.'

A heavy stillness hung over the room as each of them absorbed the implication of Faye's words. Cooper dipped her head and went to speak, but then thought better of it. Instead she pushed her chair back and headed for the door. Just as she was about to open it, she stopped dead in her tracks, turned back towards Faye and said, 'If he has done something, I promise you he won't get away with it.'

6.12 pm

The sky was growing darker by the minute. Anchored boats dinged against the marina. Sitting in an unmarked police car with the windows wound down, Detective Senior Constable Matthew Gentle breathed in the eucalyptus smell of the gum trees around Michael Atkins' unit block. It'd be a peaceful spot, this cul-de-sac in Cronulla, if it weren't for the dozens of trains that passed by on the tracks behind it.

Gentle and his colleague Constable Will Scott took in their surroundings in silence. They'd been sent to this address by Sergeant Cooper to conduct observations in the lead-up to a search warrant, which was due to be executed in a couple of hours. She'd also provided them with the registration number of Michael Atkins' vehicle, AEM 96Z, in case he turned up unexpectedly.

Gentle and Scott had only been parked in front of the unit block a few minutes when a black sports car hummed down the street towards the driveway. As it passed them, Gentle clocked the driver. He was talking on the phone and fitted the description of their man.

Gentle and Scott popped open their doors. They were dressed in plain clothes to avoid drawing attention to themselves during the surveillance task. Scott, who was tall, bald and built like a rugby player, wore a rugby league shirt. Gentle, by contrast, had a full set of hair and was dressed in a red-and-blue T-shirt. The two officers made their way over to Atkins' idling car. Gentle flashed his police badge through the driver's window, and Atkins slowly opened the door. His face turned white.

'I'm Detective Gentle from Miranda Police. Would you mind turning off your car for me?'

Atkins did what he was told and looked up at the two officers.

'Are you Michael?' Gentle asked.

'Yes.'

'Can you step out of the car for me? Just leave it where it is; we'll move it if needed.' Atkins edged out of his seat. He wore a long-sleeved hi-vis work shirt and long navy pants. On one foot he wore a work boot and on the other was a red running shoe, as though he'd been changing his footwear while driving.

'Michael, we're here in relation to the missing person report of Matthew Leveson, and as part of our procedures and investigation we are getting a search warrant to search the unit to assist with that report.'

Atkins managed to murmur an 'Oh'.

Gentle continued, 'I would ask if we can just stay out here for now, as there are other police coming down here shortly and they will speak to you then. Okay?'

Gentle observed Atkins with great interest. He appeared nervous: his hands were shaking by his side and he was starting to sweat. Atkins' eyes appeared to glaze over and his whole body slumped towards the officers.

'Quick!' Gentle yelled to Scott, who instinctively stuck his arms out to stop Atkins from falling flat on his face. Gentle steadied him, his strong hands grasping Atkins' shoulders. He'd almost fainted.

'You okay? Let's just sit you down for a sec, all right?'

Atkins mumbled something about not having eaten all day. As he plonked himself down on the concrete driveway, Gentle fetched some water and handed it to him. The two officers exchanged a puzzled look. After a time, Atkins appeared to come good, bar the profuse sweating. Gentle lowered himself to sit next him as Atkins recovered from the little episode. Gentle attempted some awkward conversation with Atkins, speaking about his job out at Girraween and his relationship with Matthew Leveson. Atkins told Gentle that he hadn't been sleeping because he was so worried about his boyfriend. The truth was, he'd pulled a drug-fuelled all-nighter in Newcastle, then driven straight into work that morning, and the night before last, Tuesday, he'd barely slept a wink after filing the missing person report at midnight. Atkins had been awake for almost 40 hours.

As they sat and talked, more and more police started arriving at the scene. Patrol cars and unmarked detectives' vehicles crowded the cul-de-sac. It wasn't long before they were surrounded.

Eventually a homicide squad detective by the name of Robert Gregory emerged from the growing pack and introduced himself to Atkins. He took over the conversation from Gentle and began to explain to Atkins the importance of him providing assistance to the police in their attempts to locate Matthew. All the while, beads of sweat trickled down Atkins' forehead and blistered on his upper lip.

7 pm
'What? He's at home?!' Cooper yelled down the phone. The audacity of the bloke. He truly wasn't helping himself. 'Whatever you do, don't let him in that unit before we start the search warrant. I'll be there soon.'

Cooper hung up and turned to her newly appointed homicide squad partner, Detective Senior Constable Mathieu Russell. Earlier she'd briefed him and his team leader Robert Gregory. They agreed they had to get going. Cooper grabbed the freshly printed search warrant document.

Like Cooper, Detective Russell was relatively young, at 36. Tall and slim with thick dark hair, he was clean-shaven and wore a crisp white shirt, pressed suit pants and carefully knotted tie. Russell was more junior than Cooper in rank but he worked more complex cases in the homicide squad.

They jumped in a car together, and Cooper's brain raced. She took the passenger seat so she had some time to think. What was Atkins trying to do at the unit? What was he trying to hide? She had to find that mattock. But she was also yet to interview Atkins, and she needed to lock him into a version of events, particularly because his retelling thus far had multiple holes, according to Faye Leveson.

Cooper fumbled through her pockets for a small flashlight and clicked it on. Hovering the torch over the search warrant, she took in the detail. The names of the authorised officers, the address and its description: *unit within blond-brick multi-level unit block, including any associated garage detached sheds, compartment and garbage bins.* The items they were searching for were listed as: *1x white/pink coloured collared polo shirt, 1x white pair of cargo pants, 1x pair of white joggers, 1x mattock (about 1metre in length) and 1x roll of cloth tape.* The next sentence made her heart sink even further. *The police officer has reasonable grounds for believing that those things are connected with the offence of Murder.* They'd have to show this document to Atkins before gaining entry to his unit, and by doing so they'd reveal their hand, namely that the police knew about the mattock and duct tape. But before anything else Cooper knew they needed to lock Atkins into a story.

As the car pulled up outside 1 Tonkin Street, Cooper's hand was already poised on the door handle. She jumped out the moment Russell applied the brake and made a beeline for Sergeant Gregory, who was hovering over Atkins. It was the first time Cooper had laid eyes on Atkins in the flesh, and there was now no doubt in her mind that this was the man in the Bunnings CCTV footage.

Speaking in a low voice – the officers had their backs turned to Atkins – Cooper explained her problem to Gregory. He nodded slowly, acknowledging her every word. He said he'd speak to Atkins. Cooper stepped to the side.

Crouching down next to Atkins, Gregory said calmly, 'Michael, we'd like to get a version off you as to Matthew's last movements. I'd like you to come back and assist us if you can.'

Atkins held Gregory's stare.

'You're an important witness, Michael. We'd like you to come back.'

Atkins nodded and heaved himself up off the ground. He walked with Gregory towards an unmarked Ford sedan, where he was offered the front passenger seat. As Gregory jumped in the driver's side, Cooper climbed in the back, sitting directly behind Atkins. She remained quiet the entire ride back to Miranda Police Station. In the front, Gregory asked Atkins about the last time he'd seen his boyfriend.

Atkins' words came out awkwardly. 'Matt was shitty because we were out at ARQ and he was falling asleep. We had a lie down in our car and he started snoring so I drove home. He was shitty and he wanted to go back to the club.' He paused. 'That was 4 am, and I saw him on Sunday and he was still shitty.' Atkins looked at Gregory. 'I've been crying at work all day . . . It's embarrassing, really.'

Cooper shook her head in disbelief in the back seat. This bloke really was something else.

15.

'I WANT TO TELL YOU, BUT I'M SCARED'

Thursday 27 September 2007

7.15 pm
The fluorescent lights were blinding after they'd stepped in from the darkened car park. Flanked by Sergeant Cooper and Detective Russell, Atkins walked through the back door of Miranda Police Station and straight up to the custody desk. It was a bland room, with lino floors and beige walls. A row of worn plastic seats lined the edges. It smelled like a hospital, a nose-tingling mixture of Pine O Cleen and bleach, though it still felt dirty.

A uniformed police officer stood waiting at the desk. 'Senior Constable Cowin, this is Michael Atkins,' Cooper explained. 'He'll be helping us with some enquiries tonight and needs to be entered into custody voluntarily.'

Cowin rifled through some papers before him and pulled out a blank document. It read *Details of Person at a Police Station Voluntarily*. He spun the paper around to face Atkins. He explained, 'You are here voluntarily at the request of police from Miranda who are investigating missing person Matthew Leveson. You are not under arrest and are free to leave anytime you wish. Do you understand that?'

'Yes.'

'You do not have to say anything if you do not want to.

Anything you say or do may be used in evidence. Do you understand that?'

Atkins responded again in the affirmative.

'If at any time the investigating police decide that you are no longer free to leave, they are required to bring you back to me and tell me what the situation is. Do you understand that?'

Atkins said he did. Cowin witnessed him sign the bottom of the page before doing the same. It was time to get started.

Inside the tiny white-walled interview room were three chairs and a small circular table. Russell directed Atkins to the seat closest to the entrance. 'I'll be back in a minute,' he said, before clanging the door behind him.

Out of earshot, in the hallway outside, Russell and Cooper spoke in hushed voices. Earlier that afternoon they'd run through the plan of attack with Detective Sergeant Gregory. It'd been decided that Atkins should be interviewed as a volunteer, not a suspect. Despite the series of suspicious circumstances that had come to light so far that day, the police really only had a statement from Matthew Leveson's mother and a bunch of inconsistencies to investigate. There was nothing solid at that point to hold against Atkins, and they had nowhere near enough to charge him with anything. But rather than simply take a statement from Atkins, as would generally be the case for other witnesses, they decided an electronically recorded interview was the best way forward.

As officer in charge, Cooper would lead the interview. Russell would mostly observe, but they agreed he should jump in wherever necessary. There was no doubt that their interviewee was nervous. There was a chance that he may even crack under the pressure. If that was ever going to happen, the time was now.

Cooper and Russell took their seats either side of Atkins, and Cooper pressed record on a video camera and audio device. She steadied her nerves with a sharp intake of air. Both Russell and Atkins were attentive as she began the pre-interview spiel, reiterating that Atkins was free to leave the interview at any time. He was there because he'd agreed to help with the investigation.

'Detective Russell and I are making enquiries in relation to a missing person who I believe is your partner . . . Matthew Leveson?' Cooper inflected up, indicating Atkins should respond.

'That's correct.'

Cooper cleared her throat. 'All right, do you agree that on Tuesday night you attended Sutherland Police Station with Matthew's mum and dad?'

'Yep.' Atkins nodded.

'Can you just tell me what that was in relation to?'

'Um, reporting Matthew as a missing perth-on . . . um, person,' he stumbled.

'Can you tell me how that came about?' Cooper asked sweetly.

Atkins' eyes darted between Russell and Cooper as though he was watching a game of tennis. 'I think we were all just worried that we hadn't seen him for a couple of days, and it'd gotten serious because he hadn't gone to work. So we were getting worried about him.' Atkins paused and watched as Cooper opened a folder on the table. 'So . . . we thought we should report him as a missing person so we could . . . find him.'

'Yep, okay.' Cooper looked up from her folder. 'Can you just go over the circumstances that led up to him being missing?'

Atkins looked at her blankly. 'On?'

'Well, you reported him missing on Tuesday afternoon?'

'Yep, yep.'

'Prior to that, obviously there's been circumstances that have . . . made you feel like that, so can you just go through them for me?'

'About like on Saturday night, the last time I saw him or whatever?'

'Yep.' Cooper looked at him. 'Whatever led to you ending up at the police station on Tuesday night.'

Atkins looked confused. It was going to be a very long interview. Two hours in total, as it would turn out. 'I'll just talk
about . . . Saturday night, what happened?' Atkins queried again.

Cooper, fed up, spoke with a sudden edge to her voice. 'Yeah,
you can start on Saturday night if you like. I understand you
went out with him on Saturday night? Is that correct?'

'So would you like to start with his parents or whatever,
or . . .'

Russell froze midway through turning a page. Cooper's
eyebrows shot up. Atkins clearly wasn't the sharpest tool in the
shed. 'Yeah, no . . .' she said.

'Sorry.' Atkins' face broke out in a fleeting grin, teeth flashing,
before he recovered and morphed back into serious mode.

'I don't want you to feel nervous, okay?' Cooper held her
hand out, a peace offering of sorts.

Atkins backtracked. 'No, no, I just wanted to know which
part you wanted me to start at?'

Cooper again explained how she'd like him to tell her how
he'd come to report Matthew missing. Atkins nodded, scratched
his head and began. 'We normally go out Saturday night, like
every Saturday night to a nightclub in the city called ARQ . . . I
don't know, we got there about eleven or twelve.'

'Yeah?' Cooper encouraged him to keep going.

'We were just there as, as normal and, yeah, Matt was falling
asleep . . . so we went outside to get some air, we went to the
car and sat in the car for a little while, and Matt fell asleep . . .'

'Mmm-hmm.'

Atkins' full account of the remainder of the weekend, in his
words, was as follows:

I drove him home and, as we're driving home, he . . . woke up
and he got really shitty, and he just said, 'I want to go back.'
I said, 'No, no, you've been falling asleep and you're snoring
your head off, and etcetera, I think it's probably time that we
go home.' And he just got really, you know, just because he

wanted to go back, so I was just like, no, we're going home, this is ridiculous, you know, you're falling asleep, you know, it's time to sort of, you know, go home . . . to get some sleep.

And then Sunday was like fairly normal, and then we sort of came home and then we watched [Australian] Idol on TV and then, umm, I . . . fell . . . asleep on the lounge, sort of watching TV. Woke up a little while later and he wasn't home. So I sent him a text and said, you know, 'Where are you', or whatever. And I didn't really worry about it too much because he doesn't work on Mondays. And he's got, you know, a group of friends that he's, you know, goes out with.

Cooper and Russell scribbled away furiously. Their lack of eye contact seemed to fluster Atkins, whose train of thought was constantly derailed. He rambled his way through a description of how he wasn't too worried, because Matt was a confident guy who had gone out clubbing on previous Sundays without him. Arms folded loosely, he explained how he became concerned on Tuesday morning when Matt didn't turn up for work. That was when he and the Levesons had decided to go to the police.

Cooper maintained an airy tone to her voice as she asked Atkins about his relationship with Matt. Atkins told her the basics: how they'd met over the internet and then in person about 18 months ago, before they started dating. Atkins told the officers that he'd identified as straight for most of his life, until about four or five years previously. His demeanour shifted as he rattled off the details of how he came to acknowledge his own 'gayness'. The topic of himself and his sexuality was safe, familiar ground. He knew that story inside out, and there was nothing he could be tripped up on here. Cooper moved through more safe topics, asking Atkins about his work, his income and the couple's living arrangements. The questions were easy, requiring little thought, and Atkins started to relax. He unfolded his arms and sat with one knee casually propped up on the other.

Cooper checked her notes. 'How would you describe your relationship with Matthew?'

Atkins' forehead crinkled. 'Close.' A scratch of the nose.

'Close?'

'Yeah.'

Holding his stare, Cooper asked, 'Was it a good relationship? Did you fight often?'

'No, we didn't sort of . . . fight often at all . . . We were, like, really close you know, it's . . . sort of like now I've got to realise, you know, how much I sort of, like, missing him.'

Russell looked up from his comprehensive note-taking, and looked back down again. Atkins was already using the past tense when it came to speaking about Matthew. We *were* close. We *didn't* fight.

'We got on really well,' Atkins finished.

Cooper asked about the time Matthew had gone missing the year before, in August 2006. Atkins said he didn't know the details, except that the disappearance had something to do with Faye Leveson. 'He sort of didn't get on well with his mother.' Atkins leaned in towards Cooper. 'Doesn't still sort of get on well with his mother . . . He says she's a control freak.'

Cooper circled back to the couple's relationship. 'Do you always know where he is, what's your relationship like – phone messages, do you see each other every day?'

'Yeah, usually.' Atkins rubbed his eyes. 'In saying that, like, he has sort of been like a bit distant lately.'

'Yeah? Since when?'

'Oh, about a month ago . . . I know he has had some sort of issue with depression before.'

And there it was, Atkins' attempt to plant the seed of a defence. Matt had depression, he'd been more distant of late. Perhaps he'd run off? Or worse.

'Okay, so when you say he's been different in the last month – how?'

'Umm.' Atkins licked his top lip. 'How do you describe it?'

His face erupted into an unexpected smile, eyes lined with crow's-feet and straight white teeth peeking out from behind his thin lips. Cooper, unsmiling, held his stare. Atkins' smile melted from his face. 'This probably isn't the right word but, umm, I would say he's been a bit more homely even.'

Cooper and Russell allowed a silence to brew. Atkins filled the space with a sudden admission that Matt had become jealous. 'Will his parents hear this . . . the interview?'

Cooper waved away the concern. 'They're not going to hear anything at this point of time, we're just trying to find him . . . I want you to be as honest . . .'

'Yep.' Atkins folded his arms tightly across his chest.

'Our concern here is Matthew and his safety, so anything you can tell us, obviously it's going to help us to find him.'

'Yeah.'

'So I hope you can be as honest and frank with us as you can be?'

Atkins rubbed his hands together. 'We sort of, like, had a threesome with a friend . . . You know, it was [Matt's] idea, and after that he just got really jealous . . . It was . . . you know, [the other guy] is like a good friend to both of us.'

Cooper nodded, even though she had no idea where this was heading.

'Matt wanted to do it, not myself. I'm really not into that, and I say to him . . . "You'll just open up a whole can of jealousy" . . . sort of thing.'

Atkins was on a roll, casting himself as the innocent bystander, the reluctant party, to Matt Leveson's threesome desires.

The interview by this point had been going for almost 30 minutes. So far Cooper had covered some of the basics, but there was much more to go. Atkins was attempting to appear helpful when he was actually being evasive on the important topics. It was unhelpful and suspicious behaviour from a man who should be doing everything he could to find his missing boyfriend.

'Does Matthew have any enemies or any problems: gambling, alcohol, drugs, anything like that that Matthew might have?'

Atkins hesitated and flicked a conflicted look at Russell. 'I just don't want to get him into trouble . . .'

'He's not going to get into trouble. We're trying to find him, okay? So if he's got a gambling problem, there might be people after him for money. If he's got a drug problem, he might have gone on a bender, you know – maybe we should widen the search and check hospitals.'

'Yep, yep, yep.'

'If you tell me he takes drugs, I'm not going to go out there when we find him and arrest him for taking drugs, if that's what you're worried about?'

'Yeah, no, like he does take drugs a lot . . . Well, when we go out.'

'What drugs are we talking about?'

'Usually just ecstasy and G . . . It's . . . why I think like Matt's been a bit more quiet because he's sort of . . . using a bit more.'

Atkins had Cooper and Russell's full attention. They paused their note-taking. 'Okay, so tell me about his using . . . like, how many would he take?' Cooper asked.

'He wouldn't really tell me.' Atkins' fingers squirmed over the table. He started rubbing his hand over the microphone in front of him.

'That's actually the microphone,' Cooper pointed out. 'Sorry – if you rub that it's going to come across all scratchy.' Atkins laughed and tucked his hands towards his body.

'Sorry!' He smiled, a moment of relief from all the tension in the room, before continuing. 'I used to say to him . . . like, "Just tell me how much you've had", because I said like if we end up at St Vincent's, I just want to be able to say to them . . . you know, you've had X amount or whatever . . .' Atkins claimed he had tried to stop Matt from taking drugs, while he himself only 'sometimes' took drugs.

Cooper asked Atkins about Saturday night. They'd had Thai for dinner, watched TV, got ready and had a rest before heading out.

'What were you wearing on Saturday night?'

Atkins squinted through one eye as he tried to recall. 'Blue jeans . . . light blue jeans . . . no, umm let me think, darkish jeans, not a blue but a dark.' He face screwed up into a yawn. 'Pardon me, sorry,' he said, his voice muffled through his hand. 'And a light blue singlet and some sort of white top.'

'A white top over the top of the singlet?'

'No, no, sorry it was . . . I think it was a like a white-coloured shirt, Industrie shirt.'

Russell noted down his evasive description. Police would later discover he'd in fact worn a black T-shirt.

'And what about Matthew?'

'I think he had some Industrie shorts on . . . and a singlet.'

'What colour singlet?'

'I think black.'

'And what colour were the shorts?'

'Like camo . . . you know the two-tone . . . sort of like a military sort of pattern.'

Cooper continued her detailed questioning. Atkins stifled yawn after yawn.

'Pardon me, I haven't been sleeping, I haven't been eating. Sorry.' He repeated his version of events. Matt had driven his car into ARQ that night, and after paying the cover charge they'd dropped into the Alexandria home of their friends Jack Smith and Sally White for a glass of wine. They parked Matt's car around the corner from the club in a little side street. Inside ARQ, they drank Smirnoff double-black vodkas from the bar and took ecstasy pills. Atkins had one at midnight and, at about 1 am, Matt took his. They socialised and danced with their friends.

Atkins stopped his story. 'Can I take my jumper off? It's getting hot now.' He pulled the fleece over his head, getting stuck momentarily inside as he unravelled his arms from the sleeves. Cooper and Russell watched Atkins as he spent another 30 seconds folding it up neatly in his lap. 'It's gotten hot in the room now,' he repeated. Cooper and Russell remained silent. They briefly caught each other's eye, then looked away.

'How did you come to leave the club that night?' Cooper asked.

'Matt was, like, falling asleep.'

'Where was he when he was falling asleep?'

'I think, like, upstairs on the balcony,' Atkins proffered. 'It was . . . you know, you see him walking around and he was, like, getting dozy.'

Atkins said Matt was drug-affected. He told his boyfriend they should get some air. They walked to the car and Matt fell asleep in the passenger's seat. Atkins started driving them home, and part of the way through the trip, at about 4 am, Matt woke up. He wasn't happy. He told Atkins he wanted to go back to the club. But Atkins insisted that they go home because Matt needed to sleep. When they arrived at the unit, Matt was angry and started talking about going out again on Sunday night. Atkins had a shower and sat down in the lounge. It was around 5 am by that point. The effects of the drugs on Matt seemed to have worn off when they both went to bed.

'And what happened on Sunday?' Cooper asked. 'What time did you wake up?'

'In the afternoon sometime, about two o'clock or something, two or three . . . We sort of just had . . . a lazy Sunday afternoon.'

'Did you wake up together?'

'Yeah, pretty much, I think.'

According to Atkins' statement, they spent the day hanging around the unit. He admitted to leaving once or twice, but only to go for a walk to the Cronulla mall around 4 or 5 pm, to get some air. Cooper's brain ticked over. There it was, Atkins' first denial of going to Bunnings. The lie had left his lips with ease.

Atkins didn't know it yet, but he'd just locked himself into a story they could prove was partly false.

'Okay, so from the time you went to sleep at five o'clock to the time you woke up at two, obviously you were there the whole time?'

'Yep.'

'And was the first time you left the unit about five o'clock on Sunday?'

'Yeah, I think so.'

'To go for a walk down the mall?'

'Yeah.'

'What was Matt's demeanour like on Sunday?'

Atkins wriggled in his chair. 'He was much better, yeah, like he wasn't happy but like he was okay. Like he wasn't . . . yelling or screaming, or . . .'

Cooper combed through the details of Matt's plans for that Sunday night. Atkins said Matt had spoken about going out with his friends Luke and Paul. After a protein shake for dinner, Atkins had fallen asleep on the lounge after watching *Idol* and bit of *Rove* on TV.

'Matthew was there?'

'Yep.'

But Atkins claimed by the time he'd woken up from his couch slumber at about 1 or 2 am, Matt was gone. He sent his boyfriend a text message. But he wasn't too worried; he assumed Matt had gone out with Luke and Paul, as planned.

The version of events was wildly different from what Atkins had told Faye and Mark Leveson only yesterday. Cooper needed to think on her feet. 'So, the last time you saw him would've been halfway through *Rove* on Sunday night?'

'Yeah.'

'Did you try and ring him, or . . .?' Atkins told her that he did. Another lie. As the police would later discover in phone records, the first time Atkins tried calling Matt was just prior to this police interview, as he had been driving home that afternoon.

As the interview approached the one-hour mark, it was becoming crystal clear that Atkins was not behaving like a concerned partner. Looking across at Detective Russell, Cooper asked if he had anything to add at that point. Atkins turned to Russell, who said they would now just go over everything Atkins had told them.

Russell assembled his notes and started right back at the beginning. He took Atkins through his version of events in meticulous detail, from driving Matt home to what time *Idol* was on TV on Sunday night.

'Who were the performers on that night?' Russell asked. 'Do you know what was on *Rove*?'

Atkins gave vague answers throughout the cross-examination. Russell took an interest in the threesome Atkins had described. 'Did that present any tension in the relationship?'

'Not really,' Atkins responded lightheartedly. 'We didn't really like do much, the whole full-on having sex thing, it was just, you know . . . How do you describe it?' He gave a little laugh. 'A just-get-naked sort of thing.' He leaned his head into the palm of his hand. 'It wasn't too bad . . . probably, you know, not tension, it just like brings up issues for everybody.' Atkins looked from Russell to Cooper and back to Russell, looking for support on the topic. 'Because Matt had a little bit of trouble with his self-esteem. Like most young gay guys have self-esteem issues because everybody you know wants to be so beautiful and yadda yadda.'

A firm knock interrupted the interview. A shadowy face peered in through the tiny window of the door. They decided to stop things there for now.

'I think so, yeah.' Russell checked his wristwatch. 'The time is 8.37 pm.'

The tape was stopped.

While Cooper stayed in the room, Russell was met by his superiors outside. They led him to a private room next door, where they'd been watching the interview from. What had they learned in over an hour? Not an awful lot, in the scheme of things. Cooper and Russell were yet to ask Atkins about Matthew's abandoned car. Atkins still had no idea the police knew about his Bunnings purchases. Gregory offered some words of encouragement.

Russell returned to the interview room and handed Atkins a styrofoam cup filled with water. Russell turned the camera back on and launched straight back in. He demanded exhaustive detail about Matt's car and the last time Atkins had seen it.

'When you state that Sunday you just had a lazy afternoon, you didn't go anywhere, did you use your vehicle at all?'

Atkins thought the question over. 'I can't remember . . . . Matt might have.' He shrugged. 'Because he likes to drive my car.'

'Did you notice, when you went to the mall, where your vehicle was, or where Matt's vehicle was?'

Atkins assumed Matt's was on the street, and his was parked underneath the building in a shared garage space.

'What were you wearing when you went out on Sunday?'

'I think some . . . long cargo pants . . . and a polo shirt, like a Cotton On one I think.' He paused and looked at Russell before repeating, 'I think.'

It was their first gotcha moment. Atkins had just perfectly described what he wore to Bunnings on Sunday. He further confirmed his shirt was a light lilac colour and his shoes were white leather lace-ups. Atkins had played into their hands. It was time to ramp things up.

The detective lay another trap, quizzing Atkins about his knowledge of the local area, in particular his familiarity with Waratah Oval in Sutherland. Atkins knew it, but not by name. Cooper nodded, directing Russell to go ahead with one of two bombshells they planned on dropping.

'Well, Michael, we just wish to inform you that earlier today we located a green Toyota Corolla [Seca], which we understand is Matthew's car.'

Atkins sat frozen in place.

'Do you understand that?'

'Yep.'

'And that car was found at Waratah Oval in Sutherland. Is there anything you can say about that?'

Atkins stared at Russell. 'Mmm, don't think so.'

'Is there anything that comes to mind when we tell you that we've located his car at Waratah Oval?'

Atkins looked down at his hands. 'Not really.' His thumb picked at the skin on another finger.

'I've become aware that Waratah Oval is a meeting point of some regard for the gay community . . .'

Atkins seemed to relax. Perhaps the police weren't zoning in on him after all. 'I've heard of that.'

'So when I say, "A gay meeting point in Sutherland", you're aware of that but just not the name – is that correct?'

'Yep.'

'Have you been to that gay meeting point before?'

'No . . . I don't go to beats.' He looked at the two officers. 'It's . . . awful in the gay community . . . It's one thing that I've sort of never done.'

Cooper asked him to describe what a beat was. He told her it was a common name for a public meeting place where people, usually closeted men, go to have random sex.

Back on safe ground, Atkins continued his line about how he didn't like what beats showed about the whole gay community, 'the randomness' of sex. He explained to Cooper and Russell that gay people were very open with their sexuality, and that was why he never liked the idea of meeting randomly and having sex. 'I think it's just awful, that's why I sort of much prefer to be in a relationship.'

Another lie. As they would discover, Atkins was a serial cheater, and he thrived on the randomness and spontaneity of sexual encounters with a revolving door of unfamiliar men.

'Now, Michael, just to let you know, we're conducting investigations in regards to his car.' Russell paused. 'Obviously we've got concerns that [Matthew is] missing and we've conducted some examinations in that vehicle. One thing that was located in the vehicle is a receipt for a purchase at Bunnings Warehouse at Taren Point. Can you offer any explanation as to that receipt?'

Shaking his head stiffly, Atkins replied, 'Um no, I don't think so.'

'Has Matt given you any indication that he would or has attended Bunnings Warehouse?'

'No.'

'The receipt is for a purchase of some items about 12.21 on Sunday afternoon. Can you offer any explanation as to why a receipt for the sale of items from Bunnings at Taren Point would be in Matt's car?'

'No . . . no.'

'No?'

'Nah.' A quick shake of the head.

'We've made enquiries in relation to that receipt and it details the purchase of two items, one being a mattock or a pick . . .' Russell gestured a hammering motion with his hand. 'Do you understand what I say in regards to a pick?'

'Yep.'

'A digging implement. And the second is for a roll of duct tape or gaffer tape. Are you aware of that? You know what I'm talking about when I describe those items?'

'I think so, yep.'

'Is there any reason why those items would need to be required by Matt or by anyone else?'

'Don't know.'

Russell stared him down. 'Did you purchase those items?'

'No.'

'In fairness to you,' Russell said, 'I wish to inform you that we've been to Bunnings Warehouse, we've conducted enquiries there and we've reviewed CCTV footage which monitors and records the sale of items over the cashiers there, and also records persons seen entering and leaving Bunnings Warehouse. Do you understand that?'

'Yep.'

Cooper sat with a hand over her mouth, eyes focused on Russell as he spoke. This was the moment they'd been building up to.

'It's our belief that about twelve-twenty on Sunday afternoon that . . . you went to Bunnings Warehouse and you were the person who purchased that pick and the gaffer tape. Is there anything you wish to say about that?'

Atkins looked away before replying, 'Ahh, don't think it was me.'

Silence. The tension in the room was palpable.

'Who do you think it could be?'

'I don't know.'

'Are you maintaining that the only place that you went to on Sunday was a walk through the mall?'

'I think so, yeah.'

Atkins reached for his cup of water, glugged down the remaining drops.

'Is there any person that would say that you went to Bunnings . . . or didn't go to Bunnings on Sunday?' Russell was running out of ideas. The guy wasn't budging a bit from his poorly constructed story. The detective decided to reveal that they had in fact viewed the CCTV footage in which the person who bought the mattock was wearing camouflage-style cargo pants, similar to what Atkins had just described to him as what he was wearing on Sunday.

'Can you offer any explanation as to that?'

'No.'

Surely even Atkins must have realised by this point that the two officers were seeing straight through his lies. Either he felt confident he could still outsmart them, or he didn't understand how bad he looked.

Russell pushed on. 'How does it make you feel knowing that

in Matt's car is a receipt for this purchase from Bunnings, and that we're telling you that the person who looks like you is in the footage at Bunnings warehouse purchasing the pick and a role of gaffer tape when Matt, at this moment, is missing?'

'Ah, surprised.'

'Do you want to elaborate on that at all?'

'Mmm, no.'

'How do you feel about our belief that it's you that made that purchase?'

'Surprised,' Atkins repeated.

'Do you wish to say anything further about that?'

'Nuh.'

'Do you wish to view the footage from Bunnings?'

Atkins raised his eyebrows. This time he was surprised. 'Oh yeah, if you like?'

Confused by his answer, Russell clarified, 'Do you wish to?'

Atkins hesitated, a blank look on his face. 'Neither . . . I suppose.'

Russell tried to understand what Atkins was trying to say. 'You're welcome to view the footage. You're not obliged to say or do anything in regards to watching that footage, but whatever you say or do when watching that footage will be recorded and may be used in evidence. Do you understand that?'

'Yes.'

'Okay . . . Are you prepared to watch that footage?'

'Ah, no.' Finally, a straight answer.

Russell gave it one last crack. 'Michael, are you in any way connected with the disappearance of Matt Leveson?'

'No.'

'Did you purchase a pick and gaffer tape from Bunnings about twelve-twenty on Sunday afternoon?'

'No . . . I don't think so.'

Russell decided to give Atkins an opportunity to come clean. 'Is it possible that Matt suffered an adverse reaction to drugs or otherwise as a result of you and him going out . . . and something has happened to him that you don't wish to disclose with us?' Russell paused for effect. 'Or that you're afraid to tell us about?'

'No . . . I'm not sure.'

'Is there anything else that you wish to say in regards to us locating Matt's car?'

'No . . . I don't think so.'

'Are you sure there's nothing you want to tell us?' Cooper said.

'Yep.'

'You are sure?' she stressed.

'Yep,' Atkins said rather chirpily, perhaps sensing the interview was nearing an end. But Russell at this point explained that the police had a warrant that gave them the authority to search Atkins' unit. They would be looking for items including the mattock and the gaffer tape, plus anything else that might indicate what may have happened to Matthew.

'Do you know where Matt is now?' Cooper asked.

'No.'

'Okay. Done.' She explained that the custody officer would come in shortly to talk with Atkins about the fairness of the conduct of the interview.

'All right, it's twenty past nine by my watch.'

The two detectives left the room. The official interview was finally complete.

Emerging into the hallway outside, Cooper and Russell were met by Detective Sergeant Gregory. They spoke quickly and quietly about the content of their interview with Atkins and his lies. They were under no illusions that he knew far more than he was telling them. With the tape now switched off, providing a less intimidating environment for Atkins, Gregory decided to enter the room himself with Cooper and Russell in tow.

He addressed Atkins in a no-frills sort of way. 'Michael,' he said, 'I have serious concerns for the welfare of Matthew

Leveson. I am aware of the version you have supplied the detectives and, from my knowledge of the enquiry, I am of the opinion that you have clearly told untruths.'

Atkins was clearly taken aback. 'I don't know what to say.'

'How about you inform us where Matthew is.' Gregory wasn't mucking around. 'If you care about him as much as you have said you do, you should advise us where Matthew is.'

Atkins was lost for words. 'I don't know what to do. I feel like I'm being intimidated.'

Gregory had heard it all before. 'That is a pretty natural reaction when you have been caught out telling lies to police about the disappearance of your partner, and are seen purchasing a digging implement and duct tape. I would be surprised if a person wasn't intimidated when I am inferring they are involved in the death of their partner.' He paused, let his words sink in. 'Have a serious think about your situation.' With that he turned on his heel and left the room. Russell followed him out. The door slammed shut.

Cooper and Atkins sat quietly after the rather intense moment. She decided to change tack in a last-ditch attempt to glean some truthful answers from Atkins. She spoke gently, and tried to use his silences to her advantage. 'Michael. Tell me what happened to Matt. I know you know.'

Atkins looked up at Cooper, his internal struggle written across his face. He went to speak, but then stopped himself just as the words were about to escape his lips. He looked at his hands, repositioned himself in his seat. Cooper didn't break her stare. She believed she was on the cusp of him telling her what had happened to Matt. 'Michael, please tell me what happened to Matt. He doesn't deserve to be left where he is.'

Atkins finally broke his silence. His words will stay with Cooper forever. 'I want to tell you, but I'm scared what will happen to me if I do.'

16.

THE DRUG DEN

Thursday 27 September 2007

10 pm

Sitting in the back seat of an unmarked police car, Atkins stared blankly out the window. Street lights and traffic whizzed by as they made their way along the spine of the Sutherland Shire's main peninsula, from Miranda to Sutherland.

Sergeant Gregory pulled them into the driveway of Waratah Oval. It was late and the sports fields were shrouded in darkness. Football and soccer practice sessions had long finished. The floodlights were off and the car park deserted. Matt Leveson's vehicle was gone too, towed hours ago for forensic examination.

Gregory had driven there with Atkins' approval. After the post-interview chats, Gregory had suggested that they show him the place where his boyfriend's car had been located, hoping it would to help jog his memory.

Gregory pulled into a parking bay facing the oval, just like Matt's car had been, and yanked on the handbrake. Cooper was seated beside him in the front passenger seat, and Russell was in the back with Atkins. Gregory craned his neck around and said, 'Michael, this is the vicinity of where Matthew's vehicle was located. I want you to indicate where Matthew is.'

'I don't know what to say,' Atkins said.

'Will you tell us where he is?' Gregory pushed.

'Maybe I should speak to a solicitor.' It was the first time Atkins had mentioned the S-word.

'I don't have a problem with that,' Gregory said. 'Is it the case that you don't want to assist us at this location anymore?'

'I don't know what to say.'

'Okay, Michael.' Gregory turned back to face the front. Releasing the handbrake, he said, 'It is late. We will have to return to Cronulla, where a search warrant is going to be executed at your residence.'

The occupants of the car fell silent as Gregory drove towards Tonkin Street.

11.05 pm

The waterside unit block was deathly quiet. Outside the door of unit four, a large congregation of plainclothes police officers surrounded Atkins.

Facing the lens of a switched-on video camera carried by a young detective called Katrina Bullock, Sergeant Cooper explained what police were looking for: a white or pink polo shirt, long cargo pants and a pair of white joggers. This was the outfit captured in the Bunnings CCTV footage, the one Atkins now admitted to wearing on Sunday. But the main items police would be searching for were the mattock and the roll of gaffer tape.

Cooper introduced her police party for the record. There was Bullock behind the camera, and Senior Constable Nicole Gallagher, a blonde woman with a wispy fringe swept across her forehead, staring coolly down the barrel of the camera. Gallagher would be in charge of collecting and filing the exhibits. Standing in the outdoor corridor waiting for the search to commence were Constables Scott and Gentle, the officers Atkins had met earlier in the driveway. They'd be doing the digging around inside. Detective Russell was also present, as well as an independent officer. Then there was Atkins himself.

'Right, if you want to open the door for us,' Cooper directed Atkins. The screen door screeched open then a jangle of keys followed as Atkins turned them in the lock of a solid brown door. Edging inside, he quickly bent down to scoop up his cat, a fluffy white moggy, as it bolted for the gap between his legs. Atkins took the cat to the laundry.

Demanding that Atkins stand against the wall of the living room, Gentle proceeded to clear the unit. He flicked on light switches in each room before checking for any hidden person who may be inside. But there was no one.

'Okay, Mr Atkins, is this your unit?'

'Yes.'

The 1980s-style apartment was tired-looking: beige walls, dark timber doorways and carpeted floors. Every room contained the unit's original fit-out, with outdated cabinets and venetian blinds, and cruddy plastic faucets in the dank bathroom. The spare bedroom overflowed with boxes of knick-knacks, a broken shower door and the couple's ironing board. The kitchen smelled stale, and looked it too.

'If you can just perhaps walk through and indicate which room is which?' Russell requested.

'The lounge room and the dining room,' Atkins said, pointing. It was a fairly large space, but the decor made it feel cramped. A timber dining table was positioned in the furthest corner, next to windows and a door that opened onto a small balcony. In another corner sat a cluttered desk and weathered timber cabinet with dirty sliding doors, crammed with bits and pieces: a model wooden ship, a miniature keg of beer, a dead plant and several framed photographs of Atkins' cat. Each wall was adorned with some sort of picture: a tiny Japanese drawing, a black-and-white print, a painting of moored boats. Hung on the wall to the left of the entrance was a two-by-two-metre poster of *The Vitruvian Man*, Leonardo da Vinci's iconic drawing of a man in two super-imposed positions with his arms and legs spread apart.

'Is this the lounge you said that you fell asleep on?' Russell asked.

'Yes, I did.'

The camera panned around to the middle of the living room, which was entirely taken up by three bright blue couches, a small two-seater and two one-seaters, pushed up against one another. A huge flat-screen television hung on the wall.

'Are any of those items that I read out to you on the warrant . . . are there any of them you'd like to disclose to me now before we start?' Cooper asked Atkins.

'I think the clothes are in the bedroom,' he mumbled.

The search party set off towards the main bedroom, shadowing Atkins. The room had white walls and carpeted floors. The centrepiece was a queen bed, low to the ground and unmade. Dark timber bedside tables were littered with empty Mount Franklin water bottles. The only window in the room was shielded by tightly shut blinds. An IKEA wardrobe was in one corner; a dirty white towel hung over its door. A chest of drawers and mirror stood opposite.

Atkins bent down to the floor and picked up a crumpled pair of cargo pants. Cooper directed him to leave them on the bed.

'I think that's the ones . . . I'm not sure,' Atkins said.

'Are these the pants you had on, on Sunday?'

'Ah, yeah, could have been.'

'Okay, we'll seize those pants.'

'The pink shirt, or the light lilac collared shirt, do you know where that is?' Cooper asked.

'Not off the top of my head.' He swung his head around the room.

'Right, we'll just start searching this room.' She looked up at Scott and Gentle, indicating they should begin.

As he rummaged around under the bed, Gentle came across something peculiar. He held it up for Atkins and Cooper to see.

'What are all these . . . swords?' Cooper asked.

'They're . . . training swords.'

The room fell silent as Gentle and Scott lined up the weapons on the floor. There were at least eight of them, some individually wrapped in cotton and taped together.

'There's no sharp ones there,' Atkins rushed to explain. That much was true. They were mostly bamboo sticks or fixed timber swords used by Atkins in his ninjutsu days.

Next they moved through to the bathroom, and Cooper stopped Atkins outside the door. Something had occurred to her. 'Michael, I'm just wondering. Because, obviously, we're investigating that Matthew's disappeared at this stage . . . If we do find him, he obviously hasn't got any DNA on the system or anything like that.'

Atkins nodded.

'I'm wondering if you'd consent to give us his toothbrush, hairbrush, something like that? That way we've got something to compare it to if we find . . . worst-case scenario . . . if we find a body or something.'

The words didn't seem to faze Michael Atkins. 'Yeah, that's fine.'

Gentle made his way over to the sink and seized a hot pink toothbrush that Atkins confirmed was Matt's. Scott proceeded to examine the rest of the room. The counter was cluttered with Matthew's hair and facial products. A hair dryer hung on the wall. Matt's hair straightener was neatly put away in a drawer. In the wastepaper bin beside the counter were dirty tissues and a bright yellow cardboard container for Minoxidil, an over-the-counter treatment for hair loss.

In the hallway cupboard outside, Gentle pulled down a pile of martial arts uniforms and belts, all of them black. 'Are you a black belt?' he asked Atkins.

'Yeah.' Atkins shrugged.

'You're a black belt in martial arts?' The fact could prove significant. 'What martial arts are you in?'

'Ninjutsu.'

They shifted their focus to the kitchen. 'Is this your meal?' Gentle asked Atkins, indicating a half-eaten plate of congealed food.

'Yes.'

'When did you have that there?'

'Last night.' A lie. Atkins had been eating soft cheese and drinking red wine at Jake McCloy's place in Newcastle.

There was the sound of a door opening behind them, then rummaging, before Constable Scott called out. 'These were located.' He held up a clear plastic bag. 'Pills.'

Cooper moved forward. 'All right, Michael. There's some blue pills that have been located above the oven. Can you tell me what they are?'

'Umm . . .' He thought for a second. 'Ecstasy.'

'Okay,' Cooper said. 'Are they yours?'

'No.'

'Whose are they?'

'They're Matt's.'

Cooper took a moment to remind Atkins of his rights. He wasn't obliged to say anything, and whatever he did say could be used in evidence. 'How long have they been here for?'

'I'm not sure.' He shrugged. 'Umm, a week or two.'

'Have they always been in that position?'

'Usually, yes.'

'Did you know they were there?'

Atkins paused. 'Yes.'

Cooper turned to her colleagues and stated the obvious for the camera recording. 'Right, we'll be seizing them . . . The time is 11.55 pm.'

Gentle called out in the background, 'Also at 11.55 pm, just this Brooks shoe container just found on the floor of the kitchen.' He flipped the shoebox over in his gloved hands. 'Size ten and a half, USA.' He opened the box. 'Also inside is a receipt from Paul's Warehouse, Miranda. The date is twenty-fourth September 2007 at four thirty-one pm.'

Cooper stared at the package in Gentle's hands. She processed the date and time. 'What time was that?'

'At four thirty-one pm on the twenty-fourth September.' Monday afternoon. The day after Matt disappeared, and the day before Atkins reported him missing to the police. Gentle continued reading from the receipt, 'One hundred and nineteen dollars cash tendered.' The shoebox was seized.

'Michael, just in relation to that box, are they the shoes you've got on your feet?' Cooper looked down at Atkins' brand-new shoes.

Atkins said they were. He claimed that he'd finished work at 3 pm on Monday, at the Coca-Cola Amatil factory at Wentworthville.

Clearly Atkins had forgotten the lie he'd told Cooper on the phone that afternoon. 'Do you agree that when I spoke to you on the phone earlier today, you told me you were working at Penrith?'

Atkins stumbled. 'Sorry, no, near . . . The workshop where my company is stationed . . . . Their workshop is at Girraween.'

'Yeah?'

'Which is near Penrith.' It wasn't. Girraween was at least half an hour's drive from Penrith. Little did he know that he'd had the eyes of two detectives on him the entire time. Cooper pondered what his intentions for his lie were.

Gentle called out to Cooper. 'Just got a potential find here, a glass of money . . . cash.'

'Michael, who owns that money?' Cooper asked him.

Atkins explained they were connected to the pills.

'Do you sell them?'

'No . . . I've always . . . That's what we usually fought about, is him doing that.'

There were bundles of cash. Each stack separated by a rubber band. Gentle counted as another officer tallied. 'Twenty, forty, sixty, eighty, one hundred, one-twenty, forty, one-sixty . . .' The counting went on and on. 'Three thousand, seven hundred and fifty-five dollars,' the officer finally announced. Cooper made a note as the cash was placed in an evidence bag.

'Would you care to give me any information on Matthew's drug-dealing?' Cooper asked.

'He'd been doing it for a while.'

'Who to?'

'People at the club we go to. That's why he wanted to go out clubbing on Sunday night . . . to, like, sell more, and I sort of, like, didn't want him to.'

'Was he selling on Saturday when you were out?'

'Um, probably.'

Cooper peered into a cupboard. She turned to face Atkins as she said, 'Michael, during our interview you told me about Matthew taking vials of G.' She pointed. 'Is that G up there in the cupboard?' Inside was a clear plastic bag filled with little soy sauce fish. There were dozens of them.

'Mmm.'

'So all those little fish, are they all containing GHB?'

'Yeah, I think so . . . to my knowledge.'

'We'll be seizing all of them.' The officers scooped up the GHB fish, and a bundle of soy-sauce-filled ones that were yet to be cleaned and refilled. As the evidence was bagged up, Cooper zeroed in on Atkins. 'Now that his, well, his drug-dealing has come out . . . who's his dealer?'

'A guy he knows from the club. Usually Benji.'

'That's his dealer?'

'Yeah.'

'Do you know Benji's last name, or is that a nickname?'

'I'm not sure. I don't know his last name, no . . . Not sure.'

As Cooper kept probing, Gentle and Scott were scouring the kitchen. Every cupboard was pulled apart. There were more drugs stored in a Louis Vuitton pouch, and a 500 ml vodka bottle was filled with GHB. As Atkins stood watching, Cooper circled back to the dodged question of his new shoes. 'Michael, with your shoes that you bought . . . What made you go and buy new shoes on Monday?'

'I just needed – I had the afternoon off and just needed new shoes . . .' His voice tapered off.

'Where are your old shoes?'

'In the laundry, I think. Maybe.'

Gentle's ears pricked up. He'd already thoroughly searched the laundry. 'There were no shoes in the laundry. You said in the laundry here?'

'Yeah, maybe. I'm not sure.'

With the kitchen search completed and the drugs bagged up, Gentle and Scott proceeded onto the unlit balcony. They looked around the tiny space with torches. Two outdoor chairs faced out towards the water view. A gas barbecue was pushed hard against the brick wall. There were a couple of potted plants on the dirty ground. There was no mattock, or any need for one in this 'garden'.

Back inside the unit, in the main room, the camera panned past the timber cabinet. A white iPod and a pair of Dior sunglasses were among the clutter on top. These were two items Matt never left home without. But their importance was not yet known by police.

Squatting down next to the couch, Gentle picked up a black backpack. 'When was the last time this was used?'

'Umm, threw it there, like, on the weekend sometime.'

'The weekend just gone?'

'Yeah.'

'So you were the last person to use it?' he said as he unzipped the bag.

'No, Matt . . .'

'Do you know what's in there?' Gentle riffled through it.

Atkins' voice became defensive as a crowd formed around the backpack. 'I'm not sure, I think it's a blanket.'

Cooper cut in. 'Did you say Matt used it?'

'Yeah.'

'But you used it on the weekend.'

'I didn't use it,' Atkins pressed. 'I just picked it up and moved it there.'

'From where?' Cooper fired.

Atkins looked towards the hallway. He licked his lips before mumbling, 'Umm, the spare room. Or, I can't remember where it was.'

'What makes you think there's a blanket in there?'

'Because I used to take it to work with me, when I did night shift at the big factory, and it used to get cold there.' He said the last time he used it was about a month ago.

'Why would it be in the bag now?' Russell queried.

'Oh, 'cause it was just never taken out.'

A white blanket stuffed into a backpack that sat randomly in the middle of the lounge room was a sticking point for police. So were the other items inside.

'I've got a black plastic bag,' Gentle said as he unzipped another section that contained a large garbage bag. Atkins said he had no idea what it was used for. Also tucked inside was a purple necktie. The police seized the backpack and its entire contents.

Gentle headed over to the coffee table in front of the lounge. Sitting in plain sight was a dark wallet filled with credit cards and ID cards in the name of Matthew Leveson. Another wallet lay next to it. It was one of Matt's prized Louis Vuitton items, the wallet that he never left home without. It wasn't seized by police, but they did pounce on an item which would provide a treasure trove of information. Lying on the floor of the lounge room was Matt's Apple laptop. Russell asked Atkins if he had any objection to them taking it.

'Well, there's nothing on it. Why do you want it for?'

Russell stared him down. 'Do you agree that, in the same circumstances of assisting the location of Matt, that we –'

'I just don't want, like, Matt coming back and then suddenly him being pissed off with . . .'

'Well, if Matt comes back then he can have the computer back.'

'Yeah, but . . . then you've looked through it.'

Russell again explained that the purpose of the search was to help find Matt. The laptop was seized.

With the living room search now complete, the officers did one final sweep of the unit for the missing joggers that Atkins had claimed were in the laundry. They were neither there nor in the bedroom.

Gentle asked, 'Did you throw the shoes out?'

'I didn't think I did.'

'When's your garbage come?' Cooper asked.

'Um, Tuesday.' They were too late.

Cooper and her team moved their search efforts outside, making their way towards the downstairs garage. Torches lit the way down a long ramp to the driveway. The beam landed on a row of five large council bins. Gentle and Scott lifted the red lid of each one. As expected, they were empty. The police followed Atkins in his hi-vis jumper down the driveway and waited as he unlocked the garage door and entered the grimy space.

'Is this all your garage, is it?' Cooper asked, looking around the expansive underground junkyard. There was stuff everywhere. Haphazardly stacked cardboard moving boxes. An old surfboard. Eskies and fold-out chairs. Rolled-up carpets. Garbage bags full of discarded possessions.

'No, it's shared between the units.'

'Do you have an allocated spot that's yours?'

'Where the car is.' Atkins gestured to his black Mazda Eunos parked in a tiny bay near one of the roller doors. Gentle flashed the torch inside the driver's seat door and asked where Atkins' phone was. Atkins said he didn't know.

Cooper indicated the officers should search for it immediately. Detective Bullock, behind the camera, circled around the front of the car to the passenger seat just as Constable Scott pulled out a lilac polo shirt, the one Atkins had worn to Bunnings. The officers decided they'd seize the entire car for forensic analysis. As Scott threw the shirt back inside, he spotted something shiny on the floor. 'There's the phone,' he announced.

Atkins' mobile was lying on the floor of the front passenger seat. Scott bagged it.

The garage door was opened, and Gentle reversed Atkins' car outside. The driveway was too narrow for the tow truck to access. Detective Bullock followed the vehicle out and filmed as it was driven up the steep driveway. Turning the camera back towards the inside of the garage, she flicked it around the space as she waited for her next instructions. The search was almost over. It was nearing 2 am, and all that was left were some formalities.

As Detective Russell spoke with Atkins at the edge of his now empty car space, Bullock panned the camera to the left. Unlike the other spaces, Atkins' neighbouring car spot was largely empty. There was only one item up the back. A big black box about a metre in length, half a metre in width. It appeared to be a bulky set of sound speakers. But its presence didn't seem unusual, considering how many other random objects littered the communal garage. The box certainly didn't grab the attention of any police at that moment. It was only in the months that followed, as the investigation slowly unfolded, that its significance would emerge.

17.
RIGHT TO SILENCE

Friday 28 September 2007

9 am

White knuckles rapped on wood. Atkins heaved himself up off the couch and made his way to the front door. It had been after 3 am when he'd finally collapsed into bed. His unit was an absolute pigsty after the police ripped through it, and he had now had his mobile phone taken away. How was he supposed to live his life?

Atkins opened the door and peered out into the glare of the morning. Two bulky figures stood in the entryway, holding the screen door ajar.

'Morning, Michael.' It was Sergeant Gregory with an officer Atkins didn't recognise who introduced himself as a detective inspector from Miranda Police.

The pair made their way inside. In the living room, Sergeant Gregory turned to Atkins with a stern look on his face. 'Michael, has your situation changed from last night?'

Atkins stood with his arms folded against his chest and left the question hanging.

'Are you willing to tell us where Matthew is?' Gregory tried again.

Atkins looked down at his feet and replied, 'I still don't know what to do.'

The officers exchanged a glance. 'How about you grab the Yellow Pages and find a solicitor,' Gregory said.

After Atkins pulled out the phone book and scribbled down the numbers for several criminal lawyers, Gregory offered him the use of his mobile. Atkins dialled a solicitor by the name of Bruce Honeyman. After speaking briefly with Honeyman and explaining his situation, Atkins handed the phone over to Gregory, who exchanged a few words with the newly appointed lawyer.

By that afternoon, Atkins exercised his right to silence, a deafening silence that would hold for the next nine years.

10.30 pm

With his arms crossed and his stance wide, Mohammed Ashraf surveyed the queue. He had a knack for smelling trouble a mile away. But as a security guard of ARQ he rarely encountered it. Working the door of a gay club was a security guard's dream; almost every person inside was high on ecstasy, and the euphoric, lovey-dovey feeling the drug produced meant they were much more likely to be huggers than fighters. At 40, Ashraf was older than most of the excitable patrons who passed through his doors. But he knew many by name, and even the ones he didn't know, he got along well with.

As he bobbed his head to the bass emanating from the dancefloor and checked a patron's ID, Ashraf spotted a familiar face. It was Michael, one of his regulars. He was alone, which struck Ashraf as unusual because every weekend, without doubt, Michael was always accompanied by his much younger boyfriend Matthew.

'Where's your other half?' he said lightheartedly as Michael came within earshot.

'Let me get a stamp and I will come talk to you.'

Michael paid the cover charge at the desk and returned to the door. He told Ashraf that he and Matt had broken up.

Ashraf couldn't hide his surprise. 'You're kidding, aren't you?' While the security guard didn't know the couple well, he'd observed them together many times now, the most recent occasion being the Saturday night just gone. They appeared to have a strong relationship as they were always together. Matt was a social butterfly and seemed pedantic about his appearance. He'd often ask Ashraf how he looked.

Michael told Ashraf, 'Matt wanted his freedom. So that was it.'

He didn't stay long that night. After about an hour in the club, Ashraf saw Michael exit. As he passed by, Michael said, 'Mate, it's not the same. I have to go.' He seemed sad. It was strange.

It became a whole lot stranger when Ashraf later noticed some posters hanging up around ARQ. Twenty-year-old Matthew Leveson was missing. Ashraf's colleague told him that some of Matt's work colleagues had come into the club earlier that afternoon asking for permission to post them. They urgently wanted to get the word out.

Ashraf's mind boggled. Michael had lied to him.

18.

'WE'RE LOOKING FOR A BODY'

Saturday 29 September 2007

3 pm

The doorbell chimed, its cheerful melody breaking the silence of the Leveson home. Mark walked with Faye towards the front door, his body moving on autopilot while his mind ran riot, from distress to confusion to angst. His 20-year-old son had now been missing for almost a week, four days of which the police investigation had been running. But he and Faye had no idea about what progress, if any, had been made so far. Hopefully this morning's scheduled visit from police would change that.

Mark and Faye swung open the door and were greeted by Sergeant Melissa Cooper, clutching a clipboard, who introduced her homicide squad colleague Sergeant Robert Gregory. His presence didn't alarm the Levesons, as only yesterday they'd been informed that Homicide investigators would be consulting on the case to ensure that no stone was left unturned. It appeared that police were taking Matt's disappearance seriously. But they lost any sense of reassurance after his first words on their front step.

'I have to inform you that we're no longer looking for Matt,' Gregory said. 'We're looking for a body.'

Faye's face turned white. Mark's hand squeezed her shoulder.

'We believe he's been met with foul play,' Gregory said.

The detective's words sank in. Faye's vision blurred, and her knees buckled. Mark, with his arm around his wife's shoulder, grabbed her as she collapsed to the ground. Neither parent could speak.

Their Matty was dead. And the police believed he had been murdered.

11.30 pm

Sitting in his parked car outside Sydney's Fox Studios, Anthony Rogers waited nervously. He was about to try GHB for the first time. He'd heard all about the party drug and its euphoric effects. But at 19 he hadn't yet plucked up the courage to give it a go. Tonight seemed like the right occasion. He felt safe. He was in the presence of an older guy he'd known for about two years. His name was Michael Atkins.

They'd met when Anthony was just 17 and still at high school. Anthony was the epitome of tall, dark and handsome, and had no problems attracting the attention of other guys. When they first met, he and Atkins had sex a few times before they lost touch, only seeing each other here and there on the club scene. That's what made it so peculiar when Anthony had received a text message from Atkins out of the blue earlier that day. Atkins told him he had a spare ticket to the Sleaze Ball and invited Anthony to come along. The annual festival was the second biggest 'gay night out' of the year. It was a fundraiser of sorts for the biggest – the Sydney Gay and Lesbian Mardi Gras. Held at Moore Park on the grounds of the old Sydney Showground, the Sleaze Ball had been running since 1982, and attracted a crowd of thousands.

In the passenger seat of Anthony's car, Atkins pulled out a little soy sauce fish. He placed it in Anthony's upturned palm and watched as the younger man unscrewed the red lid and squirted the entire contents into his mouth. It tasted foul. Grabbing an opened can of Coke, Anthony washed down the salty aftertaste.

Anthony's heart skipped a beat. Now what? But Atkins didn't wait around to explain. He hopped out of the car, eager to get going. Techno music pulsed through the night. They could feel the vibrations through the ground.

Atkins handed Anthony a ticket. He felt strange taking it. There was still something off about the situation. Earlier, at Atkins' unit in Cronulla, Anthony had relentlessly quizzed him about why he had a spare ticket. He knew that Atkins had a boyfriend called Matt. He'd even met the guy one night when they were out clubbing. Atkins had swatted the question away, saying that Matt was going to Sleaze Ball separately, with other friends.

Anthony felt uneasy. If he had a boyfriend, he wouldn't dream of going with another guy to an event. He was concerned the couple might be fighting, and he didn't want to be caught in the middle. Atkins reassured him that he and Matt definitely weren't fighting.

As they made their way through the front gates of the Sleaze Ball, Anthony tried to relax. But within 30 minutes of arriving, he ran to the bathroom to throw up. He had taken too much GHB. He spent the rest of the night in the medical tent.

Sunday 30 September 2007

12.30 am
Luke Kiernan and his boyfriend Paul had just arrived. Neither of them was in a particularly good mood. They'd questioned whether they should even go to the Sleaze Ball at all. It'd been an emotional week as they digested the news that one of their closest friends was missing. For weeks now, Luke and Matt Leveson had been planning their matching outfits for that night's festival.

As Luke and Paul tried to cheer up and enjoy the night, they worked their way through the crowd. There were sweaty, shirt-less men in every direction. Some were dressed in weird and wacky costumes. Others wore very little aside from the glitter or masks on their faces. The energy was electric. As the crowd parted fleetingly, a familiar face caught Luke's eye.

'There's Mike!' he said in surprise, pulling at Paul to follow his lead. The couple wound their way around sweaty bodies and jumped into Atkins' line of sight. He was standing with a group of about five guys aged anywhere between their late teens to mid-20s. Luke and Paul had never seen any of them before.

'Mikey . . .' Luke started. He was lost for words. His mind was racing with questions; most importantly, why on earth was Atkins here? Instead Luke said, 'Are you okay?'

Atkins stared at them both. 'Yes.'

Paul jumped in. 'I tried to call you,' he said, trying to keep his accusatory tone to a minimum. But the truth was that Luke and he were both really worried about Matt. They wanted to be kept in the loop and help however they could.

Atkins told them that he'd lost his phone. He'd come along that night because he felt like getting out of the house. He appeared reluctant to speak with them. At this point Luke and Paul didn't know he'd been claiming Matt had gone out with them on Sunday night.

Unperturbed by Atkins' lack of interest in the subject of Matt, the couple pressed on with their questioning: How was everything going? Was there any news about Matt? Had the police discovered anything?

But Atkins continued to evade their questions, cutting them off and changing the subject before he said a curt goodbye, turned on his heel and walked away.

1 am

Laser lights swept the dancefloor as Nate Patterson jumped in time to the music. He'd been out for hours but the night was young. He'd kicked things off at ARQ, paying the cover charge and getting stamped, then making his way over to the Sleaze Ball.

Skinny, with a lip piercing and dark hair, Nate was 19 and about six feet (1.8 m) tall. His height meant he could peer over the tops of all the bobbing heads, which allowed him to spot his ex-boyfriend Michael Atkins dancing nearby. The pair had been dating up until about a year ago, when Nate had broken things off. He'd suspected Atkins of cheating after finding used condoms on the floor of Atkins' bedroom. Late last year he'd seen Atkins kissing a hot young blond on the dancefloor at ARQ. He'd later learned the guy's name was Matt Leveson.

Nate hadn't seen Atkins in months. He'd basically cut all contact after the cheating revelation. But seeing him now at the Sleaze Ball was weird, not only because it was an encounter with his ex, but also because just an hour ago at ARQ Nate had seen a missing person poster with Matt's photo. He made his way over to Atkins and said he'd heard about Matt, then asked a couple of questions.

Atkins looked shocked. He said he didn't know much yet, and didn't want to talk about it. But he did say he wanted to hang out with Nate a bit.

They pulled their shirts off and started dancing. Before long Atkins pulled out a clear drink bottle with a dark blue liquid inside. He drank some before offering the bottle of GHB to Nate.

Nate declined. They danced some more before Atkins started to sway, and looked as though he was finding it hard to stand up. Atkins leaned in close and said he was staying at a hotel for the weekend.

They were interrupted by Atkins' friend Brendan Arnold, who asked Atkins why he was at Sleaze Ball. Only days ago Brendan had been at Atkins' unit helping him submit photos of Matt to the police. Atkins was severely drug-affected, slurring a response.

Brendan remained serious. He told Atkins that he'd been trying to call him to see what was happening with Matt, but Atkins told him he'd lost his phone. Brendan asked how he'd lost it; Atkins laughed, and fobbed him off by saying it was embarrassing. He walked off with Nate to dance elsewhere.

In the early hours of the morning Brendan spotted the pair again. Atkins was off his head on drugs but Brendan pushed him for his new mobile number. At one point, Atkins moved close and whispered in his ear, 'It's so hard not to jump your bones right now.'

Brendan walked off.

7.30 am

The sun was high in the sky when Atkins called it a night. He left the Sleaze Ball with Anthony Rogers, the young man he'd arrived with. Atkins got behind the wheel and drove them back to his Cronulla unit.

After several hours of groggy sleep in Atkins' queen bed, the one he'd usually shared with Matt, Anthony left and went home. It was another seven days before he found out that Matt Leveson was missing. The revelation shocked Anthony to the core. He felt sick to the stomach. Shaken and confused, he considered contacting Atkins to ask what the hell was going on, but instead he decided to delete his number from his phone. They never spoke again.

6 pm

Hours after the ex-lovers had parted ways outside the Sleaze Ball, Nate Patterson and Atkins met that Sunday night at a hotel in the city. Atkins had booked a 'Superior King' room at The Grace Hotel, a luxury, heritage-listed hotel near the Sydney Harbour and the Opera House. In his online booking enquiry, he'd written: *hello! i was hoping to book in as early as possible. And we would like to park our car! And does this include breakfast thanks very much.* He'd paid $225 for the room the day before, just before Anthony had arrived at his Cronulla unit prior to them going to the city for the Sleaze Ball.

On the tenth floor of the hotel, Atkins had sex with Nate and asked him to stay the night. It was exactly one week since Matt had disappeared.

The following morning, the pair ate breakfast together before Atkins dropped Nate at the train station. Not once did Atkins bring up the subject of his missing partner.

19.
OFF THE CASE

October–December 2007

It was a fleeting mention, a small photograph with a headline that read: *Search for missing man*. Tuesday 2 October marked the first time Matt Leveson's disappearance was made public, but it was hardly treated as big news. Buried on page ten of the local community newspaper, beside a report on a shopkeeper being assaulted and a petty theft, the article read, 'Police are appealing for public assistance to find a Cronulla man who has been missing for more than a week. Relatives said his disappearance was completely out of character.' The brief article described how Matt had been reported missing when he didn't show up for work the previous Tuesday, and made no indication that police were in fact building a case of murder against his boyfriend.

The evidence against Atkins was mounting. Police had now isolated three separate events captured on CCTV that tracked the 44-year-old's movements between Sunday 23 September and Monday 24 September. The most damning, of course, was the footage from Bunnings. But Sergeant Cooper had also secured images depicting Atkins and Matt leaving ARQ together through the front doors in the early hours of the previous Sunday. The time stamp revealed a departure time of 2.11 am.

As Cooper viewed the ARQ footage bit by bit, replaying it over and over again, she observed Matt in the foyer of the club, just inside the doors, before the couple left. He appeared steady on his feet as he pulled on a black singlet and exited into the street. He wore light-coloured shorts and white shoes. Atkins followed closely on his heels; he was wearing dark jeans, a black T-shirt and white joggers. Cooper made a note. These were not the clothes that Atkins had described to police. He claimed he'd worn a white shirt with a singlet underneath. Police would need to obtain another search warrant to see if they could find both Atkins' and Matt's clothes from the night. As the recording continued, the couple could be seen crossing the road and walking out of sight. The last frame appeared to show Matt heading in the direction of his car, but he was some distance out in front of Atkins.

Detectives had also managed to track down CCTV footage from Atkins' Monday afternoon grocery trip to Woolworths, where he had run into Pete Leveson, and from Paul's Warehouse, where Atkins had purchased a pair of new shoes. The fact that his old ones were still missing was of great concern to Cooper: What evidence did they hold? Why did he throw them out? But with his garbage bins emptied, it was looking increasingly unlikely that they'd ever be recovered.

Evidence of Atkins' peculiar behaviour in the week that had passed was also slowly becoming known. Police had received information that he'd turned up to ARQ on the Friday night just gone. He'd also been spotted at a dance festival on Saturday, partying with a new lover. During a canvass of Atkins' unit block, Cooper discovered that a young man had slept over following the Sleaze Ball. She found it hard to believe these were the actions of a man in a committed relationship, who was deeply in love with his missing partner.

More holes in Atkins' story were appearing as police began taking statements from Matt Leveson's family, and friends of the couple. Close friend Luke Kiernan confirmed that he and his boyfriend Paul had had no plans to go out with Matt on the Sunday night. They'd never even discussed it, despite Atkins' claim.

A strong theme was beginning to emerge: Matt had indicated he was unhappy in his relationship with Atkins. After speaking with Kerrieann Waud, Matt's colleague, Cooper learned that Matt had described his older boyfriend as controlling, possessive and jealous. Contrary to what Atkins had claimed during his police interview, Matt was the one who didn't want to have group sex, and he was sick of Atkins' demands for it. Matt had even revealed to Kerrieann, during their last shift together, that he intended to stand up to Atkins.

Further evidence of tension between the couple was discovered as police began trawling through Atkins' mobile phone. In a text message exchange with John Burns, Atkins had asked if he'd heard from Matt.

John had replied: *Is something wrong?*

Atkins' response read: *Been better he not been home since Sunday nite he now a missing person let me know if u hear from him or if u know where he may be. I keep on cryin at work x*

John had sent back: *I hope your okay . . . I'd be really worried to . . . Is it all about this fight . . .*

Atkins asked John how he knew about any such fight, and John replied: *On sat night he sent me messages bout a fight with you.*

The 'fight' was a significant revelation to police. John Burns later told police that he believed the group sex changed Matt's relationship with Atkins. John had personally been put off by Atkins' attempts to pay him more attention afterwards. Of particular interest was Atkins' comment to John: 'If I wasn't with Matt, I'd be with you.'

With Matt's phone still missing, John Burns provided police with his final text exchange with his friend, showing he was the last person to speak with Matt. The messages included his friend's 3.19 am text: *Mike's having a fucken cry. He is taking me home and won't let me stay! Fucken cunt!*

As the police investigation moved into forensic examination mode, Cooper was informed of some intriguing discoveries that had been made. Following the search at Atkins' unit, the seized items were transported to the crime scene department, where officer Ellen Konza photographed each piece of evidence before conducting a number of forensic tests on them.

Konza tested the white hospital blanket covered in large yellow stains, which had been found in the backpack on the floor of Atkins' living room, for blood using Hemastix. The test came back negative. But on the hem of the blanket, Konza spotted a thin red stain approximately 1 mm wide by 120 mm long. She conducted another Hemastix test, which this time returned a positive result. Further analysis suggested the blood was human. Its presence raised more unanswered questions for investigators.

The examination of Atkins' car offered the most important find. Detective Senior Constable Robert Stephens from the crime scene department had meticulously examined the seized vehicle. He had begun his visual inspection of the messy interior by bagging up Atkins' lilac polo shirt, discovered in the car, as well as a pair of underpants, some dirty work boots, a bunch of cable ties and a packet of Nicorette. Rummaging through the driver's door pocket, Stephens had collected chewing gum, receipts and a used condom wrapped in tissue. Atkins' DNA would later be discovered inside it, along with that of an unknown male, not Matt, on the exterior.

As the hours had ticked by, Stephens became aware of an audible alarm sounding intermittently. At first he'd thought the beeping may have been coming from the car, a signal that the door was open or the ignition turned on. But, when the noise started grating on Stephens, he decided to disconnect the battery. To his surprise, the alarm had continued, and he tracked it down to the front passenger seat area. It was only after he peeled back the floor mat to check underneath that he discovered the source of the sound, hidden beneath the carpet. A bright red mobile phone. A new-model Samsung that was turned on. Stephens picked it up in his gloved hand and flipped it over. The display showed dozens of unread text messages. The beeping was the alerts for new messages filtering through. Messages, as it would turn out, coming in thick and fast from concerned friends and family. This was Matt's missing phone.

The unearthing of the victim's phone in Atkins' car was yet another black mark against her suspect. John Burns' evidence confirmed that Matt had been in possession of his phone in the early hours of Sunday 23 September, as he and Atkins were supposedly driving home in the Toyota Seca. Yet the phone had been found in Atkins' black Mazda, hidden out of sight. Each time Atkins had texted his boyfriend, urging him to call or professing his love and concern, the phone had actually been in his possession.

After Cooper's review of all this evidence – which pointed to Atkins' many lies, and his suspicious actions – she strongly believed he was directly involved in the disappearance of his young partner. Cooper was confident they had their man.

But Cooper never saw the case out. Within a week of her being assigned as officer in charge of the investigation, Cooper was taken off the case. Following her promotion to sergeant at Miranda Police Station earlier that year, another officer had appealed her appointment, and in early October he won. Cooper was immediately transferred to another station. Despite having worked the most critical days of the case, she was to have no future involvement. For the Levesons, the detective's sudden departure marked the beginning of their feeling that, as the family of the victim, they were being kept in the dark.

As the weeks rolled by, it wasn't only the lack of communication from police that bothered the Levesons, it was also the lack of respect and compassion shown by one uncaring police officer in particular. From Mark and Faye's point of view, the detective made them feel as though 'it was us and them'. Mark recalls of the time, 'We were no longer on the same side. It was that bad.'

But the police weren't the only ones leaving Mark and Faye out in the cold. The Levesons hadn't seen Michael Atkins since the night they'd all reported Matt missing. Not once had he called them to check in, or to ask how they were holding up. The concerned parents tried contacting him by phone, and even tried visiting him. But each time they buzzed his unit the lights would go off inside. Instead they left letters in Atkins' mailbox asking how he was faring.

Two months after Matt's disappearance, in November 2007, Atkins showed no interest in participating in a vital media conference with police, where the family made an emotional plea to the public for help to find their boy. Sitting beside her husband and sons Pete and Jason, Faye choked back tears as she directed her message down the barrel of the cameras: 'I want my son back. He's a beautiful boy. He wouldn't harm a fly.' As Mark rubbed her back in support, Faye continued, 'Please, if you heard something that night, that morning, please come to the police and tell them.' Police told the media that a reward was available to anyone with information that led to an arrest. It was a measly $1000. No one came forward.

Matt's long-awaited 21st birthday, on 12 December, came and went without a word from Atkins. It was a horrendous milestone for the Levesons. Faye left flowers on Atkins' doorstep as a reminder of the person he too had lost. On her missing son's Myspace page, Faye wrote: *We miss you so much! We can only wonder how much Mike is hurting as I have not heard from him. I hope and pray he is coping better than we are.* The Levesons also set up a Facebook page about Matt's disappearance, and pinned up hundreds of 'Have you seen our son?' posters around the Sutherland Shire and Sydney's gay nightclub area asking for information about Matt's whereabouts. Atkins didn't offer to help.

The truth was that Atkins had more pressing matters on his mind. As police investigations continued, it didn't take long to secure a stack of statements alleging that Atkins was a drug dealer. He – and Matt – had been supplying GHB and ecstasy to his friends and other customers at ARQ for around 12 months prior to Matt's disappearance. So Atkins' claim to police that the cache of drugs seized in his unit during the first search was Matt's was yet another lie. Instead witnesses confirmed that Atkins was dealing both before and after Matt went missing, including at the Sleaze Ball. Police then charged Atkins with the drug offences, and on 18 December he faced court on four counts of supply of a prohibited drug.

During the police interview about the drug charges, Atkins took legal advice and answered 'No comment' to most questions about his drug-dealing. He claimed, 'It was always Matt's little baby . . . He thought it was exciting . . . and he just organised most things.' He could blame his young partner as much as he liked, safe in the knowledge that Matt wasn't coming home to defend his name.

Around this time, a week before Christmas, Mark delivered Atkins a batch of homemade fudge and Faye wrote a Christmas card begging for him to contact them. Atkins never bothered with so much as a thanks.

PART II
GOTCHA

20.
DIGGING FOR MATT

April 2008

Clumps of soil were thrown up into the air. Dried leaf litter flew high. Worms and bugs crawled for their lives. But there was no sparing them as the mattock pulverised the earth.

Mark Leveson grunted with each taxing swing. It was tough work digging in the heat of the day. The chore was made all the more difficult by the distressing thought ramming its way into his mind: *I'm digging for my son.*

It was a task no parent should ever have to perform: searching acres of bushland for the body of their child. But it was the gory mission Mark and Faye Leveson now lived and breathed. Their determination was unwavering. Every weekend since Matt's car had been discovered at Waratah Oval in September 2007, the couple had ventured into countless patches of scrubland, hoping to find a freshly dug bush grave.

As they ploughed, Mark and Faye dared not imagine the horror they'd encounter if they did in fact find their son's grave. How it would feel to actually see Matt's body. To plunge into the soft soil and unearth their own flesh and blood, discarded like a piece of rubbish. It was too much for Faye to bear at times, but her love for her lost son gave her the strength and stomach to push on. Matt had needed her in life, and now he needed her in death. If the police couldn't find him, then the Levesons would themselves.

Behind Mark and Faye's dogged determination to find Matt's body was their certainty that Michael Atkins was involved with their son's disappearance. Their suspicions were all but confirmed in January 2008 when police recruited the parents to play a critical role in gathering key evidence against Atkins. Mark and Faye agreed to visit Atkins at his Cronulla apartment in a bid to befriend him and, with Mark fitted with a covert listening device, they hoped to trip Atkins up.

That summer night, with a body wire taped to his chest, Mark's pulse throbbed in his neck as he banged on the door of Atkins' unit. Faye stood by his side, swallowing hard against the bile rising in her throat.

They'd have been nervous anyway, but to make matters worse, only moments before they'd embarked on the unnerving visit police had informed them for the very first time that Michael Atkins had bought a mattock and duct tape from Bunnings on the day their son disappeared. He'd lied to police and claimed he was never there, but the CCTV footage showed otherwise. Atkins' fingerprints had also been discovered on the receipt found in the boot of Matt's Toyota Seca, linking him directly to the dumped vehicle. These shocking disclosures left the couple paralysed with dread. Despite their tears and Faye's trembling bottom lip, police had urged Mark and Faye to proceed with their planned visit. They reluctantly agreed. Do it for Matt, they told themselves.

After Atkins swung the door open, Mark shook his hand and Faye kissed him on the cheek. They entered the unit behind him, and the first thing Faye noted was how spotless it was. Even though the room was cluttered with mismatched furniture, everything had a place. It was not as Faye had pictured.

Atkins made cups of coffee in the kitchen and tried to talk casually about his cat as the couple cast their eyes around the unfamiliar home. It was simply gut-wrenching for them to be in Atkins' presence, in his home. But as they each took their seats on one of the faded blue couches, it was Faye's chance to implore Atkins to tell the truth. Through tears she pleaded, 'I'm sorry but I just, I need to know, I mean, I carried him . . .'

'Yeah,' Atkins said flatly.

'. . . for nine months.' The desperation in Faye's voice was palpable. 'And we've lost him.'

As Faye wiped tears from her cheeks Mark took over, relaying the story of how they almost lost Matt as a baby seven months into the pregnancy.

'Really,' Atkins said, taking a sip of his coffee.

'I just – I've got to have him back,' Faye said.

'I know . . . Like, I want him back too.' Atkins stared into his mug and scratched his neck. He wiped beads of sweat from his frozen brow with the back of his hand.

It was time to amp things up. Mark went straight for the jugular. 'The police – we don't get much out of them,' he said. His mind jolted into overdrive as he tried to keep his voice level. 'The one thing they have told us so far is that they said on the Sunday . . . That's the day after he went missing, or he went missing that night . . .'

Atkins eyes were glued to the floor. 'Yeah?'

'They said they have got some' – Mark struggled to get the words out, not being a trained cop, and with no clue how to do this properly for the sake of the tape – 'they claim, very, very good video footage of you at the Bunnings buying a mattock and some tape.'

'Mmm.' Atkins' expression was fixed.

'And that's why they're sort of looking at you and pointing fingers.' Mark clasped his hands together and steadied his voice. 'Were you gardening, or what were you doing with that?'

Atkins had his answer ready to go. 'Matt, on the previous weeks, and it's on the balcony still, all of these punnets of a zucchini and packets in there . . .' He gestured outside. 'It's on the balcony.' Atkins shrugged. 'And there's just an old vegetable plot down the other side of the house . . . And that's just why . . . and you can have a look.'

Mark still kicks himself for never having gone outside to check while the opportunity was there. But in that moment, with a body wire stuck to his chest, he couldn't physically rip himself away from Atkins. He still had more questions; most importantly, why had Atkins lied to the police about going to Bunnings to buy the mattock?

'The police said you said you didn't buy it,' Mark pressed.

'I know . . . It was . . . I hadn't slept.' Now it was Atkins' turn to stumble over his words. 'And I didn't . . . The police were just . . . They've said I've said stuff which I never said. And I've had like five police at me just screaming at me literally, literally in the car.' Atkins studied his fingernails, refusing to look them in the eyes. 'Never believe the police like . . . 'cause they just lie.'

'If Matt wanted to do the garden . . . You bought those after he was missing on the Sunday?' Mark asked.

Atkins cut in. 'No, he was still here.'

'He was still here? So did he go with you to Bunnings?'

'No.'

'He just – he just stayed behind?'

'Yeah.'

Mark's head pounded. Atkins had given so many versions of that fateful Sunday that it was hard to keep track of all his lies.

'I thought that you said when you woke up he was gone?'

'That was in the morning 'cause I fell asleep,' Atkins replied.

Faye squeezed her eyes shut. They needed to change tack. This was all going nowhere fast. 'You don't think he OD'd?' she asked, probing as to whether there was any chance Matt had overdosed on recreational drugs.

'No.'

'He didn't OD?'

Mark cut in, 'Was he careful with doses, was he?'

'Yeah.'

Faye said, 'All these things go through your mind. I thought maybe he's OD'd somewhere, and the person that's found him has panicked and thought I'll get rid of him and . . . just try to conceal it all in a blind panic.'

Atkins mumbled his response. 'If it's just, like, ecstasy you don't OD really. It's not like . . . heroin and that sort of stuff.'

'So there's no way he would have OD'd?' Faye asked.

'No.' Atkins was firm.

'So he was here when you went to Bunnings?'

'Mmm.'

'Was he asleep or . . . drug-induced sleep?'

'No, he wasn't drugged,' Atkins said. 'I mean, Matt was usually very good. Like, he was always pretty careful really . . . He'd, you know, tell his friends what to take and how much.'

Faye made one more attempt. 'So you can honestly say that you don't know what happened to him?'

'No, I don't.'

'No?' Mark pushed, softly.

'I'd tell you,' Atkins said, staring at the floor. 'I want him back. He did mean the world to me – everything.'

A tear fell down Faye's cheek. 'He's probably dead some-where,' she said hollowly.

Atkins looked up in surprise. 'Don't say that . . .'

'Not probably,' Mark said more firmly. 'He is. He's dead somewhere.'

'And it's just so hard, every night I go home and I can't sleep,' Faye said through her sobs.

'I know, neither can I.'

'I see his face every single night.'

'I know, so do I.'

The conversation continued for a few more awkward minutes before Mark thanked Atkins for the coffee and they said their goodnights.

Outside, in the car, Mark – with the body wire still attached – spoke with Faye about their impressions of Atkins as they drove to Miranda Police Station to meet with detectives.

Mark, forever the optimist, said, 'Perhaps something out of all that was useful?'

Faye stared out the window. She wasn't feeling well. 'He's got no conscience. I could see it in his eyes,' she said. 'Crocodile tears.'

As they entered the police station, Faye clutched her stomach and ran to the bathroom. She burst into a cubicle, doubled over the toilet and vomited. Her stomach heaved at the thought of playing happy families with the man she believed, with all her being, was responsible for her son's murder.

But she and Mark had played their part exceptionally well. Their traumatic experience proved beyond useful for police. The brave parents had successfully elicited Michael Atkins' first and only admission that he had bought the mattock from Bunnings. Atkins' confession not only provided a gotcha moment for police, but also fuelled Mark and Faye's search for their son's body. Whereas at first they'd needed to find Matt to provide him with a proper burial, they were now pursuing justice as well. Matt's body was vital evidence of the crime. So they found themselves spending every spare moment digging up bushland around Sydney.

In the early days their search efforts were sporadic, as sites were chosen at random. But by early 2008, they became more methodical and forced themselves to think like killers.

'If you're going to dispose of a body,' Mark explains matter-of-factly, all these years later, 'then you want a place where you can park the car off the road and won't be seen. You also need access to the bush from the car.'

But the sheer size of the area where Matt might be buried meant the task was impossible to conquer. Anywhere up to 300 kilometres of Cronulla, and perhaps even further, was within the realm of possibility. The Levesons were never going to find their son without homing in on sites of real probability. They needed a logical plan, a system based on something more solid than a hunch.

Mark, the accountant turned detective, studied the reading on Matt's car odometer. He was armed with the knowledge that Matt pedantically reset his vehicle's odometer every time he refuelled. By obtaining Matt's bank details, he found that his son had filled up his car with petrol on the Tuesday prior to his disappearance. There was no time associated with the bank records, but Mark figured the refuelling took place when Matt was either on his way to work or on his way home.

Mark then made an inventory of the movements of his son's car after that point: the number of trips to and from work, the Saturday-night journey with Atkins to ARQ and the return home to Cronulla. Then there was Atkins' shopping spree at Bunnings on the Sunday and the one-way excursion to Waratah Oval, where Matt's car was located. Mark calculated the number of 'missing kilometres' between the car's use and the reading on the odometer.

'From that, I produced a body disposal timeline,' Mark recalls. Analysing his suspect's known movements, he came to the conclusion that Atkins had buried Matt either late on the night of Sunday 23 September or in the early hours of the following morning.

With his bookkeeping brain kicked into overdrive, Mark used the data from the timeline and unaccounted-for kilometres to highlight a search radius. It was a lot closer to home than they'd originally thought. Matt was almost certainly buried in the Sutherland Shire. Mark and Faye's gut instinct pointed them towards the Royal National Park.

Even then, there were 15,000 hectares of thick forest to search. Mark once again found a logical way to deal with the impossible task: the Levesons downloaded the weather charts from the Bureau of Meteorology, which told them that the night Atkins disposed of Matt had a seven-eighths moon, low cloud cover and no rainfall, with a temperature in the low 20s. It was a good night to be in the bush.

Armed with these details, their obsession intensified. On nights of similar weather conditions, the husband and wife began trawling the bush at 2 am to replicate Atkins' movements, searching for places that seemed the most fitting to dispose of a body. Each eerie reconnaissance was followed by an expedition with a mattock. Often, as Mark sledged into the earth, Faye would cry. Night or day, the bush felt menacing. The national park held secrets it would never give up. They felt alone and hopeless in their quest. But giving up wasn't an option for Mark and Faye.

They were the Levesons. A force to be reckoned with.

21.
CLOSING IN

May 2008

Detective Sergeant Simone Woolbank entered Miranda Police Station less like a breath of fresh air and more like a gale-force wind. Tall and fit, with sleek black hair pulled tightly into a ponytail, Woolbank could command a room without words. She was fierce, but also deeply empathetic towards others.

Woolbank had started her career at the tender age of 21 in Redfern, a gritty inner-city suburb of Sydney. Her passion was working with victims of serious sexual assaults and child abuse. She and one other female detective were the only women in the team. Woolbank quickly learned how to stand up for herself, and if a colleague tested her patience or overstepped the mark they only ever did it once. One time, early in her career, a colleague was spreading a rumour that he'd slept with her. At the pub one night, as he stood with a big group of male colleagues, she marched straight up to him and said, 'So, I hear we've had mind-blowing sex?' He turned red. No one ever tried that on her again.

By the time Woolbank was transferred to Miranda Police Station in early 2008, she was a mum of three young children. She'd worked hard to rise through the ranks to sergeant, but had decided to leave Redfern to work closer to home. Her experience in a grungy city beat plagued by armed robberies, serious assaults and murders had provided her with an impressive track record for reviewing and compiling detailed police briefs for complex court cases. Her new bosses at Miranda immediately handed her the Matthew Leveson case. She was asked to undertake a thorough review.

Despite Atkins' drug arrest providing a small win for police in December 2007, the murder investigation had since stalled. Detectives didn't feel they had enough evidence to charge Atkins, though they had little doubt he was responsible. As Woolbank read the file, the boot of Matt Leveson's car quickly became a focal point of hers. She wasn't only interested in what it had contained – the Bunnings receipt – but, perhaps more critically, what was missing. Months earlier, a senior constable had made an intriguing discovery as she flicked through crime scene photographs of Matt's abandoned vehicle. Nicole Gallagher had noted that there were a number of disconnected coloured wires in the car's boot. They looked as though they ought to be connected to something. Gallagher had called Faye Leveson and asked whether she knew if Matt stored anything in his boot. She had no idea but figured her son Pete would know. A few hours later Gallagher heard back.

Matt had kept a sound system, a subwoofer, in the boot of his car. The boom box had originally been built by Pete for his own vehicle. He'd made it from ten-inch (25-cm) speakers and chipboard, and covered it in grey carpet to match the interior. When Pete had tired of it, his younger brother took it for himself to use in his Toyota Seca. Pete had helped Matt wire it up; the subwoofer took up the entire boot space. But in the photos all that remained was the wiring.

It was a red flag for Woolbank, one of many which helped form her opinion that the investigative channels in the case were far from being exhausted. There was still plenty of detective work to be done.

For the next three months, from May to August 2008, Woolbank and her second-in-charge, Nicole Gallagher, combed through every piece of evidence collected to date. A thorough examination of the internet history on Matt's laptop revealed that on the Sunday afternoon following Atkins' Bunnings trip, there was a Google search made on 'Sleaze Ball', and a visit to the Ticketek website. Atkins had claimed to police that Matt was alive and well in the unit at this time, having a 'lazy Sunday', but Woolbank strongly suspected he was already dead, which made the next discovery even more chilling. Around 4.10 pm that afternoon, someone had trawled a website called Manhunt, an online dating and hook-up site for men who have sex with men.

A thorough examination of Atkins' phone history further revealed a man obsessed with finding sex in the hours and days after his boyfriend disappeared. Alongside Atkins' 'worried' text messages to Matt were his attempts to reignite the spark with ex-lovers or line up dates with men he'd cheated on Matt with during their relationship. On the same day Matt disappeared, Atkins had reached out to a young man who'd still been at high school when Atkins took his virginity during 'aggressive' sex. The boy told police that in May 2007 Atkins had picked him up from school and taken him back to his apartment for 'persistent and demanding' sex. The 17-year-old had felt 'vulnerable' and 'uncomfortable' during the encounter, and never saw Atkins again because he 'didn't feel safe' with the older man. Atkins' text to him on Sunday 23 September had gone unanswered.

As police pored over the records, they found a phone call at 3.11 am on Thursday 27 September from Atkins' mobile to a number registered to a Newcastle resident named Jake McCloy. When Woolbank first contacted Jake, he was a reluctant witness. He told her he was terrified Atkins would track him down if he spoke to police. It took months to secure his trust, but Woolbank finally coaxed him into making a statement that confirmed Atkins had driven to Newcastle for sex on the Wednesday after work, only three days after his boyfriend vanished, and less than 24 hours after making the missing person report to police. These were not the actions of a committed or concerned partner.

A forensic analysis of Matt's phone revealed that Atkins had accessed his voicemails and text messages in the days after he vanished. He'd read the heartbreaking pleas from Faye and Matt's close friends.

Woolbank tasked Gallagher with reviewing every second of footage gathered so far, of Atkins' police interview and the by now multiple search warrant videos, just in case they'd missed anything at all. In a dark room, Woolbank and Gallagher huddled around an old television set watching the first of the three searches. When the tape was almost at the end, they watched as police seized Michael Atkins' car from the garage. As the camera panned from the driveway to the dingy carport, Woolbank's heart leaped into her mouth.

There in plain sight was the missing boom box, resting on the concrete floor of a neighbouring car spot. It had been there the whole time.

The discovery marked a major breakthrough in the case; it was the strongest piece of physical evidence since the Bunnings receipt had been found in the boot of Matt's abandoned car. But those two elements alone weren't enough. Woolbank needed proof that the boom box was in Matt's car the night he and Atkins drove into ARQ. She found it in a new statement from Matt's colleague Kerrieann. She confirmed that the last time she saw Matt, in the car park of NRMA on the evening of Saturday 22 September, he was playing music 'so loud' in his car that 'the bass was vibrating through my body'.

This was the confirmation police had needed. The boom box had been ripped out of Matt's car sometime between him leaving work on Saturday evening at 6 pm and Atkins leaving the receipt from Bunnings in the empty boot.

Woolbank was, by mid-2008, confident she had enough to charge Michael Atkins with murder. She presented her brief of evidence and a detailed timeline of the alleged crime to her bosses. They told her to go get him.

22.

THE ARREST

Tuesday 5 August 2008

A kookaburra chortled to itself high up in a spindly gum tree, calling up the beginnings of a brand new day. A wintry chill pervaded the air. Water lapped gently against moored boats in the Cronulla marina.

Hidden inside his car, Mark Leveson drummed his fingers on the steering wheel. He could barely contain himself. It had been 10 months and 13 days since his middle son had vanished. Now justice was almost within reach.

A convoy of headlights burst into sight, and Mark ducked below the steering wheel. Half a dozen cars passed by and pulled up in the cul-de-sac, then a dozen police marched into the sleepy Cronulla unit block. Mark clenched his fists tight as this long-awaited moment unfolded: the arrest of Michael Atkins.

When Detective Sergeant Woolbank had visited him and Faye at their Bonnet Bay home some days ago, she'd come with the good news that they were going to charge Atkins with murder. Mark's eyes had glistened. Faye wept with relief. For months they'd been banking on that very outcome. Even though the detective had refused to tell them when the arrest would be, 'for operational reasons', Mark wasn't about to deny himself the chance to watch the bastard go down. Every morning since, he'd rolled out of bed at 4 am and staked out Atkins' unit block. It'd taken almost a week but, finally, it was D-Day.

With his window lowered and his ear cocked, Mark heard a firm knock on Atkins' door. 'Open up, police!' Woolbank's strong voice boomed.

Mark quietly opened his door. He wanted to creep closer to the unit block and take a look at Atkins' face, but he resisted the urge and instead leaned against the hood of his car in anticipation.

A TV crew arrived in the street. As the cameraman hauled out his camera and tripod, a reporter climbed out of the vehicle and nodded politely towards Mark. This was the sort of footage news bulletins thrived on. The arrest of an accused murderer.

Moments later, a number of police officers emerged from the building. Woolbank led the way.

The cameraman pounced. Mark strained to see the 'money shot' being chased.

And there Atkins was. Dressed in faded blue jeans and a colourful jumper with a monkey symbol, the hood pulled down over his face, he was handcuffed and flanked by two male officers. As Atkins was guided into the back of a police vehicle, he kept his head tilted towards the ground.

Gotcha.

Detective Woolbank stepped into the front passenger seat. The arrest had gone to plan. Atkins had been home alone, as hoped, and he'd agreed to leave with police quickly and quietly. She found it startling that he'd shown no emotion as she'd read him his rights.

Driving off down Tonkin Street, leaving the media behind, Woolbank glanced up just as the police car levelled with a familiar face.

Mark Leveson. He was leaning on the bonnet of his car with his arms crossed.

Their eyes locked. Woolbank shot Mark a smile. His own grin was already plastered all over his face.

23.
THE TRIAL OF MICHAEL ATKINS

Monday 31 August 2009

Faye Leveson's kitten heels clipped across the concrete pathway. A formidable sandstone building loomed ahead of her. The Darlinghurst Supreme Court, built in the 1880s, was rich with stories from Australia's dark criminal history. Situated in the heart of Sydney's 'gay mecca', the courthouse stood less than 200 metres from where Matt was last seen leaving ARQ.

With each step Faye took, the fear inside her swelled. Sensing her dread, Mark took her hand in his and squeezed it tight, a tiny gesture to let her know they were in this together. Their marriage of 31 years was rock solid. There was nothing magical about why they worked. Like any couple, they'd had their ups and downs: petty arguments, screaming matches, work and money stresses, and health scares. But nothing prepared them for the anguish they'd suffered over the past two years.

Marriages don't always survive the trauma of losing a child, particularly when it's to murder. It's not difficult to understand why when even looking at the other person is a constant reminder of loss. If it's not the intense grief that initially drives couples apart, it's often the coping methods developed over many months or years. A numbness takes hold. The death of Mark and Faye's middle son, his murder, still didn't seem real. As a couple, they'd been tested in ways they never could have anticipated. But they knew that, if not for each other, they'd never get through it.

As the Levesons walked inside courtroom three, they appreciated each other's love more than ever. It was a surreal experience to take their seats on the wooden benches and note the dark timber panelling, the heightened podium for the judge and the row of seats along the side of the room for the impending jury selection.

Shuffling through his files at the bar table was Crown Prosecutor Chris Maxwell. With a traditional wig placed over his silver hair, the Sydney silk wore traditional black robes and jacket along with his jabot, a white collar with two lengths of material hanging down the front. Maxwell, having practised as Queen's Counsel since 1989, was well respected by police and throughout the legal profession. His career had seen him prosecute some of the state's most notorious homicide trials. Perhaps the most twisted murder he had ever encountered involved a gay victim named Stephen Dempsey. In 1994, 34-year-old Dempsey was shot in the heart with a bow and arrow at a gay beat in Narrabeen, before his body was dismembered and kept in a freezer. Maxwell successfully mounted a case against the murderer, Richard Leonard, who was jailed for life.

Dealing with despicable human beings like Leonard was a weekly occurrence for Maxwell. In his line of work, he was constantly confronted with the worst of what humankind was capable of. Maxwell once revealed that he counteracted the negativity by surrounding himself with positive, creative pursuits. In the lead-up to a case, he prepared himself mentally by performing steadfast rituals: baking, playing golf and spending time with his family.

Prior to Michael Atkins' trial, Maxwell had held numerous meetings with Detective Sergeant Woolbank. Together they pored over the evidence, highlighting their strongest pieces. But the most important was still missing: Matt's body. The absence of a body was bound to be a major sticking point for any juror: Where was the proof of murder? But Woolbank was quietly confident. The evidence, albeit circumstantial, was overwhelming.

The decision to prosecute Michael Atkins in the first place was not taken lightly. Just because the family or police wanted the case to be prosecuted was not enough reason for the Office of the Director of Public Prosecutions to storm ahead. But in the trial of Michael Atkins, Maxwell believed there was a reasonable prospect of securing a conviction. The weight of the verdict would rest on the shoulders of the soon-to-be-empanelled jury.

As the first day of Atkins' murder trial swung into action, Detective Woolbank sat beside Mark and Faye Leveson in the public gallery. She watched on as, one by one, prospective jurors were called to stand up in the jury box. Each candidate was brusquely assessed by Maxwell and Atkins' experienced defence barrister, Keith Chapple, SC. Each was afforded three opportunities to challenge or reject the potential jurors they didn't want included. The process seemed harsh but was performed strategically, with little emotion.

In the public gallery, Detective Woolbank was apprehensive as the final 12 were selected. She now recalls, years later, 'I was worried when they were first picked. I didn't feel confident.' I asked her why, but she couldn't quite put her finger on it: 'It was judged on looks alone. I suppose by looking at them, I was worried about their ages – some appeared too old, which perhaps meant they'd be more inclined to be homophobic, and then the very young ones perhaps didn't seem worldly enough.' Woolbank's gut told her that in order to secure a conviction against Atkins, they needed a jury with open minds and life experience. The prosecution was about to present them with a case which involved homosexuality, promiscuity, the party scene and drug usage. But she feared the 12 men and women before her did not appear to be people who were capable of putting their own prejudices aside. But there was nothing to be done. The trial was finally underway.

Justice Peter Hidden explained how the six-week trial would unfold, emphasising the importance of the jurors approaching the case impartially, with an open mind. Atkins sat behind his lawyers at the bar table as Justice Hidden spoke. His hair was neatly combed, and a pair of spectacles was perched on his nose. Despite being on remand, he was not dressed in his usual prison greens as it was deemed prejudicial for the jury to know the accused was being held in custody. His lawyers had organised for some clothing to be brought in, and Atkins wore an ill-fitting suit, blue shirt and a purple tie.

The tie was Matt's tie, Faye realised. She couldn't believe the hide of the man; there he was, up on murder charges and wearing a tie that had belonged to her dead son.

Justice Hidden continued, informing the jury that in a real sense they were 'judges', and at no point were they to speak with or acknowledge anyone inside or immediately outside the court precincts. Even at home, they should keep to themselves. They were warned sternly not even to reveal which case they were serving on.

Justice Hidden concluded his opening address:

In real life, ladies and gentlemen, trials like this are not like American television. It is not a battle broil to the death between prosecutor and defence counsel. There is, in fact, a high degree of cooperation between the accused and the defence, which is very valuable.

When you return on Wednesday, the Crown Prosecutor will open the case to you: that is, he will address you and explain . . . what the case is about, and what it is he sets out to prove. After that, the case will get underway and you will start to hear evidence.

But, as it would turn out, one of the most significant parts of Michael Atkins' murder trial played out in the jury's absence.

24.

WHAT THE JURY DIDN'T KNOW

Wednesday 2 September 2009

'Your objection is to the whole of it?' Justice Hidden clarified.

'The whole document,' defence barrister Keith Chapple confirmed.

It was only the second day of Michael Atkins' murder trial, and already his defence team had sought to expose the flaws of a major piece of evidence in the prosecution's case: the recorded police interview with Atkins from Thursday 27 September 2007.

In the video account, Atkins was asked probing questions by Detective Sergeant Cooper about Matt's disappearance, their relationship, Atkins' movements on the Sunday, his thoughts on Matt's car being found dumped at Waratah Oval and, most importantly, whether he admitted to purchasing a mattock and duct tape from Bunnings. Atkins had denied the shopping spree, despite the CCTV evidence police already possessed. The lie was expected to bolster the prosecution case significantly. But the defence had identified a major flaw in the way Atkins was cautioned by police before the interview.

With the jury excused, so that legal argument could take place in their absence, Chapple explained to Justice Hidden that police had originally planned to execute a search at Atkins' unit on the Thursday afternoon, and the search warrant stated they were looking for a mattock and gaffer tape. However, in her statement, Detective Cooper admitted that disclosing this knowledge to Atkins before they'd had a chance to 'lock him into a story' could prove problematic. She had opted to postpone the search and invited Atkins to the police station, where he was interviewed voluntarily despite, as Chapple was now claiming, by this point effectively being a suspect.

When Justice Hidden asked whether Atkins had been cautioned at the start of the interview, Chapple's response was the clincher that Detective Woolbank had been dreading:

> Yes, but our submission is that it was improper, that he was not told he was being interviewed as a suspect; that the police were entitled to keep information like this to themselves if they wanted to, but for a person to make an informed decision about whether or not to exercise their right to silence, they shouldn't be told that they are being interviewed to assist in locating a missing person when, in fact, they were being interviewed as a suspect.

Chapple explained how police had told Atkins the purpose of the interview was to help them with the investigation, and that it would be electronically recorded to 'save time'. As a result of what the defence was alleging were the false pretences for the interview, Atkins' lawyer was pushing for the entire interview to be thrown out of court on the basis that Atkins was misled by police.

The trial of Michael Atkins had officially entered dangerous territory from the prosecution point of view. With the jury still absent, the judge would run a 'trial within the trial', formally known as a voir dire. The procedure usually takes place when it is necessary to examine an objection or application, often related to the admissibility of evidence, without the jury present. For the prosecution, it was vital that the jury hear the police interview with Atkins, particularly his lies about Bunnings.

The defence called Detective Sergeant Melissa Cooper to the witness box.

*

'What is your full name, rank and station?' Crown Prosecutor Maxwell asked.

'Melissa Anne Cooper. I'm a detective senior sergeant attached to Bankstown.'

'And in the initial stages of this case, you were the officer in charge?'

'Yes, that's correct.'

Cooper responded steadily to a number of scene-setting questions from Maxwell before he launched headfirst into the main issue at stake: 'At any stage during the interview, did you think you had enough to arrest him for the charge of murder?'

'No, not at all.'

This was the easy part. The Crown Prosecutor wasn't trying to trip up Cooper, but to help her argue her case. He too needed that evidence to be admitted by the judge.

'Do you say that, in your mind, he wasn't a suspect at the scene?'

Cooper answered, haltingly:

Yeah, he wasn't – he wasn't a suspect. I had a missing person and a frantic mother . . . who said there were some discrepancies in stories between Mr Atkins and herself, and I had some footage . . . which was, I suppose, suspicious in nature, which could have been explained. I didn't know. At that point I didn't know what I was dealing with. I didn't even know if Mr Leveson was dead. I had a missing person . . . I don't know.

Maxwell took Cooper through her reasons for delaying the search warrant, which she confirmed was a 'strategic decision' in order to allow her time to lock Atkins into a story.

'Really, what I am asking is; at the time that you conducted the interview with him, he was a person voluntarily attending, is that right?'

'Yes,' Cooper said confidently.

'And in your view, at the time you were interviewing him, was he a suspect?'

'There was some suspicion attached to some of the things I had been told and some of the things I had seen him do, but to say he was a suspect, I didn't even know if Mr Leveson was deceased.'

'Was there a time, during the interview, that you perhaps became suspicious?'

'Most definitely,' Cooper replied. It was an honest answer, but perhaps not the one the prosecution wanted to hear. Cooper said the point at which she became suspicious was after Atkins had lied about going to Bunnings.

Then it was time for the cross-examination.

Defence barrister Chapple pounced on Cooper's admission: 'When he was responding to your questions about the Bunnings receipt and you became suspicious of it, did you caution him and tell him you were suspicious?'

Cooper said she didn't think so: 'It was not until then that I thought, okay, my suspicion was really, really heightened. It was, I felt it was, a strange reaction to a question I was asking him if he didn't have anything to hide.'

Chapple pushed. 'If your suspicions were heightened, why didn't you caution him and tell him you were suspicious?'

'I don't know.'

'He was a suspect then, is that your evidence?'

'Once he denied going to Bunnings and didn't want to view the footage, most definitely,' Cooper said.

'So if you didn't caution him and tell him that he was a suspect, why is that so?'

'He wasn't saying anything.' Cooper paused. 'I don't know. I don't know. At the time I didn't – I had already cautioned him at the beginning of the interview.'

That much was true. And it was a fact that the Crown Prosecutor argued strongly in his later submissions to the judge in an attempt to salvage the all-important evidence. Atkins had been cautioned prior to his interview by the custody sergeant, who informed him that 'he didn't need to say anything if he didn't want to' and that 'anything he did say might be used in evidence against him'. He was free to leave the interview at any stage, and he knew that. And Cooper wasn't the only detective to have ever cautioned and interviewed a potential person of interest in this way. She'd even done so under the guidance of experienced homicide detectives. Under cross-examination, she told Chapple that she wouldn't pause an interview to tell someone they are a suspect unless she had firmer evidence, and was of the opinion she was likely to arrest them. At this point, even though she was suspicious of Atkins, her primary concern was still extracting information from him about Matt's whereabouts, and the caution would have been more likely to make him clam up. The defence argued that this was precisely the point; because police didn't disclose to Atkins that he was 'a suspect' in their investigation, he couldn't properly weigh up whether or not to exercise his right to silence.

Cooper's cross-examination and re-examination by the Crown Prosecutor continued for hours before intense legal argument took over and rolled into the next morning. All the while, the jury sat wondering what had become of their murder trial.

Atkins' defence team submitted to the judge that the entire interview should be excluded because Cooper had at the beginning of the interview been suspicious of him and, at the very least, she considered him a suspect by the point in the interview when he denied visiting Bunnings. The prosecution team submitted that the custody sergeant had given Atkins a warning and that, even if the judge did find there was a low level of impropriety on behalf of police, the interview should remain because of its 'very substantial probative value'. But, facing the prospect of losing the entire interview, which would be a disaster for the prosecution case, Maxwell conceded a second position: if His Honour decided that Cooper's level of suspicion increased when Atkins denied going to Bunnings, the judge could simply exclude that section.

Justice Hidden agreed with Maxwell's alternative. The majority of the police interview could be shown to the jury, but arguably not the most compelling part. 'All questions and answers dealing expressly with Bunnings and what was purchased there should be excised,' His Honour declared.

The prosecution case had been severely damaged. There were, of course, other denials of Atkins' and evidence that would point towards his involvement with Matt's disappearance – the audio of Mark and Faye's listening device with Atkins, the discovery of the receipt in the boot of Matt's abandoned car, the ripped out boom box – but nothing quite as compelling as Atkins' bald-face lie to police.

They still had the CCTV footage of Atkins buying a mattock and gaffer tape, they told themselves. There was still a glimmer of hope.

25.

SEX, LIES AND REASONABLE DOUBT

Wednesday 2 September – Monday 12 October 2009
The position of the Crown Prosecutor was blunt and unwavering: Michael Atkins was a murderer. At some point after 3.30 am on Sunday 23 September 2007, Matthew Leveson went missing. The Crown asserted that he was dead, and Atkins had killed him. The killing of Matt Leveson was the consequence of a jealous, controlling man being confronted by a much younger person trying to stand his ground. The Crown claimed that Atkins' response was an intention to cause death.

The Levesons – Mark and Faye, and Pete and Jason – didn't miss a day of the trial in its eight long, drawn-out weeks. Each morning they'd battle through peak-hour traffic from Bonnet Bay to Darlinghurst, only to arrive at court bracing themselves for an onslaught of horror. Mark, who almost never lost his cool, was a complete wreck at times. He was forced to remain outside the courtroom for weeks on end as he waited to be called as a witness. The process was so frustrating and stressful that Faye became genuinely worried for his health.

'He was under so much pressure, we were concerned he might have a heart attack,' Faye recalls. Faye encountered her own battles in the court's corridors. She took a strong dislike to Atkins' barrister Keith Chapple, who would walk past her in the corridor, whistling and chirpily wishing her a nice morning. Perhaps he was just being polite, but to the mother of an alleged murder victim, there was nothing 'nice' about the morning they faced.

Day after day, the jury was presented with evidence about the private lives of the victim and the accused. Michael Atkins stood and nodded each time the 12 men and women entered or exited the room. No one else in the room was required to do so, but it was usual practice for an accused. It was the job of Atkins' jury – their burden, their solemn duty – to decide his fate.

Crown Prosecutor Maxwell's approach throughout the trial was straightforward. He was there to deliver the cold hard facts, and he didn't believe in overegging it. In his opening he told them, 'It is a circumstantial case. There is no evidence from any person to say they saw it happen; no direct evidence.' Including a body. Unlike most other murder trials, where gun or stab wounds, strangulation marks or even blood spatter helped tell a story of how the victim died, there was no such physical evidence available for this jury to decipher. Instead, to find a guilty verdict, they needed to consider the many pieces of circumstantial evidence to form a picture beyond reasonable doubt.

It was all the Crown had to rely on. Only one person in that room knew the truth of how Matt Leveson died, and the jury would never hear from him. Atkins continued to exercise his right to silence throughout the trial. He sat stiffly in his isolated box, listening as the most intimate details of his sexual history, drug-taking and relationship problems were strung out before a bunch of complete strangers.

Through it all, the Levesons sat staring at the back of his head for weeks on end.

The victim was introduced to the jury as a young man full of life, and loved by his family and friends. He lived with the accused, and the couple were regulars on the gay club scene. They both sold prohibited drugs, ecstasy and GHB, which the prosecution couldn't ignore. Atkins' defence suggested Matt's disappearance might have stemmed from his drug dealing. But there was no escaping the fact that Michael Atkins was the last known person to see his boyfriend and hadn't always acted like a committed partner.

The jury watched the contentious police interview, or at least the parts they were allowed to view. They heard how Atkins wasn't sure of the last time he saw his young boyfriend. His varying accounts revealed to be inconsistent against the testimony of key witnesses, including Faye Leveson. He'd initially told her he'd woken 'late Sunday morning' but outside the police station he'd told her and Mark it was 'late Sunday afternoon'. The version he finally settled on during his police interview was 'Sunday evening'. The tape rolled as Atkins explained to Cooper and Russell how, when he woke up in the early hours of Monday, Matt was gone, and he'd assumed that his young partner had gone out with their friends Luke and Paul. Not true. Luke Kiernan took the stand denying those plans ever existed.

'It is a glaring inconsistency,' the Crown Prosecutor hammered. 'His credibility is very important in this case.' He paused. 'Why? Because he says that Matthew Leveson disappeared and he had nothing to do with it.'

Matt had also, according to Atkins, left the unit without taking his prized Louis Vuitton key ring and the wallet containing his ID cards. The clothes he'd worn out to ARQ on the Saturday night – a black singlet, cargo shorts and belt – were never found.

'He was buried in that singlet,' the Crown strongly suggested. 'That singlet has gone with Matthew Leveson, most likely, to his grave.'

Relationship evidence formed a major part of the case. Witness after witness was called to support the notion that Matt Leveson was getting fed up with Michael Atkins' possessiveness in the weeks leading up to his disappearance. The relationship between the couple was marred by the control and jealousy issues of an older man with one more than 20 years his junior.

Matt's former colleague Kerrieann told the court how she noticed a change in Matt's behaviour leading up to his disappearance. 'He seemed to be very unsettled . . . quite the opposite to what he always was, a very bubbly and energetic person,' she testified from the witness box. Matt had confided in her about his reluctance to have threesomes with other men and, during their final shift together, he said he'd had 'enough of Mike's bullshit'. He'd said he was going to stand his ground.

It was a recipe for conflict, the Crown submitted. And text messages from the night, from Matt Leveson to key witness John Burns, told that very story. 'The terms are, "Mike's having a fucken cry. He is taking me home and won't let me stay, fucken cunt," Maxwell explained. It was clear, Maxwell said, that there was conflict on the night, and that Matt was being told to do something that he didn't want to.

Aside from Atkins, one of the last people to see Matt Leveson was their close friend Jack Smith. In his first police statement he had claimed that the last time he saw Matt Leveson was between 2 am and 3 am, when the couple left ARQ because 'Matt was not feeling very well as he was well affected by GHB'. But during Woolbank's review, police discovered a text message from Atkins to Smith at 3.07 am, almost an hour after CCTV captured Matt and Atkins leaving the club. Smith told police the text had prompted him to leave ARQ to say goodbye to his friends. What he witnessed outside was potentially crucial information to the prosecution case.

But in the box, Smith proved to be somewhat inconsistent. He came across as either cagey or forgetful, claiming he couldn't be sure what he saw actually occurred on the night in question.

'So what you say is that, on this occasion, whenever it was you went to Matt's car, you saw Mike in the driver's seat and Matt in the front passenger seat, correct?' Maxwell asked.

'Going off this, yes . . . yeah,' Smith replied, referring to his statement.

The Crown Prosecutor corrected him: 'Going off this? This is your statement that you signed. It is not just coming out of thin air.'

Maxwell put to Smith that he told police 'Matt was pulling faces' in the car.

'Yes,' he accepted.

'And you explained by pulling faces, you said "pulling manky" – is it "manky" or "monkey"?' he clarified.

'Manky faces.'

'What does that mean?' Maxwell asked.

'Taking G.'

Maxwell clarified with Smith that 'manky' faces were silly, childish ones. But Smith wouldn't commit to having seen this happen on Sunday 23 September. The reason Atkins took Matt home against his will remained unknown.

There was no body. No weapon. No blood. Nor any physical evidence as to how the alleged killing had taken place. But there was an important link between the accused and the disappearance of his boyfriend. Michael Atkins had made a cardinal error: he had left the Bunnings receipt in the empty boot of Matt's car. The piece of paper strongly linked Atkins to the dumping of Matt's car at a known gay beat. The Crown argued that Atkins had driven the car to Waratah Park in an attempt to make it look as though Matt had met some foul play by someone there.

The jury also heard how Matt's much-loved subwoofer was ripped from the boot and found in the shared garage space at Atkins' unit block.

Maxwell put to the jury:

Why would he remove the subwoofer? Combine that with the fact that he bought the mattock and Norton tape on the same day. It is because, the Crown says, he used that car to get rid of Matthew Leveson's body. He needed space in the boot to take Matthew Leveson's body to wherever he took it, and to bury the body.

The words sent shivers down Faye Leveson's spine as she sat in the public gallery. The image of Atkins walking through the hardware store with a mattock swinging by his side was etched freshly in her mind after it had been played over and over to the jury. She hoped the CCTV footage haunted them as much as it did her. And while they weren't able to hear Atkins' denial of going to Bunnings, they did hear Atkins' account to police that he and Matt woke up at 2 pm or 3 pm on the Sunday, even though Atkins had been strolling around Bunnings by noon that day.

The Crown also relied heavily on the evidence collected by Mark and Faye Leveson during their secret listening device mission. As the muffled audio played over the courtroom speakers, every ear strained to hear their covert conversation. Some parts were difficult to decipher as the wire had been embedded in Mark's clothing, but one thing was clear: Atkins admitted to the parents that he'd lied to police about buying the mattock, and claimed he'd only bought it to plant a garden.

A show-and-tell at 1 Tonkin Street, Cronulla, dispelled that claim. As the jury toured the apartment block, Detective Sergeant Woolbank told them how she'd investigated Atkins' claim. He told the Levesons that he'd bought the mattock in particular to plant a couple of tiny zucchini punnets, which Matt had picked out a few weeks earlier, in pots on his small brick balcony. Yet the mattock he'd purchased was top of the range, and the largest one available from Bunnings. Woolbank further ruled out any suggestion Atkins may have envisaged a garden bed in the shared yard of the block, which was mostly covered by a lawn. Tenants needed to ask permission from body corporate, and she confirmed there was no such request from Atkins or Matt.

All smiles. Matt at age one, and as a teenager. *Courtesy Mark and Faye Leveson*

The wedding of Faye's cousin, where she and Mark (front row, right) met in 1977. They hit it off straightaway. *Courtesy Mark and Faye Leveson*

The happy couple. Faye and Mark after they'd announced their engagement, a year later.
Courtesy Mark and Faye Leveson

The ever-expanding
Leveson family:
Mark, Faye and
the boys. Matt is
furthest right in
all three photos.
*Courtesy Mark and
Faye Leveson*

The three musketeers: Jason, Pete and Matt. The Leveson brothers remained close into their teenage years. *Courtesy Mark and Faye Leveson*

Matt with his best friend Rachel Sanki. The pair dated briefly in high school before Matt came out. *Courtesy Mark and Faye Leveson*

Matt the party boy. *Courtesy Mark and Faye Leveson*

At the same family function, Matt brought along his older partner, Michael Atkins. *Courtesy Mark and Faye Leveson*

A mother's love. Faye and Matt, with his newly platinum-blond hair. *Courtesy Mark and Faye Leveson*

Matt with one of his best friends, Luke Kiernan.
Courtesy John Burns

The Levesons had their reservations about Atkins, who told 20-year-old Matt he was in his 30s. They later found out there was a 25-year age gap between the couple. *Courtesy Mark and Faye Leveson, and John Burns*

Who is Michael Atkins? As a young man in Sydney's Sutherland Shire, he was known to his mates as 'Smike'. *Supplied*

Sensei Michael Atkins
Rank : Sandan ..... 3rd Degree
City : Sydney N.S.W.
Started Ninjutsu : 1987
Previous experience : Tai Chi
Occupation : *Restaurant Owner*
Comment : Since I started my training I have achieved goals and skills that I had not even dreamed of. I have heard many top speakers and motivators, but none can match the personal development offered by Sensei Roy.

In his late 20s, Atkins became a ninjutsu instructor, and in class he befriended many younger men. Here he is profiled in *Ninjutsu Today*, a quarterly newsletter written by Sensei Wayne Roy. *Courtesy Keira Tanko*

Matt with older brother Pete. This photo was taken at a friend's place before the brothers went to ARQ on Matt's last night alive. *NSW Police*

Matt and Atkins leave ARQ. The security footage is time-stamped 2.11 am – though the actual time was around 2.20 am – on Sunday 23 September 2007. *Courtesy* 60 Minutes

The day of Matt's disappearance, Atkins is seen purchasing a mattock and gaffer tape at a Bunnings Warehouse near his Cronulla apartment. *Courtesy* 60 Minutes

After many missed calls and messages from worried family and friends – including Atkins – Matt's phone was found by police under the passenger seat in Atkins' car. *NSW Police*

 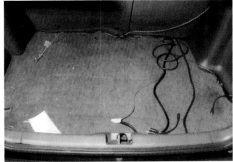

Matt installed a subwoofer in the boot of his car (above left) – but when police discovered the abandoned vehicle at Waratah Oval, the speakers had been removed (above right). *NSW Police*

The receipt recording Atkins' purchase at Bunnings, which was found in Matt's car boot. *NSW Police*

In his initial interview with police, four days after Matt went missing, Atkins' story of his night out with Matt was revealed to be inconsistent. But because police didn't properly caution him about their suspicions, critical parts of the interview were excluded at the murder trial. *NSW Police*

A crushing outcome. After Atkins was acquitted by a jury in October 2009, Faye's devastation was written all over her face. *Dean Lewins/ AAP Image*

(Above and below) 'Pool party for porn stars'. After the trial, Atkins moved to Brisbane, where he hosted an annual clothing-optional Australia Day bash. *Facebook*

Atkins with younger friends, including his new boyfriend, at Brisbane gay nightclub The Beat. *Facebook*

(Above, and below left) Atkins dressed as Peter Pan for a party. *Facebook*

On the dancefloor with another friend. *Facebook*

(Right) For years, Mark and Faye spent their weekends digging at sites throughout southern Sydney in the hopes they would find Matt's body – to no avail. *Courtesy* 60 Minutes

(Left) Atkins after giving evidence at the coronial inquest. Before this time he had exercised his right to silence for the better part of a decade. The inquest, which was heard between November 2015 and December 2017, came about after years of tireless campaigning by the Levesons. *Paul Miller/AAP Image*

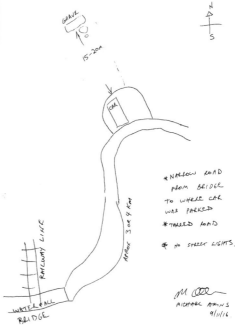

After Atkins made his deal with police – immunity from prosecution in exchange for revealing the burial site – he hand-drew this map. The site is shown to be three or four kilometres from Waterfall Station, in the depths of the Royal National Park. *NSW Police*

(Left) The cabbage-tree palm under which Matt's body was eventually found, in the final hour of the police search, on 31 May 2017 – nine years, eight months and eight days after Matt had disappeared. The palm is now tended to in the Levesons' garden. *Courtesy Mark and Faye Leveson*

(Right) Detective Chief Inspector Gary Jubelin, (second from left), who oversaw the four-year reinvestigation of the Matthew Leveson case, shows Mark and Faye the burial place of their son. *Dean Lewins/AAP Image*

(Left) Mark and Faye react to the news with Jubelin and Detective Senior Constable Scott Craddock. Looking on is Mitch Lombe, the driver of the earthmover that uncovered Matt's remains. *Kate Geraghty/Fairfax*

(Right) Jubelin, Faye and Mark at a press conference in the Royal National Park after the discovery. *Simon Bullard/ Newspix*

After delivering their family impact statements to the Coroner, the Levesons show the media what had happened to their son. Faye holds a photo of Matt taken shortly before his death, and Mark holds a photo of Matt's skeletal remains, which had been pieced together like a jigsaw puzzle. *Dan Himbrechts/AAP Image*

Telling their story. Mark and Faye in a *60 Minutes* interview with Tara Brown. *Courtesy* 60 Minutes

Proud parents. Mark and Faye marching in the 2017 Sydney Gay and Lesbian Mardi Gras. *Courtesy* 60 Minutes

(Top, middle) Emotions running high at Matt's funeral, which took place on Friday 9 March 2018. Mark said, 'Today we can do what we set out to do. We can give our Matty the proper send-off he so justly deserves, in front of his family and his friends.' *(Top) Janie Barrett/Fairfax (Middle) Dean Lewins/AAP Image*

(Left) At the wake, gathered left to right: the author; forensic psychologist Dr Sarah Yule; Faye Leveson; Detective Senior Constable Damien Bateman; Gary Jubelin; Scott Craddock and Mark Leveson. All wearing purple, Matt's favourite colour. *Courtesy Rachel Sanki*

Importantly, the mattock in question was never found by police in their many searches. Neither was the duct tape. If the items had in fact been bought for 'innocent purposes', the Crown asked, then where did they go?

Perhaps one of the easiest concepts the jury had to consider was the bizarre conduct of Atkins after his boyfriend went missing.

On the Monday, he embarked on a shopping spree at Paul's Warehouse to buy a new pair of running shoes. His old ones – the pair he supposedly wore on the Saturday night – were never found. On the Wednesday, three days after Matt's disappearance, he drove to Newcastle to have sex with Jake McCloy. On the Saturday, he bought tickets to the Sleaze Ball and took along a hot, young date. On the Sunday, exactly a week from when he was alleged to have murdered Matt, he had sex with his ex-boyfriend Nate Patterson in a hotel room Atkins had booked online.

Then there were the countless text messages to love interests, ex-lovers and casual sex partners, which the Crown argued was behaviour inconsistent with that of a grieving lover.

Even Atkins' multiple messages of concern to his boyfriend's phone proved a lie. He knew Matt would never receive them because his phone was hidden in the passenger footwell of Atkins' car.

As the weeks dragged by, the Crown submitted a list of 54 circumstances in total to prove the charge of murder. The sheer density of material was enough to make anyone's head spin. Faye Leveson clearly remembers certain jurors nodding off to sleep at times. On top of that, they needed to consider the defence case.

Keith Chapple was short and sharp in his approach. He did his best to relate to how they may feel hearing 'an awful lot about relationships between gay men'. As a straight man himself, he said, 'It may be awkward for you to have listened to some of this evidence.' He showed them a photograph of Atkins and Matt at ARQ, taken only hours before the accused was said to have murdered his boyfriend. They were cuddling and smiling. 'If two men cuddling each other like that offends you, may I ask you just to move beyond that for a moment,' he said. 'What does it tell you? They appear to be happy in each other's company . . . the picture, we suggest, tells you an awful lot.'

Chapple suggested the lack of physical evidence against his client spoke volumes more. The police had combed through Atkins' unit, his car and Matt's car many times, and yet the DNA evidence amounted to nothing. There was no trace of a body having been in the boot. 'It has been swabbed, it's been inspected, it's got fingerprint powder all over the outside and the inside.' And taking a body out of the unit was a huge risk, he proffered. There was the stairway, neighbours and a shared garage space.

Then there was the burying. No shovel or pick, just a mattock and some tape. 'What has it got to do with this case? The tape?' Chapple asked the jury. 'He bought it at the same time he bought the mattock – big deal. Big deal. He's in Bunnings.'

There was the white hospital blanket that was found in the black backpack during the first search. The spot of blood on it didn't belong to Matt or Atkins but to an unknown person.

And so Atkins' defence continued, gnawing away at the prosecution's claims. There were so many unknowns in this so-called murder case. Most importantly, Chapple said, 'We don't know if the man is dead. Yes, it is a sad fact that Matthew Leveson is not talking to people. Of course it is a sad case. We submit it is actually sad for this man as well. Because this man' – at this the barrister gestured towards Atkins – 'Matthew Leveson, the missing person, was his partner.'

According to the defence, it was possible that Matt was simply missing. He'd disappeared before. And there was a side of Matthew Leveson that few people knew about, certainly not his parents or his friends outside of ARQ. 'The secret life of Matthew Leveson' included the fact that he was selling drugs, which meant, the defence argued, that Matt was involved with some shady characters. 'What if he did go to Waratah Park to meet somebody? It's a lonely old place at night,' Chapple said.

The jury considered the defence's suggestion that Matt took the boom box out of his car because he was worried about his security down at the oval. Maybe he met with foul play at the hands of a drug deal? Or another gay man? Maybe he even faked his own disappearance, ran away to teach Michael Atkins a lesson? Chapple posed the likelihood that Melbourne had a great gay community too. The possibilities were endless. Chapple didn't fully commit to any one in particular but he raised them, one after the other.

There had been dozens of apparent sightings of Matthew Leveson since September 2007. A young blond male fitting his description had been spotted at a number of locations, including Sutherland train station, Hamilton Island, Darwin and Alice Springs. Members of the public who were familiar with Matt's photo from missing person posters or articles in the media had called Crime Stoppers to report what they'd seen. Could any of these sightings be definitively ruled out?

To make matters more complicated, as Justice Hidden summarised the case, the jury had another option for their verdict: manslaughter. If they were not satisfied beyond reasonable doubt that Michael Atkins intended to kill Matthew Leveson, they were open to consider their alternatives.

26.

A FREE MAN

Tuesday 20 October 2009

The 12-person jury panel sat through a harrowing 28-day trial before they retired to the secrecy of the jury room to deliberate. They were faced with a God-almighty task: to convict or acquit. No one but those 12 will ever know what went on behind those tightly closed doors.

Within a day of being sent out, Mark and Faye Leveson received word that the jury was returning. With their hearts in their mouths, the couple sprinted back to court and took their seats. Faye held her breath as the jury filed in. Surely this was a positive thing; they'd come to a verdict so fast.

But it was a false alarm. They'd reached an impasse, the young foreman told the judge. Faye released the air trapped in her lungs. Justice Hidden ordered the jury to return to their deliberations. Not nearly enough time had passed.

As the Levesons waited anxiously in a coffee shop nearby, Detective Sergeant Woolbank paced up and down the corridors of the Supreme Court. Her anxiety levels had been through the roof in the lead-up the trial. They weren't much better during the proceedings, and the jury's drawn-out deliberations were torture. Every night she returned home to her children in a state of stress.

The false alarms were terrible for the nerves of the Levesons and Woolbank. Twice more the jury returned with questions for Justice Hidden: Could he tell them what 'reasonable doubt' meant? What was the difference between murder and manslaughter? Faye Leveson took the latter question as a good thing; at least they seemed to be considering both options?

But on day five of the deliberations, the jury once again returned only to tell the judge they could not reach a unanimous verdict. Enough time had passed by now, so Justice Hidden decided to give them the 'Black direction': permission for the jury to return a majority verdict, whereby all except one juror could agree.

As the deliberations continued, news reporters standing out in the street told Mark and Faye that they could hear yelling and screaming coming from one of the back rooms. There were apparently two jury panels in deliberations at the Supreme Court at the time, but the Leveson family strongly suspect it was the jury in their case causing the commotion.

But by the end of that day, they finally made their decision. The wait was over.

The Levesons trained their eyes on Michael Atkins as he was brought up to the courtroom from custody, his handcuffs unlocked before the court came into session. As the jury entered the room, they each looked at the ground. Not one of them made eye contact with the family.

As the foreman stood before the court, he was addressed by the judge's associate, who asked if the jury had agreed upon a verdict.

'Yes.'

'Do you find the accused, Michael Peter Atkins, guilty or not guilty of murder?'

'Not guilty, Your Honour.'

Faye flashed Mark a stricken look. But she held herself together. Not all hope was lost. There was still the alternative of manslaughter.

'Do you find the accused, Michael Peter Atkins, guilty or not guilty of manslaughter?'

'Not guilty, Your Honour.'

Silence fell. Mark's breath stopped. The words hit Faye hard; all she can remember thinking is, 'He's got away with it.'

Seated beside the Levesons, Woolbank lowered her head. She'd tried to brace herself for this result, but it was no use. After more than a year behind bars, Atkins was a free man.

Faye shuffled one foot in front of the other as Mark held her up and helped navigate his wife towards the door. Her world had just gone black. Atkins would walk and the Levesons would be left floundering without answers, and without their middle son.

In a mediation room off the hallway, the Levesons were joined by Detective Woolbank, Crown Prosecutor Chris Maxwell and an associate of his. The group stood in silence. Maxwell's associate cried as she continually apologised to the Levesons. 'I'm so sorry, Faye. I'm so sorry, Mark.' Heavy tears rolled down Woolbank's tanned face, and she wiped them away. For Woolbank, the most devastating part of the verdict was her belief that just because Michael Atkins had been found not guilty didn't meant that he was innocent. For her, the acquittal didn't change a thing. Only one person knew what had happened to Matt Leveson, and he was about to be released back into the community.

Outside the courthouse, a horde of cameramen and journalists waited for the Levesons to emerge. They asked what had happened as Mark and Faye shuffled into the sunlit courtyard.

With microphones poised in front of them and their sons standing behind them in solidarity, Mark and Faye mechanically answered each question put to them. They felt numb. They'd believed in the court system. They thought the evidence presented was overwhelming. They'd hoped the trial would provide them with answers and justice for Matt. Instead, it had left them feeling even more confused.

The whole press conference was a blur. In a softly spoken voice, Mark told the media, 'We don't know what's gone on in that jury room.' He shrugged. 'Only they can answer that question.'

Her shoulders rounded in defeat, between sobs Faye said, 'He was such a beautiful boy. He didn't deserve this.' Pete placed his arm around his mother's shoulders. 'We need Matty's body back,' Faye pleaded down the barrel of the camera. 'There must be somebody out there who knows where he is. Someone who saw him that night.'

Detective Sergeant Woolbank marched towards the privacy of her own car, parked in a back street a few blocks from court, then climbed inside and slammed the door. Years of pent-up emotion poured out of her. She cried and cried. It was all over. Waves of relief and disappointment crashed over her.

The Matt Leveson case would be her last as a cop. She was utterly exhausted. Before the trial finished, she'd booked six weeks' annual leave. She planned on spending much-needed time with her young children. But instead of enjoying her case-free life, her post-traumatic stress, which had been bubbling under the surface for many years, finally boiled over. Woolbank couldn't sleep. Every time she closed her eyes, a slideshow of every horrible case, every torturous crime scene she'd ever been to, flickered through her mind. The Leveson case had been the final straw.

Mark and Faye Leveson didn't allow themselves time to come up for air. They too were at risk of mental breakdown, particularly if they paused for even a moment to fully comprehend the monumental pain they felt about losing their battle against Michael Atkins.

But they refused to let him win. Over the coming weeks and months, through their tears and sense of hopelessness, they hatched a plan together. They were the Levesons, and quitting was not an option. Michael Atkins had picked the wrong family.

Their fight wasn't over. Hell no. It had only just begun.

PART III

UNPRECEDENTED TERRITORY

27.

DETECTIVE CHIEF INSPECTOR JUBELIN

February 2014

Desk phones rang incessantly. Fingers tapped noisily across keyboards. Piercing voices called out from across the room. So was the nature of an open-plan office, where dozens of colleagues were thrown together in a melting pot.

The reality was no different in the shared office space of the Unsolved Homicide Team. The unit, which comprised almost 30 detectives, was formed in 2007 to reinvestigate hundreds of cold-case murders, mostly by using advances in technology and DNA science. The Unsolved Team was an offshoot of the NSW Homicide Squad, and both were on the same floor at Police Headquarters in Parramatta, in Sydney's west.

Crammed into a row of desks overflowing with paperwork, coffee cups and leftover lunches, Gary Jubelin attempted to block out the noise as he tried to concentrate. Frustrated, he ran a hand back and forth over his closely shaved head. As a Detective Chief Inspector, Jubelin had grown used to the quiet of his own office over the years. But having recently returned to work after 12 months' leave, he'd not only lost his office, but his team of detectives too. For the first time in his 30-year policing career, Jubelin was at a loose end. He'd been told to work on his own until something else came up. And so he found himself turfed into the general throng of the office.

More so than the white noise around him, what annoyed Jubelin now was the file in front of him. A file that had remained untouched in the year he'd been absent. That hadn't been the plan.

Before he went on leave in early 2013, Jubelin was one of three senior homicide detectives who'd met with the determined parents of a victim. Their names were Mark and Faye Leveson. They'd wanted their son's murder investigation reviewed, and they weren't taking no for an answer. They were angry about the quality of the original investigation. Despite their misgivings at the time, they'd blindly followed the advice of local detectives and they believed opportunities were missed due to incompetence.

The Levesons' request had followed the announcement of a $100,000 reward for information leading to the discovery of Matt's body. By that point in 2012, three years had passed since the acquittal of Michael Atkins, but he remained the prime suspect, not only for the Levesons but also from a police perspective. Detectives were aware of a possible lead that had filtered through Crime Stoppers. The tip-off claimed Atkins had made a chilling confession over social media. Jubelin believed that, if the information checked out, the investigation into Michael Atkins should be reopened in a bid to potentially charge him again with murder under the reformed double jeopardy laws. The long-held legal principle that someone couldn't be charged for an offence after being acquitted of the same offence was changed in 2006 by the NSW legislature. A suspect could now be retried if 'fresh and compelling' evidence was uncovered.

But Atkins' acquittal meant the case wasn't considered a high priority. During Jubelin's leave of absence, it appeared to have fallen through the cracks. It annoyed him that no one else seemed prepared to pick it up and run with it. As he prised open the file, Jubelin made a commitment to see the case through. It would be an uphill battle, but it wouldn't be his first.

Describing himself as someone who has either 'volumes of tenacity or volumes of stupidity', Jubelin admits his strong work ethic stems from his fear of failure. As a kid, he always played hard at sport not to win, but to ensure he didn't lose. That inner grit most probably came from his late father, who regulated the construction industry at a time when the unions were tough as nails.

Jubelin grew up as one of four children in Epping, a suburb in Sydney's north-west. Whereas Jubelin's father was tough, his mother was a compassionate and quiet woman. Jubelin is hardly shy, but throughout his career many colleagues and criminals alike have tended to assume that they can walk over him. But try to do so and you'll met the real Gary Jubelin: stubborn, abrasive and unrelenting.

Jubelin's peculiar status as an 'empathetic hard-arse' has made him a stand-out cop. He never dreamed of joining the force as a kid, but he instantly knew he'd found his calling when, as a misguided 22-year-old working on a building site, he witnessed police chasing a 'bad guy' down the street. It seemed to be the kind of thing he'd like to do. He signed up the very next day and never looked back.

As a young copper, Jubelin was headhunted to join the 'Stick-Ups', Sydney's infamous armed hold-up squad. In a baptism of fire, he faced off with some of the state's most violent crooks and worked alongside some of New South Wales' best and most notorious detectives. But Jubelin took the good lessons and left the bad, well before the controversial squad was disbanded following allegations of corruption.

It's as a homicide detective that Jubelin has felt most at home. Since joining the department in the early '90s, it's been his undying passion. His battle against injustice involved him committing more than 20 years of his career to the Bowraville murders.

When Jubelin first worked on the case, in 1996, five years had passed since Aboriginal children Colleen Walker, Evelyn Greenup and Clinton Speedy-Duroux had disappeared within months of each other from a small town on the mid-north coast of New South Wales. It was his job to reinvestigate the murders following the acquittal of a local man. At the time, Jubelin was married with young children of his own. He was contemplating leaving the Homicide Squad, as work had hijacked his life.

But when Jubelin met the families of the Bowraville victims, his heart broke, he became furious, and he relented. The way he saw it, three children had been murdered, and there was a serial killer on the loose. Yet no one seemed to care: not the public, or the media or, for the longest time, the police. The families told him when he first met them that the lack of interest was because they were Aboriginal.

When Jubelin delved into the Matt Leveson file, he was struck by how similar the case was to his Bowraville reinvestigation. Both involved missed opportunities by police, marginalised victims and an acquitted person who remained the only suspect. That final point bolstered Jubelin's confidence that he was the right man for the job. Through his work on the Bowraville case, he'd become somewhat of an expert in New South Wales' double jeopardy laws. The tireless campaigning of the victims' families had been one of the main driving factors behind the 2006 reforms. It was their belief that because separate trials had been held against the accused child killer, evidence that could have linked all three crimes was not considered by the court. Had the cases been heard together, there may have been a stronger chance of the suspect being convicted. Even so, after the reforms were made, by 2014 every application for a retrial that Jubelin and the families had made had been knocked back. The families and their supporters, with Jubelin by their side, had responded to the most recent blow by marching angrily on parliament in 2013.

There's no doubt that Jubelin is a polarising cop. On the one hand, he's shown immense compassion and dedication to victims' families. On the other are the claims from his critics that he's too opinionated, and too ruthless in his pursuit of justice. Jubelin says that's simply a cop-out from people who aren't prepared to pay the price he is. Even the detective's most sceptical colleagues hold a grudging respect for him. They admit that if – God forbid – their own loved one were killed, they wouldn't want anyone else but Jubelin on the job. He's appeared on television screens around the nation as the lead investigator on some of the state's most infamous crimes, and makes no apologies for using the media as a tool, or at times a weapon, in the art of crime solving. In 2012, he was also depicted in the fifth season of *Underbelly, Badness*, as the detective who led the investigation that brought down Australian kidnapper, murderer and drug-dealer Anthony Perish. His new-found fame resulted in a whole new wave of raised eyebrows around the workplace, not that it worried him much. He says his profile has only come from hard work.

As Jubelin embarked on reopening the Matt Leveson case, his marriage – his second – was in strife. He'd taken the 12 months' leave to prioritise his love life over his career, moving in with his new wife, an Aboriginal clinical psychologist, in her hometown of Perth. But the comedown from the intense daily routine as a big-city homicide detective was simply mind-numbing. By the end of his year off, Jubelin was desperate to get back to work. He returned to Sydney alone, and the distance deepened the emerging rift in his marriage. With his closest friends back in Perth, Jubelin lacked both companionship and a social life.

But for Mark and Faye Leveson, they'd secured Jubelin on Matt's case at the perfect time. With a fire in his belly and a personal life in tatters, the detective channelled his energy into achieving one goal: chasing Michael Atkins.

28.

'POOL PARTY FOR PORN STARS'

Early 2014

'Never have I ever . . . had a threesome!'

The statement was met with squawks of laughter as a handful of young men reached for their glasses and drank. There were about ten of them seated around Harry Jones's dining table. It'd been the 21-year-old bartender's idea to play a round of the drinking game to break the ice at his party. He often hosted pre-drinks at his tiny apartment in Brisbane's inner city before he and his friends hit the clubs. Tonight he'd been short on numbers, and had invited along a random or two. One of them had arrived right on the dot at 7.30 pm. Punctual as ever. Perhaps a sign of his age? He was, after all, the oldest of the group by far. But that didn't make him any more mature. The drinking game, full of sexual innuendo, was giving him great enjoyment. Every time Mike Atkins drank to a statement, he smiled flirtatiously around the group of young men.

Harry had met his guest in 2011. They weren't the closest of friends, but almost every weekend they partied together at their favourite gay club, The Beat. Atkins lived close to the club in the heart of Fortitude Valley, Brisbane's party precinct. After moving up from Sydney that same year, he'd bought a stylish split-level apartment where he lived with his new boyfriend, a slim, over-tanned, blond-haired, blue-eyed 20-year-old. The mismatched couple was often the subject of the gay rumour mill, with plenty of other clubgoers questioning what on earth such a young, attractive guy saw in Mike Atkins. Some gossiped that he was only doing it to live somewhere nice. They bitched that their relationship was less about love than Mike being his 'sugar daddy'.

Still, these rumours stopped neither Harry nor plenty of other young guys from hanging around the muscly, singlet-clad older male. Using his hot boyfriend as a 'honey pot' of sorts, Mike Atkins thrived on the activity that surrounded them as a couple. He often shouted rounds of cocktails at the bar, which did wonders for his popularity. His juvenile audience thought he was a smooth operator, charming and worldly.

On the Brisbane gay party scene, Atkins was perhaps best known for his annual Australia Day celebration, which he hosted in the shared pool area of his luxury apartment complex. Dubbed the 'Pool party for porn stars', an invitation was the hottest ticket in town. An exclusive gathering of 20-something gay guys – and Mike Atkins. The dress code was strict, and involved very little clothing. Budgie smugglers were in, but shirts and pants were a no-no.

From Harry's own interactions with Mike Atkins, he knew him to be a real party boy. Recently Harry had started dealing drugs; nothing too crazy, but he had his loyal customers. Atkins was one of them. On a night out, he'd usually buy about $100 worth of drugs from Harry, which equated to four ecstasy pills. But Atkins chose his timing carefully. He would never purchase drugs when his boyfriend was with him, picking the nights when his partner was studying at home. On those nights, Mike would often move in close to Harry on the dancefloor. He'd get handsy and Harry would push him away, flirtatiously telling him to behave. But Mike was persistent, and never hid his attraction to other guys. Harry believed he wasn't a faithful partner but, then again, he didn't know the terms of the couple's strange relationship.

29.

GOING UNDERCOVER

Saturday 27 September 2014

Andrew Danvers had never felt so nervous in his life. Standing on the street in the middle of Fortitude Valley, he felt completely at odds with the Saturday-night revellers and drunken loud-mouths swarming around him. Andrew was completely sober, but he felt drunk on adrenaline. Giddy with anticipation. He was outside an expensive apartment block only metres from the doors of Brisbane's gay dance clubs, waiting for his target.

'Jesus Christ!' Gary Jubelin cried out with a start. Danvers was fidgeting, and had accidently grazed over the body wire discreetly attached to the inside of his shirt. The interference had almost burst the eardrums of Jubelin and his small team of detectives listening intently on the other end. Sitting in unmarked cars or standing in position throughout the street, plainclothes police kept their eyes and ears on Danvers. The undercover operation had been months in the making.

After examining the tip-off to Crime Stoppers, Jubelin had determined that the source alleging Michael Atkins had con-fessed to him was in fact his ex-lover. Since 2010, Danvers had made three separate reports to the Crime Stoppers website in varying stages of detail. He claimed Atkins, under the username of 'MikeyBoi Atkins', had confessed to him on Facebook one night about Matt's death, the weapon, the disposal of Matt's body in bushland and his motive: Matt had threatened to go to police about Atkins' drug-dealing. The most chilling extracts of 41-minute conversation included:

9.36 pm MikeyBoi
I found some of matts stuff the other day.

9.36 pm Andrew Danvers
Really

9.37 pm MikeyBoi
So I dropped it off to him

9.37 pm Andrew Danvers
What do you mean you dropped it off to him?

9.37 pm MikeyBoi
Left it where he is

9.37 pm Andrew Danvers
?

9.37 pm MikeyBoi
Where he is residing doesn't matter, I will show u when u come back

9.38 pm Andrew Danvers
R we talking about matty?

9.38 pm MikeyBoi
Yep
Maybe I should stop, I am drunk

9.39 pm Andrew Danvers
Where is he residing?

9.39 pm MikeyBoi
He lives in the bush now

9.44 pm Andrew Danvers
Hes still alive then?

. 9.45 pm MikeyBoi
In spirit yes, in physical being, no
Dead men tell no tails

9.46 pm Andrew Danvers
Lol

10.01 pm MikeyBoi
U wanna know how he died?

10.01 pm Andrew Danvers
Yeh?

10.01 pm MikeyBoi
He called me a dog, and I hit him
His head hit the passenger side window of the car
And he was unconscious
Then he just OD'd
Serves him right

Jubelin believed the tip-off was a legitimate line of enquiry, and police needed to prove or disprove that Michael Atkins and 'MikeyBoi Atkins' were one and the same. Jubelin had sought consent from the Director of Public Prosecutions to reinvestigate Atkins, as was required by double jeopardy laws. After receiving the green light, Jubelin found himself a new team: Detective Senior Constable John Mastrobattista, from the homicide squad; and two young guns from Miranda Police Station where the original murder investigation was run. Detective Senior

Constable Damien Bateman looked straight out of central casting, brawny and attractive with a trendy haircut. In contrast, Detective Senior Constable Scott Craddock looked far from your everyday copper. At over six feet (1.8 m) tall, if the 28-year-old's impressive height didn't catch your eye then his shock of red hair almost certainly did.

With his team assembled and hard at work, Jubelin informed Mark and Faye Leveson that their son's case was being reopened to examine information that was potentially 'fresh and compelling'. But for operational reasons, at that stage he couldn't divulge exactly what the possible lead was. Regardless, the Levesons were ecstatic that perhaps, finally, justice was in sight. They speculated together that Atkins must have slipped up, providing them with the breakthrough they'd been searching for all these years.

After taking a detailed statement from Andrew Danvers, who was now based in Canada, Jubelin seized his laptop computer for forensic examination. It revealed the conversation had taken place on 8 June 2010, less than a year after Atkins' acquittal. But a technical analysis of the username 'MikeyBoi Atkins' didn't reveal whether the account belonged to the real Michael Atkins, and it was also no longer in use.

If the social media confession had any chance of standing up in court, Jubelin needed more. They had to find Atkins and plan a sting, a strategy to elicit more admissions from him. To devise the best possible operation, he sought expert advice from the senior forensic psychologist for NSW Police, Dr Sarah Yule. The criminal profiler became the fifth member of his squad.

Unlike a traditional evaluation, where a forensic psychologist might interview their subject, Dr Yule's criminal profiling was based on an indirect assessment of Atkins. She studied witness statements from ex-lovers and friends to decode his personality traits. She evaluated what impact Atkins' strict Catholic upbringing may have had on him coming out late in life. Then there was his behaviour throughout the original police investigation:

his strange conduct in the days following Matt's disappearance, his video interview and the listening device recording with Mark and Faye. It was plain as day to Dr Yule that Atkins was no skilled mastermind. His version of events was weak, riddled with inconsistencies and lacking in sophistication. There were also conflicting aspects of his personality to consider. While he could be domineering and possessive in his romantic relationships and sexual encounters, he also tended to be socially awkward, unengaging and fairly passive. He was no psychopath, despite his lack of empathy. Instead his superficial relations with others seemed to stem from his diminished emotional intelligence.

Dr Yule formed the opinion that Atkins was highly motivated by self-preservation and, due to his limited emotional capacity, tended to compartmentalise his life. He could easily shut off a chapter and move on. His drug-taking also allowed him to be the outgoing, party animal he so desperately wanted to be. Above all else, Dr Yule advised detectives that Atkins appeared to be overly concerned with how others perceived him in all areas of his life.

Dr Yule's character assessment helped Jubelin get inside Atkins' head, and allowed him to make the strategic decision to wire up Andrew Danvers and send him in to confront Atkins. It was a big ask of the softly spoken and, at times, timid Danvers, who now needed to be assertive and provide Atkins with an ultimatum: that he couldn't live with the confession Atkins had dumped him, and if he was going to keep his secret he would need to know exactly what happened or he would take it to the police. Luckily Danvers was eager to help, despite his former close bond with Atkins.

In planning the sting, the strike force established that Atkins, now 51, was living it up in Brisbane. It wasn't hard to figure out, based on his new boyfriend's social media photos, that Atkins had well and truly moved on from – or perhaps 'compartmentalised' – being charged and acquitted of Matt Leveson's murder.

It also didn't seem to faze him that his new lover looked just like his dead boyfriend.

More unnerving than that, Jubelin thought, were the photographs of Atkins' annual Australia Day pool party: dozens of young guys, some of whom didn't appear a day over the age of 16, excitedly posing for photos in their budgie smugglers around the pool. Their hairless chests and hairpin legs contrasted with the old bloke standing between them, a chunky arm around their tiny waists. Atkins seemed to have hidden his past from his new Brisbane friends. It probably helped that most of them were still in school when he was acquitted of murder.

Jubelin printed out one of the photographs and blu-tacked it to the side of his computer. It served as motivation for him, a constant reminder of the type of man he was pursuing.

It wasn't until the night of the undercover operation that Jubelin finally laid eyes on Michael Atkins in the flesh.

From the driver's seat of his unmarked car, he watched as the stocky Atkins, wearing a singlet, rounded the corner of the street with his young boyfriend in tow. Jubelin and Dr Yule leaned towards a small set of speakers, listening live to Andrew Danvers' heavy breathing. He'd clearly clocked Atkins as well.

Atkins spotted Danvers from a few metres out. 'Andrew?' he said with surprise. They hadn't seen each other in eight years.

'Hi Mike.' Danvers smiled, his nerves subsiding at the familiar face.

'What are you doing here?' Atkins seemed taken aback, but also pleasantly surprised at the unexpected appearance of his Canada-based ex-lover. He introduced him to his new boyfriend, who left the pair to catch up by skulking upstairs. They appeared genuinely stoked to see each other. Danvers got so involved in the conversation that he seemed to forget why he was there.

Watching from the roof of a parking station across the road, detectives Craddock and Bateman could tell by Danvers' body language that it wasn't going well. The ex-lovers looked far too comfortable and friendly.

Jubelin and Dr Yule became breathless, agitated. Danvers, perched on a low brick fence next to Atkins, was catching up with him about what they'd each been up to since they'd last seen each other. Ten minutes passed. Twenty. Drastic action was needed.

'I can't believe you did that!' a voice screamed, as an irate woman stormed down the street towards Danvers and Atkins. She'd come from the direction of the pubs and bars. A tall bloke chased after her, yelling back. The couple, in the middle of a heated domestic, stopped right in front of the ex-lovers. At the top of their lungs they squawked at each other.

'I'm giving you an ultimatum!' the woman shrieked. The bloke started marching off. She grabbed him by the arm. 'I said, I'm giving you an *ultimatum*!'

She had light brown hair pulled back in a ponytail. He was tall, with an athletic build and a shaved head. It was Jubelin and Dr Yule.

Danvers was confused. Jubelin, in his desperation for Danvers to confront Atkins, had launched into the spontaneous drama. But it didn't work. Danvers took it as a cue to wrap things up. He said goodbye to Atkins and made plans to talk later on.

Back in the car, Jubelin was frustrated. That wouldn't do at all.

'Come on, mate!' he implored Danvers. 'You need to get angry at him. Get fucking angry! This is your one chance. You're pissed off – he's potentially murdered someone!'

Danvers nodded. He was ready for take two. He fired off a text to Atkins, asked to him to come down and talk in the pub at the end of his street. Atkins agreed.

As the pair walked towards the Wickham Hotel, a crack of thunder signalled an impending drenching. Detectives Craddock and Bateman ducked for cover as a downpour smacked the pavement outside, while Atkins and Danvers each plonked down on a bar stool in the busy pub.

This time, to Jubelin's great relief, Danvers was far more direct. He cornered Atkins about the confession.

'I don't even have a Facebook account,' Atkins claimed, before proceeding to deny the confession had ever come from him. He stressed to Danvers that he was innocent and had nothing to do with Matt's disappearance. He even said that Matt had been seen out on the Sunday night after he left home. After 45 minutes, the pair bid farewell and went their separate ways.

The operation hadn't gone completely to plan, but Jubelin was happy. The team had a few well-earned celebratory drinks in the motel that night. Even though Atkins had denied the confession, sometimes a denial could be just as good as an admission.

The detective decided it was time let the Levesons know what they'd been working on. Jubelin called them and launched straight in, explaining how he and his team were currently up in Queensland for an operation. But he didn't get much further. As he explained how Atkins had confessed to Andrew Danvers, under the username 'MikeyBoi' on Facebook, Faye exclaimed, 'But Atkins doesn't have a Facebook!'

Faye knew this to be a fact. Since Atkins' acquittal, she and Mark had made it their business to keep tabs on him. They knew all about his new life up in Brisbane, where he lived, the clubs he went to and the new boyfriend he was dating. Mark had once anonymously called the young man's parents to warn them of Atkins' history. He'd even sent the couple newspaper clippings about Atkins in the mail. Faye also regularly checked the boyfriend's public Facebook page. She'd scoured social media for any trace of Atkins' own Facebook page, but he'd never set one up.

'Have you checked to see if this Facebook page was set up by Kevin Britten?' Faye enquired. She was referring to a man whom she and Mark could only describe as some kind of nut job. Kevin Britten, an alias, was obsessed with the case, and with Michael Atkins. It was alleged that back in 2011 he'd broken into Atkins' car and stolen property before setting up a mobile phone in Atkins' name. He'd also once pretended to find Matt's body in the Royal National Park. Britten was only one in a long line of pests who constantly harassed the Levesons with theories and speculations about Matt's murder.

It was the first time Jubelin had heard any of this information. He vividly remembers the life draining out of him. He said he'd call them back, and hung up. *Fuck.*

The detective broke the news to his team, and they set out to find any past police reports on Britten. There were plenty, but not one had been linked to either Atkins' name or Matt Leveson's in the police computer system.

Jubelin and his team pounced on Britten, a 45-year-old with an extensive criminal history. He made full and frank admissions that he'd set up the 'MikeyBoi Atkins' Facebook page, and forensic examinations of his computer confirmed it.

It was all a lie.

Jubelin relayed the full story to the Levesons, which meant the police now had nothing new on Atkins. The family was devastated, and Jubelin felt particularly responsible for having given them what he now realised were false hopes. In a way, it felt like Atkins had walked free all over again. As for Britten, they felt as though they'd all been made fools of by a clown, whom the police couldn't even charge with public mischief due to the statute of limitations.

The easy way out for Jubelin would have been to apologise to the Levesons and walk away. But he felt awful for them. And, more than that, he was royally pissed off, which made him all the more determined.

30.

FUNERAL ENVY

Tuesday 21 October 2014

As I walked towards the front door of Mark and Faye Leveson's house the afternoon I first met them, my heart was beating quickly. I couldn't help but momentarily take in their home's spectacular view, with the bright blue water of Bonnet Bay glittering below. The quiet suburb, best known for its Christmas light displays, sits on the eastern banks of the Woronora River, close to the mouth. By the time fresh water has made it there, it's travelled 36 kilometres from the river's source through Sydney's Royal National Park. The streets are all named after former American presidents – Washington Drive, Kennedy Crescent, Nixon Place – a quirk most locals will likely tell you about.

As I pressed the Levesons' doorbell that day, its melody echoed through the house, causing an eruption of barking from above. I listened as two sets of footsteps rumbled down the stairs. I took a few deep breaths in a futile attempt to settle myself.

It's never pleasant reaching out to the family of a murder victim. That's the understatement of any journalist's career. Most often an approach is met by insults, hurled with the aim of knocking the wind from your lungs. It's a response I've come to expect if I'm the one daring to stand on the front step of a shell-shocked family. Unfortunately, it is part of the job, and it's hoped that the end result is giving parents, siblings, children and close friends of lost loved ones an opportunity and platform to speak out, if they so desire.

Still, whenever I've knocked on a door I've always felt complete and utter dread. I can't think of anything worse than disturbing someone, no matter how much time has passed, with the sole purpose of asking them to speak with me about the most gut-wrenching moment of their life. For me, it will always feel an awful intrusion, one I experience with my head spinning, palms slippery with sweat. Door slams and failed attempts are often followed by my own tears in the car afterwards. But that is nothing on what the people behind those firmly shut doors are going through: the insurmountable anger and that crushing, panicky, heart-searing pain, white hot and never-ending.

My Tuesday afternoon meeting with Mark and Faye had been arranged a month prior, so when I stood at their front door I knew I was hardly making a cold call but, as usual, I felt pretty uncomfortable.

My initial email to the Levesons had been sent out of the blue. I'd forced myself to write to the couple after reading about their son's disappearance in a book of unsolved crimes by Australian author Justine Ford. I figured by that point, September 2014, the case was technically considered 'cold'. I'd never even heard of Matthew Leveson before, and while my unfamiliarity might have had something to do with me hailing from Queensland, I was still shocked that the case didn't have a higher profile. If the family would agree to it, I wanted to use the national platform of 60 Minutes, where I was working, to bring it to wider attention.

The way I saw it was that this gorgeous young man had disappeared in highly suspicious circumstances; he was almost certainly dead, and the evidence that his much-older partner Michael Atkins was involved with Matt's disappearance was compelling. Yet Atkins had walked free when a jury found him not guilty of murder and manslaughter in 2009. The case captivated me and I just knew 60 Minutes had to tell this story.

Looking back now at what I ended up writing in my email to the Levesons, I couldn't have been more direct. Fortunately for me that was exactly how Mark and Faye are too.

16/09/2014 5.10 pm:

Dear Mark and Faye,
Thank you for taking the time to read this email.

I am a researcher at *60 Minutes* and recently I have been reading about your son's unsolved murder.

Firstly, can I please offer my deepest sympathies for the loss of your son. I can only imagine it is still very difficult to speak about the circumstances surrounding his death.

I was hoping to touch base with you both to have a chat about the investigation. I'd also like to see if there's any potential for us to do a story with you, depending on your thoughts/the current state of the investigation.

I only have a work number for you and would prefer not to bother you during work hours. Would it be possible to email me a home or mobile contact?

Look forward to hearing from you.
Kind regards,
Grace Tobin

Mark and Faye responded in no time at all, generously thanking me for my interest in Matt's circumstances but asking for some time to themselves for a few weeks. It was coming up to the anniversary of Matt's death, and that year marked the seventh year of losing him. It's said that time heals all wounds, but I've witnessed for myself that there are some wounds in life which are far too deep and infected to come even close to healing. For the Levesons, every year September 23rd rolls around is even more painful than the one before. Not that their pain is by any means restricted to one day of the year. The loss of Matt is all-consuming, and waves of anger, heartache and frustration wash over each of them on every single day of the year.

Despite the enduring impact Matt's loss has had on his parents, and my nerves as I stood on their front step that October afternoon, Mark and Faye embraced me with the warmest of welcomes from the instant they swung open the door. As I followed the couple into their home, I took in my surroundings. Sky blue painted walls decorated with a seaside theme. Dainty seahorses hung from hooks. Shells dangled from ceiling lights. Up the stairs and through a child safety gate at the top, we were ambushed by two overexcited dogs. It was quickly apparent that Bundy and Buster, two Maltese shih tzus, were Mark and Faye's pride and joy. The prized pooches escorted the three of us into the living room, where I was invited to take a seat at the dining table. As Mark brewed us each a cup of coffee in the kitchen, I cast my eyes around the living room. Matt's face beamed out from almost every direction from framed family portraits that adorned the walls, remembering a family of five.

I never knew Faye Leveson before she lost her son Matty, but I can see how her pain has taken its toll on her in the way she holds herself in times of despair, her shoulders rounded and her arms folded across her slender, petite body, as though the weight of the world, at least as she knows it, is dragging her down. Yet Faye radiates warmth, and she's a mother through and through, a caring woman who will never stop being mum to her three boys. She has a soft voice but at times it's strained. Like so many women of her stature, she's not to be under-estimated as her bite is in fact far worse than her bark. Her rage can be shocking and hurtful. In the years I've now known her, I've seen her dress down experienced homicide detectives and senior solicitors with scathing criticism that drains the words from their mouths. Her anger, when unleashed, strikes at the heart of her target like a deadly brown snake does, unexpected and with a slow-burning venom. Detectives have told me they have lain awake at night with her words burned into their minds. But Faye's anger has only ever been in the name of Matt.

Mark, on the other hand, is a measured man. He's the family rock, forever working towards their ultimate goal, to find Matt and to chase down justice. The first things you notice about Mark are his kind eyes and his smile, which is always ready to go. Mark's words of wisdom keep everyone around him on track. Just when the rest of the family is truly losing hope, Mark will come through with another plan, another way forward. He's also the last person you'd expect to be covered in tattoos. But up and down each arm, as well as on his back, his skin is inked. Look closely though and you'll see each of his 12 tattoos revolves around Matt. It was as close as he had to a tomb for his son. On his forearms are the words: *Death leaves a heartache that no one can heal*, and *Love leaves a memory that no one can steal*. On his bicep is a tattoo of his son's face encircled with: *May you now rest in peace. Matt 12.12.86 – 23.09.07. Your memory will never die.*

But there's more to Mark's tattoos than remembrance; there's a strong sense of wanting retribution too. Mark has an inner grit that isn't at all obvious upon meeting him, but analyse his inked skin and you'll appreciate that side of him pretty quickly. *It's always too soon to quit* is tattooed on the inside of one arm. On the other: *Winners are losers who don't give up.* Perhaps most telling is the tattoo inscribed *Fiat Justitia*, Latin for 'Let justice be done'. But Mark's favourite saying about his family's experience with law and order is that, 'It's not a justice system, it's just a system.'

Faye also wears her grief on her skin. One of her tattoos is her favourite photo of Matt. It's on her upper thigh, just low enough for the ink to show when she sits down in a knee-length dress. Over her heart are her children's names in their own handwriting: *Pete, Matt, Jase.*

Of course, many of these impressions, which have been cemented by my years of knowing the Levesons, were fleeting when I first met them on that Tuesday afternoon. But what struck me as I sat with them at their dining table, coffee in hand, was that these were two parents who truly loved their boy in life, and now in death. There was nothing polished or practised about what they said. Over the years they'd met with countless journalists, given numerous interviews and quotes for different newspapers and news bulletins, and yet that afternoon was no easier than any other time they'd told the story of how their son was taken away.

Surrounded by piles of documents and photos, I sat silently holding a notebook with a pen poised in my hand. Faye looked at me and smiled. She knew what was coming. Mark clasped both hands together, elbows firmly on the table, and leaned forward. He had something important to say, and I could tell by the look on his face that he wasn't one to mince his words.

'As parents to Matthew we are one hundred per cent committed, until the day we die, to finding out what happened to our son. We do not want to leave this earth not knowing and passing that burden onto our other two boys.'

But then came Mark's words of warning. A cautionary tale. He said they'd been contacted by a number of journalists over the years, just like me, who had wanted to tell Matt's story: 'They've come here and sat around this table, just as you are today. We've spent hours upon hours helping their research or filming elements for TV. They've made promises. And we've been let down.'

Many of these news or feature stories had never made it to air, which explained why Matt's case wasn't on the radar. Each of these empty promises had hurt Mark and Faye badly. They wanted some reassurance that I wasn't going to muck them about. I didn't yet have the green light for the story back at work – I hadn't even pitched it yet – but I knew I couldn't let them down. I made them a promise right there and then to tell Matt's story. Little did I know how hard that would be.

I hadn't realised it at the time, but my pledge had come at a fitting moment for the couple. The Levesons were still reeling from the let-down of the bogus Facebook confession, revealed four weeks earlier, and they were looking for a new outlet to chase justice. They found it in the prospect of a *60 Minutes* story exposing the full circumstances of Matt's disappearance and Atkins' suspected involvement.

Once the ground rules were set, Mark and Faye spent hours with me detailing their torment over losing their son while the man they held responsible for his death was free to walk the streets. Their obsession with Michael Atkins was palpable – and why shouldn't it be? He was the one other person on this earth who should have loved their son as much as they did, and he'd shown nothing but contempt for their boy, the truth and the law.

That afternoon they told me one of the most heartbreaking confessions I've ever heard. Mark peered across the table at me and admitted that he and Faye suffered from 'funeral envy'. I asked him what he meant.

'When we see a hearse driving past or a chapel overflowing with mourners, we feel envious.' The ache showed in his face. 'I mutter under my breath, "lucky buggers", because we wish we could have a funeral for Matt too. But we don't even have his body. And only one person can resolve that for us.'

As soon as I left the Leveson home that afternoon, I wrote an email to my senior producer at the time, Stephen Rice. We often co-produced crime stories and, as a researcher, I was keen for his support before taking the story pitch to our executive producer. I told him about the acquittal of Michael Atkins in spite of the captivating evidence against him, and how Mark and Faye now spent their weekends searching and digging for their son's body by moonlight in the bush.

There was so much more to learn about the case. With Rice's backing, I embarked on the research assignment to trace the investigation from the very beginning.

There was no way of knowing back then the twists and turns to come. How the case would consume me, becoming my obsession and Australia's too. After years in the shadows, the death of Matt Leveson was about to resurface as one of the country's most bizarre, mind-boggling, heart-wrenching and intriguing mysteries.

31.
TICK, TICK, TICK

January 2015

It was only a few months after I'd first met with Mark and Faye, having since been given the green light to go ahead with researching the story, but already I was encountering some serious bumps in the road. As I made my way through 1300 pages of court transcripts from Atkins' trial, I read with interest the discussions held on voir dire, when the jury was absent from court. It became abundantly clear to me and senior producer Stephen Rice that our *60 Minutes* story needed to be built around the evidence the jury didn't hear. Michael Atkins' cold-blooded lies in his police interview were outrageous, particularly combined with the compelling Bunnings CCTV footage. His denial of ever having gone to Bunnings, which was kept from the jury, would form the backbone of the story. But there was one major problem: we didn't have a copy of the police tape. And neither did the Levesons.

I started with Detective Chief Inspector Gary Jubelin. After several attempts to track him down for a meeting, I finally locked him in for a coffee in Parramatta. I remember feeling slightly daunted; the Jubelin name was well known in media circles. But his friendly demeanour put me at ease, and Jubelin was keen for the story to go ahead, not only in order to expose Atkins' lies but also because he and the Levesons were now working towards a new goal: a coronial inquest into Matt's death.

Unlike a criminal trial with a prosecutor and a defendant, an inquest is an enquiry led by a Coroner who investigates certain kinds of deaths in an attempt to find out the manner and cause of death. It's an inquisitorial process rather than an adversarial one. Persons of interest can be named in an inquest, but the Coroner cannot find someone guilty of a crime. Instead, if at any stage the Coroner forms an opinion that a person has committed a crime in connection with the death, an inquest is required to be suspended and referred to the Director of Public Prosecutions.

The likeliness of Atkins being referred to the DPP during an inquest into Matt's death was close to zero. He had already been tried and acquitted of the crime, which made the premise of an inquest highly unusual in itself. It was basically unheard of for an inquest to be held after a murder trial, with the acquitted person remaining the only person of interest. The Levesons had already been knocked back once in 2010, but this time they had Jubelin's backing. He was more than willing to take on the judicial system to help Mark and Faye in their fight to find the truth. The Coroner's Court was also a strategy to put pressure on Atkins.

Jubelin arranged a personal meeting with the State Coroner, Michael Barnes. He recalls telling Barnes 'that this was the last throw of the dice for the family. They'd put their faith in the justice system and they still had no answers.'

In a letter to the Coroner dated 17 December 2014, the Leveson family poured their hearts out in an account of their ongoing anguish:

> We turn to you as the State Coroner to help us find out what happened to our son, our brother. We feel an inquest would provide answers as to what happened to Matt: Is he dead? How he died? Where he died? When he died? Who was responsible for his death?
>
> Without those answers our lives are a living nightmare. We are hoping your Court could help us find those answers. If not, where else do we turn?

The Coroner conceded there was nothing to prevent an inquest in the case. He granted the Levesons' wish, to their relief. 'We don't get many victories,' Mark said to me, when he delivered the news. 'It makes ones like this all the more significant.'

The inquest was due to commence at the end of 2015. The clock was ticking. From a police and journalistic point of view, it would be ideal for our *60 Minutes* story to air prior to that date. Casting a national spotlight on Michael Atkins and exposing the circumstances surrounding his behaviour would provide one last opportunity for new witnesses to potentially come forward, or for 'fresh and compelling' evidence to be gathered.

But by the middle of that year I was still no closer to obtaining a copy of Atkins' original police interview. Jubelin was unable to help; there's a strict process for police to follow in order to hand over exhibits to journalists. My applications to the Supreme Court and the DPP were rejected; neither department had kept copies of the exhibits following Atkins' acquittal. They'd been returned to the NSW Police, and the official line there was that the matter was now before the Coroner's Court, so it would be best for me to apply there.

We had one shot left, and it was a shot in the dark. When I made a detailed application to the Coroner's Court for access to Atkins' police video in its entirety and the Bunnings CCTV footage, I was told that exhibits were rarely, if not ever, released to the media prior to the commencement of an inquest. Sure enough, weeks passed without a response. By the end of October 2015, we were running out of time to air something before the inquest started.

I met Channel Nine's in-house lawyer, Maureen O'Connor, who told me in no uncertain terms not to give up. She had an idea. A directions hearing had been set for the first week of November. We would hire a barrister and take our fight to court.

October 2015

The phone on Sharon Ramsden's desk sprang to life. It was late in the day and the Sydney law firm Marsdens was emptying of her colleagues and their clatter.

Ramsden answered, and the softly spoken voice of an older man came over the line. His name was Michael Atkins. He'd been referred to Ramsden by Legal Aid, who had advised him he didn't fit the criteria for taxpayer-funded legal representation. But he needed a lawyer, and fast. He explained his situation: he had been subpoenaed as the only person of interest in an upcoming coronial inquest, despite being acquitted of the murder six years earlier. There was also an urgent media application by Channel Nine's *60 Minutes* team to access key evidence featured in his trial. If the application was successful, he risked national exposure before the proceedings even started. Needless to say, he wanted Ramsden to fight it.

Ramsden had never heard of the Matthew Leveson case or Atkins' alleged involvement before that first conversation with him. At 30 years of age, Ramsden had still been completing her law degree at Newcastle University at the time of Atkins' murder trial. Not that his history bothered her as, like any lawyer worth her salt, Ramsden believed every person is entitled to procedural fairness.

Following her conversation with Atkins, Ramsden called a trusted colleague to work the case. At 37, Claire Wasley was fairly young for a barrister, particularly such a successful one, but she had strong experience in coronial matters. Yet not even she had ever encountered a situation quite like Atkins' before. As she and Ramsden would soon discover, their client's position was unprecedented.

Tuesday 3 November 2015

Within a week of assembling, the young defence team found themselves going head to head with us at Channel Nine. The argument put forward by *60 Minutes*, backed by the Leveson family and the NSW Police, was that a story containing the 'evidence the jury never heard', specifically Atkins' lies about buying the mattock and tape at Bunnings, could prompt new witnesses to come forward, or prompt witnesses who may have been misguided as to the true nature of Atkins. Jubelin's point of view, supported by the Police Commissioner, was that the story was part of an 'investigative strategy'.

But Atkins' legal team hit back by claiming that the television program's interest in the police video was only to point out Atkins' lies and inconsistencies, which constituted a 'trial by media', undermining the jury system and the impending inquest. Under instructions from Atkins to do whatever it took to protect his exposure before the inquest, Ramsden and Wasley upped the ante by attempting to suppress the actual transcript of his murder trial, specifically the voir dire sections. Sitting beside Mark and Faye in the public gallery, I felt crushed. That was the entire basis of the story I'd pitched over a year ago. We were treading water in dangerous seas.

Thankfully, Deputy State Coroner Elaine Truscott granted access to the CCTV footage and specific parts of the police interview with Atkins. But she didn't allow it for the sake of *60 Minutes*. Instead, it was the compelling position of the Leveson family that was strongly taken into consideration. 'They need to be able to say that everything that could have been done has been done,' the Coroner stated in her ruling.

The story would go to air.

Sunday 22 November 2015

Suburban Australia was settling in for the night as over a million viewers tuned in to the final episode of 2015 for Channel Nine's flagship current affairs program.

'This is a duty no parent should ever have to perform,' *60 Minutes* reporter Michael Usher told the audience.

Mark and Faye Leveson held a shovel and a mattock as they trudged through the dense bush of the Royal National Park. In a heartbreaking introduction to their hell on earth, the Levesons showed both Usher and the nation how, each weekend, they searched and dug for the body of their son. For the first time, the full and extraordinary circumstances of the case were detailed over 14 minutes of television, from Matt's disappearance to the Bunnings CCTV footage, the lies contained in Atkins' police interview, and Atkins' acquittal and new life in Brisbane.

As the story drew to an end, Faye furrowed her brow and looked at Usher with a haunting stare. She said, 'The truth's going to come out. One way or another, the truth is going to come out.'

The iconic ticking clock filled the screen. Its *tick, tick, tick* now captured the situation Atkins found himself in. He had just been exposed across Australia as the man who knew the truth about Matt Leveson's death and refused to tell his grieving parents. The public, and other media outlets, were shocked and appalled.

The inquest hadn't even started yet but, after the program was aired, life as Atkins knew it began unravelling. The horrible secret he'd held close for all those years was now a ticking time bomb ready to detonate under the scrutiny of the law.

32.

THE INQUEST

Monday 7 December 2015

Walking along the footpath hand in hand with her husband, bile burning the back of her throat, Faye Leveson had a sense of déjà vu.

It was a warm morning. Heat shimmered up from the worn pavement outside the State Coroner's Court in Sydney's inner-western suburb Glebe. For more than 40 years, the dreary complex had hosted the families of the deceased in its first-floor courtrooms while downstairs, on stainless steel tables under fluorescent lights, the lifeless bodies of their loved ones were examined by pathologists in the morgue.

A small throng of cameras rolled and snapped away as Mark and Faye, flanked by their Pete and Jason, entered the ageing building. The infectious smile of their missing son beamed out from a custom-made handbag slung over Faye's shoulder. As Faye says, one side is all Matty, covered with photos including the last snap of the whole family together, Matt wearing a paper party hat, and another of Faye hugging him tight. The other side is covered with photos of all three Leveson boys.

What few realise is that part of Faye's fixation on finding answers stems from a promise she made her youngest, Jason, many years ago.

'He broke down one night, just before the trial,' she relays to me. 'He wanted his brother back and, as his mother, I tried to promise we'd do that.'

One of Mark and Faye's greatest fears has always been that they'd reach the end of their lives without finding Matt's remains. They've said a number of times that they never wanted to leave Jason and Pete with that burden. The impact of Matt's death on his two brothers is often skipped over in media reports. Both shy away from the public spotlight, Jason more so than Pete, but their grief is still just as strong. Jason feels let down by a system and a process he thought could be trusted, and his frustration often means he lashes out at authority. Pete, on the other hand, deals with his demons in the same way his father does, by putting on a brave, cheery face to the outside world.

Mark Leveson smiled as he entered the courtroom the first day of the inquest, dragging a small black suitcase behind him. He embraced me in a hug, warm and familiar, before greeting a dedicated group of supporters in the front row, the long-time friends who'd stuck by Mark and Faye through their most horrendous times. There was also Howard Brown and Peter Rolfe, two victims advocates who had both been personally affected by murder. Each was dressed with a splash of purple, Matty's favourite colour.

Instead of a Crown Prosecutor, as there had been in the Supreme Court trial, there was Counsel Assisting the Coroner, barrister Lester Fernandez, and his instructing senior solicitor Ian Lindwood. They were to assist the Coroner by leading the inquest, lending their advice throughout the proceedings and cross-examining witnesses.

Halfway along the bar table in the centre of the room, Mark Leveson took his seat. He would not be a silent observer as he had been at the trial, and neither would his family. The account-ant turned bush lawyer had been granted leave to appear on behalf of the family. In the months leading up to the inquest, Mark would return home from work only to study texts for court late into the night. At the inquest he'd be in the thick of the action and would have the chance to cross-examine wit-nesses who took the stand.

Beside Mark Leveson sat Pat Saidi, the barrister for NSW Police. Directly behind him was Gary Jubelin and his dedicated team: Dr Sarah Yule and Senior Constables Scott Craddock, John Mastrobattista and Damien Bateman.

Sharon Ramsden and Claire Wasley took their seats at the far end of the bar table. Atkins, although named as the person of interest, was not yet required to attend. Instead, he sat waiting in a dingy motel room in the city. Both Ramsden and Wasley had been to see him that morning, and Ramsden had explained she would take notes throughout the proceedings and call him at the end of each day with the latest.

A silence fell over the court and everyone got to their feet as Deputy State Coroner Elaine Truscott entered the room. Her Honour had a presence to be reckoned with. Truscott had a track record of 30 years' experience in law, and an impressive background as a barrister and solicitor before she had been appointed as a magistrate.

As the inquest got underway, Her Honour perused the court-room through a pair of spectacles balanced on the tip of her nose. Her severe expression, combined with her cutting delivery and noticeable eye rolls, made her seem rather intimidating.

The tone of the inquest was set early. 'The purpose of this inquest is to assist the court to come to findings as to manner and cause of death,' Lester Fernandez stated. He continued, 'It is acknowledged by everyone that there is only one person who can fill in the gaps of what happened to Matt from 23rd September 2007 and onwards. That one person is Mr Atkins.'

Fernandez added a note of warning: 'This inquest is only going to be as good as the evidence before it.'

Tuesday 8 December – Thursday 17 December 2015

While the inquest looked and felt similar to the criminal pro-ceedings of Michael Atkins' murder trial in 2009, this time there were far fewer rules. The inquisitorial nature of an inquest allowed for all manner of evidence, as long as it was considered reliable, which meant personal observations and even opinion could be heard. It made intriguing viewing for the dedicated group of court reporters turning up day by day. Their presence represented a significant step up from the waning media interest Mark and Faye had experienced during the trial. This time, daily articles covering the inquest were published in the *Sydney Morning Herald* and *Daily Telegraph*, as well as nightly news reports on each television network. Public interest had certainly skyrocketed following the *60 Minutes* story, and it now continued to grow by the day.

In the early stages, Detective Senior Constables Scott Craddock and Damien Bateman each took the stand. The evidence in their police brief consisted of facts gathered through the original investigation as well as their re-examination of the case, which had uncovered previously overlooked evidence. The detectives, alongside Gary Jubelin, didn't shy away from the harsh reality that opportunities had been missed during the original police investigation. They'd studied Atkins' vague and inconsistent responses to key questions during the initial police interview compared with his succinct answers when the topic did not revolve around his boyfriend. Despite the shortcomings of the interview, all two hours of which was played to the court in full, it was Craddock and Bateman's opinion that Atkins had been on the verge of giving police information about his involvement. At no point was this more obvious than when he told Sergeant Melissa Cooper after the tape was turned off, 'I want to tell you, but I'm scared what will happen to me if I do.' The new strike force believed this admission demonstrated Atkins' willingness to choose self-preservation over telling the truth.

The inquest also heard how the young detectives had discovered additional CCTV footage from ARQ on the night Matt was last seen. The images were not presented during the trial and may have been missed altogether by the original investigation.

The footage captured Atkins returning to the entrance of the club alone at 3.06 am to complete a drug deal, almost an hour after Atkins and Matt had first left ARQ together.

Minutes later, the footage showed Atkins' close friend Jack Smith also leaving the club, which seemed to fit with his confused evidence during the trial that he'd gone to say goodbye to his friends out at Matt's car. But when Smith was called to give evidence at the inquest, he proved again an unreliable witness with a poor recollection. Smith told the Coroner that when he arrived in the back street where Matt's car was parked, Matt was sitting in the front passenger seat and 'flailing his arms around' in a drug-affected way, an observation that was contrary to earlier evidence he'd provided to police and at the trial. He even conceded, once again, that perhaps this memory didn't relate to the night in question.

The Coroner heard that evidence was missed in the early stages of the investigation and that key evidence was now missing. The audio tapes from the all-important listening device operation the Levesons undertook to record Atkins were nowhere to be found. Hard copies of crime scene photographs and the unedited search warrant video were also misplaced. Each piece had been shown at trial but had inexplicably disappeared afterwards.

Over ten drawn-out days, the stand was a revolving turnstile of police and civilian witnesses. Mostly their evidence repeated what the trial had heard, and it was becoming apparent that the case was no further along from where it'd started. The thought that the inquest would yield no further answers weighed heavily on Mark and Faye. As Mark aptly told the court during his own evidence:

They're macabre questions, but we want answers to these. We want to know why [Matt] was murdered, how he was murdered, did he suffer, where he was murdered, when.

These things we need answers to. We hope the inquest will answer this for us.

The Counsel Assisting asked, 'Do you want to find out who murdered Matt and if other people were involved in his murder?'

'No,' Mark responded, deadpan. 'I don't need to know who. I know that. If others were involved, well, then yes, I want to know that as well.' The weight of his accusation hung in the air. He continued:

This is really our last chance. We need to get answers here for ourselves and our family. So our goal is to find these questions out and, if yourself and the Coroner help us with these matters, that's our goal, to bring Matt home.

Mark looked up at the Coroner. 'Otherwise, where to from here?'

There was nowhere else to go besides the one person who knew the truth. The man who had exercised his right to silence since September 2007. There was no other way around it; Michael Atkins must take the stand.

33.

THE FIRST DEAL

Thursday 17 December 2015

'No!' Faye Leveson exclaimed, her arms folded tightly across her chest. 'Absolutely no way.' She closed her eyes in a futile attempt to shield herself from the extraordinary proposal that was being put forward to her.

Jubelin had anticipated a pushback. What he and Lester Fernandez were suggesting to the Leveson family felt like blasphemy, but they'd been left with no other choice. They were standing at a crossroads. Michael Atkins would soon be called to give evidence but, as all persons of interest had the right to do, Atkins would almost certainly object to answering any questions on the basis that the evidence he may give would tend to incriminate him in an offence. Generally speaking, if there were reasonable grounds to the objection, a Coroner would simply thank the person of interest for coming along and excuse them from the stand, which would essentially mean game over for the family, the police and the Coroner.

The inquest had been a last-ditch attempt to find answers, but the evidence so far had failed to produce a smoking gun. Through their reinvestigation, police knew that the likelihood of gathering any 'fresh and compelling' evidence which might lead to a retrial was extremely slim. Discovery of Matt's remains was really the only scenario that might result in new charges being laid against Atkins. But, short of a dazed bushwalker stumbling across his burial site or, God forbid, Mark and Faye digging him up, the prospects were not good. There was only one option left but it was highly controversial, and legally unprecedented.

'Hold on, let's hear them out.' Mark's voice of reason struck a chord with his family. Pete and Jason were gathered with him and Faye around the table in a tiny back room at the Coroner's Court. Jason and Faye were totally against the proposal, but Pete and Mark were starting to see the reasoning behind it.

Jubelin hated the position he was putting the Levesons in, but if he thought for one moment there was any other way he could catch Atkins, he'd do it. He ran through the proposal again: 'When Atkins objects to giving evidence, there is an option available to the Coroner to grant him a certificate under section 61 of the Coroners Act.' Jubelin paused, letting the detail sink in. The Levesons were familiar with that certificate; many of Matt's friends who'd given evidence during the inquest about their drug use had been granted protection against self-incrimination.

But here was the clincher: 'In Atkins' case,' Jubelin continued, 'that certificate would provide him with immunity from prosecution for murder, and every other criminal offence for that matter, except perjury and contempt of court.'

Faye shook her head. *Immunity for murder.* How could they ever agree to such a thing? Atkins could theoretically hop into the stand and fess up to Matt's murder – *I shot him, I strangled him, I buried him here* – and face no legal consequences. But Faye also knew the predicament they were facing as a family.

Jubelin summed their dilemma up perfectly when he asked, 'Let's break it down, what do you ideally want out of this inquest?'

'To prosecute Atkins and to find Matt's body,' Mark and Faye replied.

Jubelin paused before asking what was perhaps the most unfair question he'd ever put to a family. 'What if you could only achieve one of those things – what would you choose?'

Their response was immediate. 'We want Matt's body back.'

It was appallingly unfair that the Levesons were forced to choose between two options that the justice system should have allowed them to achieve. The system was letting them down yet again. Jubelin didn't shy away from these failures. He also couldn't change what had happened, but he could push the boundaries of the inquest as far as legally possible.

It was a torturous decision but, after taking time to consider their limited options, Mark, Faye and Pete reluctantly agreed it was the only way forward. Jason remained against it, deeply so. He wanted Atkins locked away and he wasn't prepared to give up on that hope, however distant.

His parents, however, were forging ahead with their children's interests at the forefront of their minds. 'It was a double goal,' Mark reflects. 'To bring Matt home, and secondly, to not let this problem fall on the two boys after we die.'

The offer of the certificate under section 61 was a bombshell Atkins and his legal team hadn't seen coming. The goalposts had shifted, and drastically so.

In Sharon Ramsden's mind, there had been no indication that their client might be compelled to give evidence. When the notice was forwarded to them that the Coroner was seriously considering the option, Atkins' instructions were to fight it. Even under the protection of the certificate, he did not wish to give evidence willingly.

By this point, it was a week before Christmas. Court listings were winding down for the year, as was the legal fraternity. The Matthew Leveson inquest had been one of the final matters of 2015 for both Ramsden and Wasley. When they first took on the matter, they'd anticipated the whole proceedings would be wrapped up within a few weeks, but now their client had entered dangerous territory, in circumstances entirely unfamiliar to them.

Over the next two months, Ramsden and Wasley prepared themselves for an almighty challenge: to keep Michael Atkins from testifying.

Thursday 18 February 2016

As I made my way towards the front entrance of the court, I could see Mark and Faye were already waiting in the foyer. We'd arranged to meet early, eager to watch the arrival of Michael Atkins together. As predicted, he would be required to enter the witness box that morning. The Levesons had told me that for them this would be a bittersweet moment. I'd grown close to Mark and Faye over the previous 16 months, as we found ourselves bonded by our mutual goal, to expose Atkins' lies. They'd discussed with me in detail the double-edged sword of advocating for Atkins to be given immunity in exchange for testifying.

When the court doors opened, I took a seat beside Mark and Faye in the public gallery. Pete, Jason and the police joined us, while the man we'd all come to see slunk in at the very last moment. After Atkins was invited into the witness box, he focused his stare straight ahead.

'Where is Matt's body?' Fernandez put to him.

'I wish to object to any questions on the grounds I may incriminate myself,' Atkins replied. It was a global objection to all questions, and the Coroner told the court she was satisfied there were reasonable grounds for his objection. That part was fairly standard. Normally, beyond that point, a person of interest would be excused. But the Coroner now asked Atkins whether he would be willing to answer questions under the section 61 certificate. He still wished to object to giving evidence willingly. As Atkins stepped down, a hearing was convened in which the Coroner took submissions from each party. The combined strength of the Leveson family, the police and Counsel Assisting, who were all in favour of Atkins being compelled to take the stand, was a powerhouse of persuasion.

With more experience in the double jeopardy legislation than any other police officer in New South Wales, Jubelin confirmed to the court that any evidence Atkins gave in the witness box could not be used against him in any future retrial. And, as the situation stood, it was extremely unlikely Atkins would ever be charged again due to the lack of new evidence. From a police perspective, the section 61 certificate was their final chance to get to the truth.

With their son's former boyfriend as their audience, Mark, Faye and Pete Leveson each took the stand to prove to the Coroner that they each understood the consequences of such a deal. 'We came to the Coroner's Court with two objectives,' Mark explained softly, 'to bring Matt home, and secondly . . .' His voice hardened. 'To see Michael Atkins suffer and rot in hell for what he has done.' I remember flinching at the venom in Mark's words. 'Our main goal is to bring Matt home,' he concluded. 'If the second objective can't be achieved, so be it.'

Faye spoke to the court through her tears:

As a mother, as a parent, you shouldn't have to bury your children. And I can't even do that. Until we bring him home, our lives – even when we do bring him home – our lives won't be the same, but at least we'll have somewhere to go and see him, and to lay him down where he belongs.

It was during Pete Leveson's evidence that a painful lump formed in my throat. He is a thoroughly decent young man, much more concerned with the feelings of those around him than his own, and it was confronting to hear him talk about the personal pain he suffers from the death of his brother. 'We feel let down by the system and our hands are tied,' he said. 'We know who did it . . . yet we're not allowed to speak to him, we can't touch him, we can't do anything about it. If we were to go after him, then we'd be charged with an untold amount of criminal charges, and in this case, we've done nothing wrong.' He paused, collecting himself. 'I just feel so bound . . . The sheer frustration is insane.' He looked towards his mum in the public gallery. 'And seeing mum break down all the time is not pleasant. It's difficult.' Staring at the floor, he finished, 'Yeah, I just feel so bound and frustrated and angry. Very, very angry.'

But the argument from Atkins' barrister Claire Wasley was legal instead of emotional. She argued a dangerous precedent would be set if a person who exercised their right to silence, and who was acquitted at trial, was compelled to give evidence at an inquest. Wasley also submitted that the public confidence in the administration of justice would be significantly damaged if a witness was given immunity from prosecution for murder.

The Coroner adjourned the court until 23 February, but said she would continue considering the submissions over a number of weeks. There was much at stake.

It was a tenuous time for the Leveson family, made even more memorable by a startling late-night phone call one evening. On the line was former police officer Nicole Gallagher, who had worked on the original investigation. She explained how she and her husband had discovered a box of evidence in the roof of their home that contained the missing pieces of the case. Shocked and, quite frankly appalled, Mark and Faye drove to Gallagher's house. As they packed the box into their boot, they asked why Gallagher had kept the evidence. She told them it was an innocent mistake. She'd been involved in preparing an earlier brief for an inquest that never proceeded, and had taken boxes of evidence home so that she wouldn't be disturbed. Somehow, she'd never returned one of the boxes to police. Years had passed and she'd left the force, and it was only through media coverage of the inquest that her memory was jolted. The mystery of the missing evidence – the listening device recording from Mark and Faye and the unedited search footage – was finally solved. But its re-emergence didn't change the need for Michael Atkins to take the stand.

The Deputy State Coroner ultimately decided to compel Atkins to provide evidence to her court, putting herself on the line. But she too knew that without Atkins' evidence, the inquest would conclude with an open finding, and the truth would never come out. In her ruling, Her Honour stated that she was satisfied the circumstances of the case were so exceptional and compelling that immunising Atkins from potentially being tried again for Matt's murder would not cause damage or disrepute to the administration of justice.

Her judgement was immediately appealed by Atkins' defence team. He had exercised his right to silence since September 2007, and he wasn't about to break it if he could help it. Under no circumstances did he wish to get into that witness box. He took his battle all the way to the Supreme Court, where Ramsden not only appealed the Coroner's decision, but also challenged the entire basis of the inquest.

The appeals process dragged on for months. It was torture for the Levesons as they were suspended in thin air.

But, in the end, the law was on their side. On 12 October, the Supreme Court dismissed Atkins' challenge, and he now had no choice but to take the stand.

34.

LIES, RIDICULOUS LIES

Monday 31 October 2016

Microphones twisted uneasily in the hands of news reporters. Cameras burdened the shoulders of their operators. Necks strained as they looked up and down Parramatta Road, eyeballing every pedestrian within cooee of the Coroner's Court. The media pack was hungry that day. With the evidence of 26 witnesses now complete, journalists were waiting for the arrival of witness number 27. It was D-Day for Michael Atkins.

'Here we go!' a reporter exclaimed.

The cameramen turned in unison, positioning their viewfinders over their right eyes. With a crash zoom, they focused quickly on their target. Dressed in his signature court get-up of an ill-fitting suit, deep blue shirt and his deceased boyfriend's purple tie, Michael Atkins lumbered down the narrow pavement with his face tilted towards the ground. All the cameras managed to get was a shot of his thinning, greying hair. Atkins bowed his head even lower and walked faster, a futile attempt to shield his face from view. He was flanked by Sharon Ramsden and Claire Wasley, and the trio were smothered by the media pack until they sought refuge inside the court's sliding doors, beyond which point cameras were not allowed. But inside they came face to face with the Leveson family.

Faye's eyes bore into the back of Atkins' head as he made his way into the witness box. Standing before the Coroner, he took an oath rather than an affirmation, perhaps a sign that he was still somewhat faithful to his Catholic upbringing.

'He's wearing Matt's tie again!' Faye whispered angrily to Rachel Sanki sitting beside her. Armed with a notebook and pen, I sat behind Faye and her dozen-odd devoted supporters. The excitement surrounding me was profound, from the bar table to the public gallery and the police. This was a day to remember.

'Did you see his shoes?' Rachel whispered back to Faye. 'He's wearing sneakers, and they're covered in bird poo!'

I'd noticed them too as we'd waited in the foyer for court to commence, in an awkward jumble of parties standing far too close to one another for anyone's liking. Atkins had lingered as far away from the Levesons and their support crowd as possible. As I looked him up and down, taking in his outfit of choice, I couldn't help but wonder why on earth he'd shown up to court, on the most critical day of his life, wearing a cheap suit and white joggers covered in droppings. He was meant to be a clean freak.

But the sight of his dirty shoes brought a rare smile to Faye's face as the inquest got underway.

Launching to his feet, Counsel Assisting Lester Fernandez started with some housekeeping: he reiterated to Atkins that the evidence he would give was protected under a section 61 certif-icate, but the immunity didn't apply to false evidence. In other words, if Atkins lied and was found to have lied, he could still face prosecution for perjury.

Raising his voice dramatically, Fernandez began what would become an interrogation of four and a half days. 'You know that Matt is dead, don't you?' he hurled at Atkins.

'No.'

'Could Matt be alive?'

'He could be.' Atkins shrugged.

'When was the last time you saw Matt alive?'

'It was afternoon, on the Sunday.'

'What time in the afternoon was it?'

'I'm thinking it was about two or three.'

'Was that before you went to the Bunnings Warehouse, or after you went to the Bunnings Warehouse?'

'After.'

The questions and answers volleyed back and forth like a high-speed tennis match.

'Where do you think Matt went to?'

Atkins shrugged and delivered perhaps his most ridiculous lie to date. 'I always thought that he went to Thailand.'

The public gallery erupted in groans. *He couldn't be serious!* Mark Leveson, sitting at the bar table, gave no response.

'Why would he go to Thailand?'

'To start a new life.'

'What would be the reason Matt would need to start a new life?'

'Could be many reasons.'

Faye clenched her fist.

'You've just mentioned "many reasons". Let's have one?'

Atkins stuttered, 'Sorry. Like, starting afresh. Like, I think I just – say – I'm not sure, really. I just . . .'

Fernandez crossed his arms. 'I'm going to give you some time just to think about the answer you gave, so I'll stop and you let us know when you've got some reasons.'

A hush fell over the courtroom. All that could be heard was the tiny *tick-tock* of a clock on the wall. The court held its collective breath.

'Okay,' Atkins said finally. 'He just liked to travel and I just assumed, if he wasn't here, that's where he'd be, or may be.'

The courtroom was beginning to feel like a pressure cooker. One moment Atkins was being asked about his relationship with Matt – 'very loving, close and beautiful' – and the next, questioned on how many men he'd slept with immediately after Matt's disappearance – 'two, I think'. Trapped in the witness box, Atkins made a series of wide-ranging excuses for his behaviour: he suffered from depression that stopped him from searching for Matt; his young boyfriend could be a 'princess' at times; it was Matt's idea for them to deal drugs. Atkins said he held a 'tiny bit' of hope Matt might still come back one day as he missed everything about him, especially Matt's face. But he also confessed he couldn't remember Matt's final words: 'I think it was something about the TV.'

'Who drove home from ARQ?' Fernandez asked.

'I did.'

'What was the reason that you left the ARQ nightclub?'

'Matt had too much drugs.'

'How did that make him feel, having those drugs?'

Wasley jumped to her feet. 'Objection!' The reason behind it was clear; how was Atkins to know how the drugs made Matt feel?

Fernandez rephrased his question: 'What did you observe about Matt as a result of him having too much drugs?'

'He was – had – pulling faces and scrunching his face.' It was the same description of 'manky' faces that Atkins' friend Jack Smith had given. Yet Atkins and Smith's recollections appeared to directly contradict several other pieces of evidence. If Matt was so drug-affected, why had Atkins waited more than an hour to take him home? In the box, Atkins could shed no light on this.

There was also the mobile phone evidence. Text messages showed Matt Leveson was clearly coherent enough at 3.19 am to text his friend John Burns: *Mike's having a fucken cry. He is taking me home and won't let me stay! Fucken cunt!* Text messages from Atkins to Matt also revealed an earlier argument between the couple inside the club: *I said sorry 3 times!*

When asked what they were fighting about, Atkins told the court, 'I'm just totally speculating here . . . It might have been I didn't compliment him on his hair.'

Faye Leveson's eyes rolled into the back of her head.

The only possible tiff Atkins would admit to was a stand-off with Matt, during their drive home, over the volume of the stereo.

'The one thing I do remember is him turning the stereo up,' Atkins volunteered. Matt probably did it to annoy him, so Atkins said he turned it down.

'Was Matt upset?'

'A little bit, still cranky, yes . . . I think he wanted to go back.'

Fernandez kept it light. 'You think Matt wanted to go back? Did he have his "manky" faces when he was saying that?'

'A little bit; like, he wasn't completely normal.'

But Atkins refused to take the 'shitty' Matt back to ARQ because he was drug-affected, and Atkins was worried about him. Instead, Atkins took his young boyfriend home to 'make him safe'.

Fernandez steadied his stare and took aim at his subject. He spat out a provoking series of questions in rapid succession.

'While you were in the car with Matt, did you lose control?'

'No.'

'Did you have a fight with Matt?'

'No.'

'Did you hit Matt?'

'No.'

'Did he hit you?'

'No.'

'He wanted to annoy you, didn't he?'

'I don't know.'

'Things weren't going well in that car, were they?'

'They were fine in the car.'

On the edges of their seats, in a row directly behind the bar, Detective Chief Inspector Gary Jubelin and his team could barely breathe. This was the moment they'd been waiting for; if Atkins was ever going to break, the time was now. The pressure Fernandez had successfully built up felt unbearable enough to observers in the court, let alone for Atkins up there in the box.

'You were bigger than Matt, weren't you?'

'Yes.'

'Stronger than Matt?'

'I don't know about that.'

'You were the one with the ninjutsu training, weren't you?'

'Yes.'

'If you wished, you could subdue Matt in any number of ways, couldn't you?'

'Possibly.'

Fernandez continued the high-speed grilling. 'Did you subdue Matt?'

'No.'

'Did you lose control?'

'No.'

'Was Matt really alive when you arrived back at your address at Tonkin Street?'

'Yes.'

It felt as though a crescendo was coming, a nail-in-the-coffin question. But, for reasons unknown, Fernandez appeared to let his foot off the accelerator. He changed the subject. Frozen in my seat, I suddenly exhaled the air I hadn't realised I was holding on to. Even after all that, the truth was still trapped deep inside Michael Atkins.

During the second and third day of Atkins' examination, as Fernandez switched the subject of questioning to Atkins' Bunnings trip, the lies surpassed the point of ludicrous.

'Why did you make a trip to Bunnings?'

'Because I always wanted to have a garden . . .'

My eyebrows shot up.

'You always wanted to have a garden?'

'Yes. I've always been a keen gardener.'

Well, prove it, was the challenge.

Atkins reiterated the story that he had 'seedlings germinating' out on his balcony. They'd grown so tall that the little zucchini, bean and tomato plants were starting to topple over from their punnets. He bought the mattock because he wanted to dig a vegetable patch around the side of his apartment block. But why did he need the duct tape?

'I was going to use it – I'd seen it on a TV program, where they tie it around plants as they're growing, so, as they grow, it doesn't cut into them.' Little did Atkins know that the Coroner was a very keen, and well-informed, gardener. She'd never come across this mysterious 'duct tape technique'.

After court adjourned for the day, Mark Leveson couldn't stop thinking about Atkins' ridiculous lies. He should be made to prove it, Mark thought, so when he was home he jumped on the computer, went straight to the Bunnings website and confirmed that the exact type of duct tape Atkins had bought was still being sold. The next morning, he arrived right on opening and purchased a couple of rolls of the tape.

When Mark got to court, he put it to Fernandez that they should ask Atkins to demonstrate his technique. It was a brilliant idea, and Fernandez took it even further. He gifted to Detective Senior Constables Damien Bateman and John Mastrobattista the all-important task of buying two punnets of tomatoes and a mattock for the surprise demonstration. But as the two cops set out to make their gardening purchases, they realised every nearby nursery was shut. For an hour, they drove around in an absolute panic. There was no way they were turning up at court empty-handed. But they eventually found some baby plants in time, and their excursion proved to be worth it when court finally resumed.

'I've just got some items that I'm going to be showing you,' Fernandez said casually.

The public gallery tried to take a peek at what was hidden below the bar table.

'I'm going to show you two punnets of tomatoes. You know what tomatoes look like, don't you?'

'Yes.'

Presenting the plants, Fernandez asked, 'Were your tomatoes that you had similar to those?'

'Yes, I think so. Yes.'

Fernandez had Atkins right where he wanted him. 'How were you going to help those seedlings or the seeds you had for the tomatoes in terms of growing? What were you going to do? How were you going to tie them? Were you going to tie them onto something?'

'Yep.'

'What were you going to tie them onto?'

'Onto some sort of stake.'

'What were you going to affix the branches there of the plants to in terms of the stake? How were you going to tie it together?'

'I was going to use the cloth tape to do that.'

Perfect. Fernandez asked Atkins to show the court how exactly he was planning to use the tape. The public gallery's laughs began as a low snigger, but they soon erupted in incredulous squeals as they watched Atkins pull free a ten-centimetre length of the tape and attempt to wrap it around a tiny seedling.

It was black humour, given the dire circumstances of the inquest, but even Faye Leveson burst out in laughter. The scene before her was infuriating, ridiculous and hilarious all in one, and she'd have gone mad long ago without her sense of humour intact. For Mark, seeing his plan work out was his own 'gotcha!' moment. Atkins had once again shown what a liar he was. It also gave Mark pleasure to witness the usually stony-faced Deputy State Coroner Elaine Truscott appear amused by Atkins' preposterous demo. She was fighting a smile that twitched at the edges of her mouth.

Worse than the tomato plants was Atkins' demonstration of how he planned on using the heavy-duty metre-long mattock.

As Fernandez handed Atkins a replica, he asked him to hold the mattock in his hand and lift it up. 'That's a fairly heavy item, isn't it, yes?'

'Yes, it depends what you mean by heavy,' Atkins said, standing awkwardly before the court with the mattock item in his hands.

'Could you demonstrate how you were going to do the digging?'

'Like that, with two hands.' Atkins had positioned one hand down the end of the wooden handle and the other close to the metal head.

Fernandez slanted his head, taking in the strange technique. 'So in an overhead kind of way, you're digging down and then pulling across, is that right?'

'Yeah,' Atkins replied, with a background chorus of the chuckles still coming from the public gallery.

But as ridiculous, insulting and at times hilarious as Atkins' lies were, the inquest was still by this point no closer to learning the truth of how Matt died and where he was buried. That fact alone caused Dr Sarah Yule, seated next to Gary Jubelin, to worry that they'd never find answers. She was growing more and more concerned with every passing hour that Atkins was further locking into his lies. He wasn't reacting well to a public and aggressive grilling. Instead, this man, whose mind she knew well by then, was providing childlike responses to the most serious accusations. As a mother of two toddlers, Dr Yule likened Atkins to a kid caught red-handed with chocolate smeared all around his mouth, who was still denying he'd been in the cookie jar.

It was Dr Yule's strong opinion, at this stage of the proceedings, that Atkins was not going to fess up out of the goodness of his own heart. To her mind, he'd been getting away with the crime so far not because he was skilled and calculating, but more likely because he had dumb luck on his side. That said, Atkins could conceal a secret, whether it was his sexuality for almost 40 years or the circumstances of Matt's death. Dr Yule believed the immunity provided by the section 61 certificate was not motivation enough to convince him to come clean.

'There are no negative consequences for him,' she explained to Jubelin, Craddock and the NSW Police barrister, Pat Saidi, during a court adjournment. 'He's maintained this lie for nine and a half years, and because of his need for self-preservation, that's not going to shift without something else happening – something potentially jeopardising to him.'

Dr Yule was thinking of the carrot-and-stick approach. They had the carrot – the immunity certificate – but now they needed the stick: some sort of threat to Atkins' self-preservation. There was only one way forward; they needed Michael Atkins to perjure himself on the stand.

35.

THE SECOND DEAL

Friday 4 November 2016

10 am

The fifth and final day of Michael Atkins' evidence opened in spectacular fashion.

'Each day this week, you have stood up and you have faced Her Honour and sworn by almighty God to tell the truth, the whole truth and nothing but the truth, correct?' Fernandez began.

'Yes.'

'Have you taken the oath that you have made every morning seriously?'

'Yes.'

The public gallery leaned forward in their seats. The focus in Fernandez's voice was razor sharp.

'On Monday, you gave evidence that you relied on the police to find Matt, so you told them the truth in order to help them, do you recall that?'

Atkins tapped his foot on the floor. 'Yes. Vaguely, yes. Yes.'

'I asked you, when you spoke to the police about Matt, whether you told them the truth, do you recall that?'

'Yes.'

This was the moment Dr Yule was counting on.

'Your evidence was, you did tell the truth to police. That's your evidence here in this court.'

'Yes.'

'You agree that in your interview to police you told them lies, don't you?'

'Yes.'

'You've lied in your evidence in this court, haven't you, on Monday, when you said you told the police the truth?' Fernandez said. 'That's right, isn't it?'

A pause. A beat of silence, before Atkins replied, 'Yes.'

Heads wobbled from side to side in the public gallery as the Levesons' supporters and gathered journalists searched each other's faces for answers. Atkins had just admitted to lying to the court – now what? To confuse matters even more, the Counsel Assisting proceeded as though nothing had happened, launching into his most memorable stunt. 'Do you believe in forgiveness?' he started.

'Yes, I suppose.' Atkins shrugged.

'Do you believe in compassion?'

'Yes.'

'You've never had the chance to say to Mark and to Faye something about losing Matt, have you?'

Atkins remained silent. Pen in my hand, I felt goosebumps dart up my arms. Things were about to get intense.

'Have you ever had that chance?'

'No.'

With a sweeping movement, his black robes billowing around his arm, Fernandez swivelled his body to face Mark and Faye Leveson.

'I'm going to give you that chance now. Please stand up, Faye. Please stand up, Mark.'

Mark got to his feet at his assigned spot at the bar, as Faye swiftly joined him from the public gallery.

'Here are the parents of Matthew Leveson. Their son is dead, and they believe you killed him.' The drama of the courtroom had just reached dizzying heights. 'What would you like to say to Mark and Faye Leveson?' Atkins stared blankly at Fernandez, frozen in horror.

'Look at them, not me!' Fernandez bellowed. 'Look at them.'

Atkins made eye contact for a split second with his former boyfriend's parents. 'I want to say . . . sorry, I suppose,' he faltered. 'Sorry . . .'

'"Sorry, I suppose",' Fernandez mimicked. 'Sorry for what? Sorry for what? No! Look at them! Not me.' Atkins rounded his shoulders, barely looking at Mark and Faye. Fernandez barked, '"Sorry, I suppose", for what?'

'For your heartache.'

'Do you have any idea how much heartache they go through every day?'

'No,' Atkins said, swivelling his eyes back to Fernandez.

'No! Look at them, not me. I don't need any apologies. Do you have any idea what their lives are like, not knowing where their son is?'

'No.'

At that point, Pete and Jason Leveson rose to their feet in the public gallery. Side by side in solidarity, they made their way to the bar table to stand alongside their parents. The family's supporters wept, and their eyes and noses streamed. I looked up at the ceiling to keep the tears at the back of my eyes. The lump in my throat cut like glass.

'"Sorry, I suppose" – that's what you'd like to say to them. Is there anything else you'd like to say to Mark and Faye, and here's Peter as well, is there anything else you'd like to say? Here's Jason.'

'Yes.'

'This is the Leveson family. What would you like to say to them about Matt's loss?'

Atkins bowed his head and stared at his sneakers, covered in bird poo. 'I'm very sorry.'

'What are you sorry for?'

'Their loss.' He paused. 'If he's gone.'

A round of incredulous scoffs burst out of the public gallery.

'*If* he's gone!' Fernandez said.

'Yes.'

'The Leveson family believe you killed Matt. Can you look at the Leveson family and tell them whether you killed Matt or not?' Atkins' gaze remained fixed on the ground. 'Look at them!'

'No,' he said, snapping his head up, 'I did not kill Matt.'

Pete Leveson exploded with rage and resentment. 'That's bullshit!' he yelled at Atkins.

Fernandez continued, 'Would you like to say anything else to the Leveson family, who are right here in front of you, who you've never said anything to before about Matt's loss?' Atkins remained silent. 'Would you like to say anything else to them about Matt's passing?'

'I'm very sorry . . . I'm sorry Matt's not here.'

Pete called across the courtroom, 'Where is he?'

'I don't know.'

'You know you have the chance here to end the suffering that the Leveson family go through. You know that, don't you?' Fernandez pushed.

'Yes.'

'All the Leveson family want to know is where Matt's body is. Are you able to tell them where Matt's body is?'

'No.'

As the court adjourned for lunch that day, Detective Chief Inspector Jubelin grabbed Craddock and headed for the door. By this stage Craddock was considered Jubelin's right-hand man, after a recent promotion into the homicide squad. They both lived and breathed the case. In that moment, they were faced with a thrilling breakthrough.

Michael Atkins was exactly where they wanted him: cornered and facing prosecution.

1 pm

The sun was perched high above the expansive grounds of the University of Sydney, the unforgiving heat belting down from a milky blue sky. The jacarandas were starting to blossom around the campus. It was lunchtime on a Friday and hundreds of students were out in force, scuttling from tutorials straight into an early weekend.

The hype went unnoticed by a pair of detectives standing in a private nook within the university campus. Gary Jubelin and Scott Craddock had bolted there from the Coroner's Court across the road with Pat Saidi, the barrister for NSW Police. Away from the cameras and prying eyes, the trio had convened this impromptu meeting with Sharon Ramsden and Claire Wasley.

Jubelin pointed out that their client had now perjured himself. It was checkmate. He'd been caught lying, an offence that wasn't protected under his section 61 certificate, and now faced charges that could attract a ten-year prison sentence.

But the Levesons and the police remained focused on their shared ambition: to bring Matt home. The way police saw it, Atkins' perjury placed a new option on the table, a bargaining tool. A stick as well as a carrot. Jubelin told Atkins' lawyers that if their client was willing to share information that led to the recovery of Matt's body, police could consider pushing for an indemnity from prosecution. Such an approach was unheard of. They were talking about a murder suspect here. The deal would not only require the seal of approval from the NSW Attorney General, but also the strong backing of the Leveson family and the NSW Police Force, right up to the Commissioner.

Atkins' defence team played it straight, not committing either way. At this stage the discussion was still hypothetical, and they'd need to take instructions from their client before giving an answer. In the meantime, the detectives and their barrister would find out whether the potential deal held any chance of gaining approval.

*

'It was a deal with the devil,' Faye Leveson says to this day. Her family was forced into a corner by a legal system that couldn't provide them with anything even remotely resembling justice. By this point in 2016 it was more than nine years since she'd lost her precious Matty, and she and Mark had tried every possible route.

The Levesons knew there was nowhere left to turn, but that knowledge didn't make the decision any less excruciating. It felt worse than the first round of immunity offered to Atkins to take the stand, because now the choice was to lock him up or let him walk in exchange for Matt's body. Around their dining room table, over generously poured glasses of bourbon and Coke, Mark and Faye examined their impossible choice with their sons. Jason couldn't believe his parents were even considering the deal. Neither could they.

'We thought this was the last throw of the dice. If we didn't do this, we'd end up with little more than we already had. It was a gamble,' Mark Leveson admits. He and Faye know that outsiders will struggle to comprehend the choice they ultimately made – to do a deal with the most evil person they knew – but their children came first. Having Matt's body returned to their family was a prospect they simply couldn't turn down. No matter the cost.

Monday 7 November 2016

Three days after granting the police permission to push ahead with the deal, Mark and Faye received an unexpected phone call at their Bonnet Bay accounting practice. The NSW Attorney General was on the line. Gabrielle Upton was gentle and compassionate. She was calling because she wanted to check, to hear with her own ears, that the Levesons fully grasped what they were signing up for. Already the Commissioner of Police and the Commander of the Homicide Squad, Michael Willing, were on board. But Upton needed to confirm the Levesons' position before giving her final tick of approval.

'We were already full throttle anyway,' Mark reflects. 'We knew what was going on, so we thanked her for her time and her help in the matter.'

With that, the deal was done. Atkins was granted indemnity from any prosecution for the perjury and contempt of court offences he'd committed in the witness box, on the condition that he provide information to the police that resulted in the recovery of Matt Leveson's remains. But he must deliver. It was a case of no body, no deal.

Gary Jubelin conveyed the news to Atkins' defence team. The 'hypothetical' of a few days ago was now a reality.

36.

THE CONFESSION

Wednesday 9 November 2016

Gary Jubelin's shiny black shoe jiggled impatiently on the plush carpet. He checked the clock for the umpteenth time. It was 10 pm. He and his colleague Scott Craddock had now spent over six hours in the foyer and conference rooms of Marsdens Law Group.

The detectives, along with the Counsel Assisting, Lester Fernandez, and the barrister for NSW Police, Pat Saidi, were attempting to thrash out with Atkins' defence team the minutiae of how he would reveal what he knew. Sharon Ramsden and Claire Wasley were refusing to start the interview until two additional layers of protection were issued to their client, one from Michael Willing, Commander of the NSW Homicide Squad, ensuring that no information from the statement would be used against Atkins unless it was false, and another from the Counsel Assisting that Atkins would not be recalled to give evidence at the inquest so long as he provided a 'full and complete' statement about the location of Matt's body, and the manner and cause of his death.

At 11 pm, after Jubelin and Craddock had waited another hour, they heard the clip-clop of Sharon Ramsden's heels down the hallway. She told the two detectives they were now ready.

As Jubelin took a seat opposite his interview subject, he felt particularly confident. He knew how Atkins ticked. He'd staked him out covertly, listened to his private conversations, critically examined his lies in the original police interview and under cross-examination. He'd also assessed his demeanour at the times Atkins had told the truth; Jubelin had a point of reference. Jubelin also took expert advice from Dr Sarah Yule, who suggested that creating a non-judgemental environment would provide the best chance of extracting the truth.

As Ramsden and Wasley took their seats either side of their client, Craddock opened his laptop. The induced statement taken from Michael Atkins was never recorded or filmed, another of his defence team's conditions. What follows was taken from a typed version made by Craddock as he followed his boss's line of questioning.

They all looked at Atkins as Jubelin delivered his first question: 'Can you tell me your knowledge as to what happened to Matthew Leveson?'

'Yes.' Atkins exhaled. 'He had a drug overdose.'

The claim was hardly surprising. Jubelin had half-expected it. Still, it disappointed him to hear those words. He'd wanted a full murder confession.

'Did you have an argument when you were at ARQ?' Jubelin enquired.

'No, we didn't have an argument that I can remember. I told him we were going home . . . but I don't know if that means we were arguing.'

'Can you describe to me, in detail, your observations of Matt both physically and mentally during your trip home?'

Atkins responded:

He was sitting in the car normally, but he wasn't scrunching his face all the time, but you could see he was affected by G. He was looking a bit glazed over and occasionally blinking his eyes and moving slower than usual. He was just generally a little bit slower. Matt and I weren't talking much – he was more just turning the radio up, and I would turn it down. There wasn't a fight when I adjusted the radio, I would just turn it down after Matt turned it up. Matt was upset that he was going home.

Atkins said that after they parked in the street outside their unit block, Matt walked towards the front door without waiting for him. Inside, he and Matt didn't speak, and Atkins tried to leave him alone. Atkins thinks he turned on the TV and opened the balcony door to let some air in. Matt went into the kitchen for a couple of minutes before walking into the bedroom and lying on the bed.

'Did you have any intent to sleep in the same bed with Matt that night?' Jubelin asked.

'Yes, I was going to sleep in the bed with him.'

'Did you attempt to have any intimacy with Matt that night?'

'No.'

Atkins said he went out for a cigarette on the balcony before watching TV and falling asleep on the lounge.

'Did you sleep on the lounge the whole morning, from the time you fell asleep on the lounge?'

'Yes . . . I think I woke up around 9 am.'

'What did you do then?'

'I went into the bedroom and saw that Matt was lying on the ground with his eyes open, and he was not breathing and he had a funny colour . . . and he was dead. I didn't know what to do, and I just sat there with him.' Atkins' barrister and solicitor were frozen in their chairs. It was the first time they'd heard these details too. 'Later, when I was lying next to him, I told him that I loved him . . . I didn't know what to do.'

'Can you describe to me the exact position and manner in which Matt was lying when you first saw him?' Jubelin pressed.

'He was lying on the ground near the end of the bed . . . Matt was lying on his back with one arm down the side of his body and one arm over his body. His legs were with his knees bent but his legs were a little bit twisted. I saw Matt's eyes were open, Matt's mouth was slightly open.'

'What clothing was Matt wearing?'

'The same clothing he went out in the night before.'

Jubelin's mind was ticking over at a thousand miles per hour, thinking of ways he could trip him up. 'When did you form the opinion that Matt was deceased?'

'I don't remember the exact moment, but I remember looking and thinking it was not right. So fairly quickly . . . His face was a funny colour.'

Jubelin applied pressure by firing a succession of quick questions at Atkins about how he knew Matt was dead. No, Atkins said, he didn't check Matt for any vital signs such as breathing or pulse, but he did have a lot of first-aid training and he knew when someone wasn't breathing. Matt's eyes were glazed over, his chest wasn't moving and he felt cold.

Jubelin's eyes narrowed. 'Why didn't you call an ambulance?'

'I was panicking. I was freaking out . . . I was drug-affected. I was in shock and I could not believe this had happened. I don't know . . . I was just sitting there and I thought I would get blamed and I thought about the drugs.' His answers were softly spoken. Atkins was still awkward and stilted, but his manner was miles apart from the person Jubelin had observed under cross-examination.

'How long were you lying with Matt after you came to the conclusion he was deceased?'

'I think about half an hour. I just sat there looking at him. I was just in shock. I don't know if I was thinking about anything in particular.'

'How did the shock affect you?'

'It was numbing. I just couldn't think; I was totally overawed. I just couldn't think; I was paralysed.'

'When did you decide to cover up this situation?'

'I'm not sure . . . It was probably half an hour after I stopped lying with Matt. I wasn't thinking straight.'

Jubelin changed pace yet again, his words now slower and sharper. 'Did you cause Matt's death?'

'No.'

'Why did you cover up Matt's death?'

'Because I thought I would get blamed.'

'Why would you think that?'

'Because we were dealing drugs, and everyone thought I was the more responsible one so I should be the one caring for him.'

'Who were you concerned about blaming you?'

'Everybody, I think. Matt's parents. I thought everybody as in society, I suppose.'

Atkins claimed that he assumed Matt had died of a drug overdose when he found their bulk quantity of GHB left out on the kitchen bench. The old vodka bottle was usually kept in a cupboard opposite, where the ecstasy pills and cash were stored. He said on occasions he and Matt had free-poured G into a glass and drank it without a mixer.

'Do you know if Matt took any more G when you got home on the night he died?'

Atkins said he couldn't be sure. 'I assume he did, because he was trying to piss me off because I made him come home.'

Atkins' answers to the next series of questions were particularly revealing for Jubelin.

'Can you tell me your actions once you decided that you were not going to inform authorities of Matt's death?'

'I thought I could bury the body and nobody would know. I thought it would make it all better.'

Jubelin tried to keep the judgement out of his voice. 'How would you think burying Matt's body would make it all better?'

'I was not thinking very clearly. I thought people would think he has just gone away or is missing because he had done that before.'

'What would that achieve?'

'I thought the problem would all go away in some weird way.'

Jubelin held his stare. 'To describe the death of someone as a "problem that would go away" is very unusual. Can you explain to me what you mean by that?'

Atkins responded:

I don't really understand what I was thinking at the time. I look back now and I don't understand it. I just don't know. I thought I was going to be blamed and be shamed. I've always thought of myself as a good person, I would do anything for anyone. I know it's wrong. I was looking out for myself.

'So you buried a person that you loved in an unmarked grave to protect your reputation. Is that correct?'

In his husky voice, Atkins replied:

I think so. The whole thing about being blamed and the guilt. I did not want the drug thing to come out so I was trying to protect that, and I was worried what my family would think of me. I was worried about what my mother would think of me . . . She didn't know I was gay. Me having a younger partner and people judging me.

As incomprehensible as Atkins' reasoning was, Jubelin believed this admission was genuine. He reflects, about what Atkins revealed:

By him saying that he was worried about what his mother thought of him, it made me realise how pathetic he was. Of all the reasons for a 40-something-year-old bloke to bury his partner, he was worried about what Mummy thought. It was too stupid to be made up. Life experience tells you that.

But the most critical details were yet to come. For Atkins to hold out any hope of avoiding prison, he needed to reveal exactly where he'd buried Matt.

'Can you talk me through what was going through your mind, and what you did after you made the decision to get rid of Matt's body?' Jubelin sat back in his chair and let Atkins talk:

I thought I would bury the body so I needed something to dig a hole, so I thought a mattock would be a good thing to do that in the bushland . . . That was my plan, so I drove to Bunnings in Matt's car . . . and walked around there and window-shopped, for want of a better word, and bought a mattock. While I was there I thought of the idea to get tape to cover up the body so I bought some gaffer tape along with the mattock, and I paid for it and put it in the back of Matt's boot.

Once Atkins was back home, he stayed indoors for several hours waiting for night to fall. Then, he recalled:

I covered Matt with a blanket and tucked it underneath him. I don't know if it was a blanket or doona cover but I wrapped him in something . . . from his neck to his feet. I would go from sitting in the lounge room back to the bedroom to look at him. I stayed home and watched some television and sort of planning what I'd do next.

The forensic examination of Atkins' computer had also showed that at this stage in the afternoon he was not only watching TV, but was also on Matt's laptop searching Ticketek for Sleaze Ball tickets and trawling men's sex and dating site Manhunt. By his own admission, he'd done this as his boy-friend's body lay in the other room.

Later in the evening, about 10 or 11, Atkins took his car from the driveway and parked it on the street. He then drove Matt's car from the street to the garage and closed the door. Atkins said, 'I took the subwoofer out of the boot, and went upstairs and wrapped Matt's body fully. I can't remember if I used the tape but I think I did.'

The apartment complex was busy that night. Atkins said he was forced to wait until around midnight before the coast was clear to carry Matt's body downstairs to the garage. His description of this process booted Jubelin's brain into overdrive. The devil would be in the detail. 'When you carried Matt's body from the unit, can you describe to me the state of his body?'

'It was very stiff. That's what made it easier to carry, I thought.'

Craddock transcribed the word Atkins used to refer to the body of his boyfriend. *It.*

Jubelin continued, 'What do you mean by stiff?'

'It was stiff like a plank.'

'Can you describe to me how you carried Matt's body from the apartment?'

Atkins responded:

I stood him up as best I could and picked him up by wrapping my arms around his chest and carried him like a mummy . . . It was heavy, hard and awkward. I would carry him for a bit, pause, and had to put him down to open the garage door. I carried him like that to the car.

Prompted, Atkins said he pushed Matt as far forward into the car as possible, on a diagonal, so that his head was close to the passenger door. Atkins covered Matt with a blanket, the white hospital one later found in a backpack on the floor of his lounge room during the first search of his unit. Atkins closed the door of the car and drove out. He recalled having left his phone at home. When Jubelin asked why, Atkins said it was because he knew phones could be traced.

Atkins drove towards the Royal National Park, where he looked at a few different spots before settling on an area at Waterfall, not too far from the train station:

I drove until I found a stopping bay with gravel. I reversed in, then, and went up the hill and had a look around and found a spot near a big tree on the up part of the tree. I went back to the car and got the mattock and dug a hole. I went back and got Matt's body and buried it. I put a little branch over it.

'How long did it take to dig the grave?'

'Half an hour to an hour.'

'Can you describe the hole you dug?'

'It was a rectangular hole approximately two metres long by almost a metre wide. About a metre deep or 800 mm deep.'

'Did you say or do anything when you put Matt's body in the hole?'

'I said, "I love you."'

On his way home, along the Princes Highway, Atkins said he stopped the car and flung the mattock as far as he could into some thick scrub. He thought the tape went in too. After dumping Matt's car at Waratah Oval, he caught a taxi to Cronulla and walked the remaining distance home. It was early morning by then. He got ready and left for work.

'You were sending text messages to Matt's phone from your phone after you knew Matt was dead; in fact, after you had buried his body. What was the purpose of sending those messages to a dead man's phone?'

'I was trying to cover up the fact I had involvement in it.'

'It is my understanding that you accessed messages sent to Matt's phone after he was dead. What was the purpose of retrieving those messages?'

'I was looking to see who had sent him messages. I was just curious, I think.' He shrugged. 'I don't know.'

Jubelin pushed a piece of blank paper across the table to Atkins and handed him a pen. 'Could you please draw for me, as best you can, the area in which you parked Matt's car and carried his body to the gravesite?'

Atkins drew a childlike diagram of a windy tarred road that led down from the railway line at Waterfall. In a bay to the left, he drew a car reversed in towards the forest. He marked a rectangle with the word 'grave' as 15 to 20 metres from the car. A circle represented a large tree shielding the burial site.

Jubelin can remember Atkins' demeanour clearly. He seemed committed to leading police to the exact location of Matt's body. Jubelin hadn't expected to form an opinion by the end of that night that Atkins was telling the truth, but his instincts were telling him that was the case.

'I didn't form that opinion readily,' Jubelin says, rather defensively, because he knows his stance will be shouted down. This is the first time the experienced detective has given his full account, warts and all, on how and why he came to believe Atkins' version of events. After three years doggedly pursuing a man he believed to be a murderer, Jubelin changed his mind during Atkins' induced statement. He says:

> It was a process; I'm watching his body language, listening to the way in which he answered questions . . . Is he looking at me, does his speech flow? I played with the way I communicated with him; the tone in which I asked the questions; the way I stared him down. I'd apply pressure and then release it by being nonchalant. I let him talk and, in my experience, he didn't look like someone making it up. He appeared to be unburdening himself.

Jubelin tells me that there was no eureka moment for him during the interview. Instead, the more Atkins opened up, the more believable his version became. Jubelin doesn't consider Atkins was smart enough to manipulate that situation. The history of the case had shown that Atkins wasn't even capable of thinking two steps ahead, and he'd evaded prosecution because he'd been blessed with a whole lot of dumb luck.

'Emotionally, I was really pissed off,' Jubelin says. He reflects on what he saw unfold that evening:

> For me to come out of that interview room believing a guy that he buried his boyfriend because of a drug overdose goes against my very nature. It's detrimental to me as a homicide

detective; I actually pride myself on being a hard arse. But our job is to find out what happened.

2 am

The roads were empty of traffic, and the night was still and silent.

The late-night car trip was unlike anything the occupants had ever experienced. With Gary Jubelin behind the wheel, Sharon Ramsden and Claire Wasley were crammed into the back seat of his unmarked police car, sitting thigh to thigh with their client. Craddock was in the front passenger seat, his long legs against the dashboard.

Attempts at small talk were futile. The majority of their 45-minute drive from the Sydney CBD to the Royal National Park passed with few words exchanged. To make matters worse, Jubelin's efforts to create a relaxed, non-intimidating environment, to assist Atkins' memory recall, fell flat. He played chilled-out music softly from his iPod, and at one point, unforgettably so for Atkins' lawyers, James Blunt's haunting ballad 'Goodbye My Lover' wailed through the speakers.

When they wove their way into the dark, eerie national park, Jubelin followed Atkins' directions past Waterfall Station and down McKell Avenue. They pulled up at two areas of possibility pointed to by his hand-drawn map, but Atkins dismissed them. One felt too open, he said, and in another spot the car park was too small.

McKell Avenue was pitch black, save for the high-beam headlights of the car. As they continued down the snaking road, Atkins watched intently through the windscreen, his head darting back and forth. He then pointed to a small gravel bay to the left and said, 'I think this is where it was.'

Jubelin pulled up and jumped out of the car. He and Craddock watched as Atkins edged his way into the bush. There was something about the location that seemed to resonate with him. 'He had a spring in his step,' Jubelin remembers. They left Atkins alone to ponder the site: 'Due to his impressionable nature, we wanted him to walk out to where he thought Matt's body was buried, without us making any suggestions which might cloud his judgement.'

Four sets of eyes strained in the dark, watching as Atkins trekked through the dense forest. Ten metres, 20 metres, 40 metres. They were beginning to lose sight of him, so they began to follow him at a distance. Atkins kept moving, stumbling over tree roots and shrubs, before he came to a halt some 70 metres in the bush. He pointed out two trees that looked familiar to him. Craddock made a mark on each.

The small party returned to the car park, where another vehicle shortly pulled up beside them. Detective Senior Constables Damien Bateman and John Mastrobattista had arrived, armed with high-powered flashlights to properly inspect Atkins' two nominated locations.

But Atkins wasn't done. He asked to re-enter the bush from a different angle, and once again he stopped about 70 metres deep. The third site wasn't at all far from the first two, and the location of all three caused the detectives concern. It was a long way to drag a body from the car, even with the added benefit of adrenaline.

But Atkins was confident. Somewhere here, in a shallow grave, lay the body of his boyfriend. The man who had buried Matthew Leveson was finally giving up his secret.

37.

THE CHASE

Thursday 10 November 2016

The mood was electric at the Coroner's Court. It had been a week since the sudden adjournment had brought Michael Atkins' questioning to a halt, and every crime reporter in town had been talking since. Speculation was rife as to what might be going on behind the scenes. The scent of a scoop hung heavily in the air.

I made my way towards Mark and Faye Leveson through the bustling crowds. They stood in the court's foyer surrounded by their committed supporters. Partway through kissing cheeks and exchanging hugs, I looked at Mark enquiringly but he only smiled and shrugged politely. He hadn't heard anything, but court was to start at 10 am, as planned.

I spotted Jubelin and Craddock huddled in a corner, speaking in low tones. Their faces were stony and unreadable. I didn't know it at the time, but their tired, puffy eyes were evidence of the sleepless and eventful night they'd just endured. After completing Atkins' induced statement as the sun came up that morning, the two detectives had raced home, showered, changed and headed straight to court.

As ten o'clock came and went, the doors to the courtroom remained shut. Atkins' defence team had arrived but he hadn't. His absence was starting to rouse suspicion among the media. Later I found out he was safely tucked away in a motel room in the city and had no intention of attending that day. The plan, as far as Ramsden and Wasley were concerned, was for Atkins' induced statement to be tendered to the inquest as evidence but within a closed court, meaning neither the media nor the public would be privy to the proceedings. That, Ramsden thought, would mark the beginning of the end. As long as Matt's remains were found, Atkins had upheld his end of the bargain.

Reporters hovered like hawks around the Leveson family and the detectives, taking turns to question them about the delay. Both parties refused to breathe a word. Another hour passed before a staff door flew open, and Lester Fernandez walked past with his legal team in tow. He approached Mark and whispered something in his ear before gesturing for the rest of the family to follow him down the hall. Before anyone could react, the Levesons were locked away in a mediation room.

There was an eruption of chatter among the gathered supporters and court-watchers. The crowd was desperate to know what was happening. Journalists' thumbs punched out text messages to news bosses, and a few of the regular court reporters streamed outside to make private phone calls to their police contacts. The race was on.

My friend Ava Benny-Morrison was next to me as I sat on the sidelines. At the time a crime reporter for the *Sydney Morning Herald*, she'd already quietly approached Jubelin and Craddock to try her luck, but they'd refused to give up their secret. As it neared midday, Benny-Morrison became fed up and jumped to her feet. She speculated that there must have been a search underway and, rather than wait around, she was going to drive around the Sutherland Shire until she stumbled across something.

I sighed, conflicted. Much like Benny-Morrison, I too could take an educated guess that the police were probably searching for Matt's remains by that point. But the location was a complete unknown. Knowing the case as well as I did, I felt the odds were in favour of the Royal National Park, and told Benny-Morrison as much. She agreed it was the surest bet and, with that, she set off on her mission.

11 am

Tucked inside the mediation room, Fernandez revealed little about when a potential police search would begin. His spiel was brief. He confirmed that Atkins had accepted the deal with the Attorney General and led police to a spot in the Royal National Park overnight. They'd needed Atkins to come clean and, now he finally had, he would walk free. That part at least was expected. But the next blow was not.

Fernandez handed over a photocopy of all 21 pages of Michael Atkins' induced statement. Even all these years after Matt's disappearance, the family remained hopeful that Atkins might tell the truth.

Faye's eyes bulged as she skimmed over Atkins' very first answer. *Drug overdose.* A wave of revulsion instantly hit her and she swallowed painfully, willing the bile to stay down. After all this time, Atkins was blaming her son for his own death. Faye had been horrified, back in 2007, to find out Matt was involved with recreational drugs, but Matt's friends had told her how careful he'd been with his dosages. Besides, her mind screamed, why would Atkins go through with this cover-up, with the near-decade of lies it involved?

Her eyes blurry with tears, Faye read Atkins' claim that he didn't contact an ambulance or the police because he was 'freaking out' and 'panicking' about the drugs, and being blamed for them. But she felt his actions were cold. He said he loved Matt, yet he left him dead on the floor, went to Bunnings, buried Matt in the bush, then had sex with multiple partners in the week after.

Mark was equally disgusted, but he refused to allow his emotions to overrun the logical part of his brain. Atkins was afforded more than nine years to think of a story that left him in a good light. If he'd been so worried about the drugs in their apartment, why didn't he hide them before the police searched the place? History told him that Atkins was a pathological liar.

Once Faye and Mark had finished reading the statement, they passed it to their sons. When Pete read Atkins' claim that his little brother died of an overdose, he reacted forcefully. 'Bullshit!' he cried.

Faye's head spun with the 115 answers Atkins had given in his statement. With her arms folded tightly across her body, she felt sick to her stomach. Fernandez wouldn't allow them to keep a copy or read it a second time. After the Counsel Assisting reclaimed the document, he reiterated to the family how critical it was that none of them breathe a word of its contents. As he swung open the door, Fernandez told them he'd be back at some point with an update. There they remained, trapped in a tiny room.

12 pm

A cloud of tension hovered over Ava Benny-Morrison and photojournalist Kate Geraghty as their sedan hurtled into the Royal National Park. Soon, the thick scrub surrounded them on both sides of the road, and their tunnel vision narrowed. They needed to find that police search site, but the magnitude of their mission started to hit home. They were completely on their own, without a bar of phone reception, and the search site could be anywhere within the 15,000-hectare area.

Geraghty pulled in towards an opening to a fire trail. As she manoeuvred the sedan along the bumpy track, gravel crunched under the tyres and tree branches scraped against the windows until it became too narrow and they were forced to reverse out.

Back on the main road they forged on, darting down more fire trails. Down one track, Benny-Morrison spotted through the trees two bushwalkers who told them they hadn't seen any police officers or marked cars during their walk.

The Royal National Park was quiet that afternoon, and few cars passed them. The only sounds were the calls of local birdlife high up in the trees and, every now and again, the odd motorbike shuddering past.

More than an hour into their pursuit, the reporters hit a lonely intersection where they could keep going straight or turn left up a windy hill. They took a punt and chose the latter. A kilometre in, Benny-Morrison's heart skipped a beat. She noticed a blue-and-white perimeter of crime-scene tape fencing off a secluded gravel inlet. There was no time to waste. They pulled over, and the pair burst out of the car, Benny-Morrison with a notepad and Geraghty with her camera.

Two detectives in suits and R. M. Williams boots emerged from the bushland. Benny-Morrison recognised them as Damien Bateman and John Mastrobattista, two members of Gary Jubelin's strike force. They disclosed nothing. But their presence in the middle of that lonely bush clearing spoke volumes. Geraghty took a few shots before they made their way out of the national park and pulled up near Waterfall Station.

Poised over her laptop, Benny-Morrison stopped for a moment to consider what she was about to do. It was the sort of scoop crime reporters thrived on, but she'd also be breaking the news prematurely, perhaps even well before the police and the Coroner wanted it known that an official search for Matt Leveson's body was underway. She weighed up her options: to write or not to write. The information she was sitting on was huge – Michael Atkins had led police to the site where he believed his partner to be buried. That headline alone was enough to create a media circus of monumental proportions. She took a deep breath and started to write.

1 pm

In the foyer of the Coroner's Court, a cry reverberated through the waiting crowd. There was a commotion down the end of the hallway. A journalist had sprung to her feet. She gripped her smartphone. Benny-Morrison's article had gone live. Everyone within earshot reached for their phones and loaded the *Sydney*

Morning Herald website. The headline read: 'Missing man Matthew Leveson's boyfriend leads police to possible burial site'.

It was the development the Leveson family had longed for. As journalists darted outside with their phones plastered to their ears, barking instructions down the line, the foyer fell silent. Along with everyone who remained, I read the opening paragraphs of the article:

> A man acquitted seven years ago for the murder of his then-boyfriend has led police to his possible grave site in rugged bushland south of Sydney after being granted immunity from prosecution.
>
> In a sensational development in a long-running case, the inquest into Matthew Leveson's disappearance nine years ago was adjourned on Thursday.
>
> Police are now searching a location in the Royal National Park, not far from where Mr Leveson lived before he disappeared in 2007, for the 20-year-old man's body.
>
> Officers have been led there by his former partner, Michael Atkins, who was found not guilty of the murder and manslaughter of Mr Leveson following a trial in 2009.

Oblivious to the hullabaloo outside in the corridor, Mark sat hunched over his own phone inside the mediation room and distractedly scrolled through his Twitter feed. Much like the rest of his family, he was sick of waiting and having the truth withheld from him. The induced statement was the single biggest breakthrough they'd had in Matt's case since Atkins was first charged with his murder all those years ago.

Mark refreshed his feed and a new tweet popped up from Nine News. His breath caught in his throat as he read the headline. There was a link attached, and he quickly opened it. A live feed from the Nine News helicopter was loading. He let out a surprised cry.

'What is it?' Faye asked. Lost for words, Mark spun his phone around to his family as a live aerial shot began to play. The chug of the helicopter's blades hammered through the phone's speaker. A news ticker, rolling across the bottom of the screen, announced that NSW Police were searching Sydney's Royal National Park for the body of Matthew Leveson.

The door flew open in such a violent manner that it caused Faye to jump in her seat. Fernandez slammed it behind him. He asked the Levesons whether they had told the media what was happening. They said that of course they hadn't – they didn't even know the specifics of the police search. Moreover, while the fact Atkins had led police to the Royal National Park was now public, it was still by this stage not known to the media and public that Atkins had said he assumed Matt overdosed before burying him.

Mark and Faye were allowed to emerge from their confinement in the mediation room. A media pack awaiting them on the steps outside asked a flurry of questions, but there was very little the Levesons could say.

'We've been asked not to speak with the media at this time,' Mark told them, an apologetic look on his face.

'At the moment, you probably know more than we do,' Faye added as she grabbed Mark's arm and they headed up the street together.

I trailed Mark and Faye at a safe distance, while the cameramen finished capturing their footage, and found them waiting for me around the corner.

'Grace, do you want to come with us?' Mark offered. I jumped in the back seat with Rachel Sanki, and the four of us travelled south to the crime scene in Mark's bright blue Hilux ute. Conversation flowed freely despite the intense development. Faye spoke of her annoyance at having been cooped up in a tiny room all day as the real action played out 30 kilometres away in the Royal National Park. Mark's mind, however, was firmly centred on the search site. He was curious as to where exactly Atkins was claiming his son had been buried. He and Faye had been meticulous in their own searches, and chances were they'd recognise the location the moment we arrived.

Nearly an hour later, we pulled up at Foster's Flat, the official name for the area. A helicopter buzzed overhead. Media vehicles and satellite link trucks were parked haphazardly along both sides of the road. The shutter of a half-dozen cameras could be heard as Mark and Faye got out and made their way towards the police tape. When they reached the perimeter, Faye left on her sunglasses, the only layer of privacy between her raw emotion and the outside world. She and Mark hugged each other and stared into the dense bush before them.

As predicted, it wasn't their first time in this place. While Matt Leveson's parents refamiliarised themselves with the area, they told me that they'd been here before. They'd happened across the gravel stopping bay years ago during one of their weekend expeditions. It had looked like the sort of place Atkins might have come, but when they discovered a bushwalkers' track through the nearby scrub, they'd discounted it. The parents explained to me that they hadn't thought he'd bury a body right near a walking trail.

Mark and Faye stood and recalled their nearly ten-year fight, and soon dusk started falling around them. The search for their son would begin at daybreak.

38.
SEARCHING FOR MATT

Friday 11 November – Thursday 17 November 2016
The bright yellow excavator grunted to life, startling a flock of black cockatoos sitting high in the trees. The heavy machine powered through the bush, bowling over shrubs, ferns and small palms. Cameras mounted on tripods, hard up against the police tape, tracked the backhoe in their viewfinders until it became nothing more than a colourful blob through the leaves.

On the orders of the crime scene officer, Richard Crimmins, the three areas nominated by Atkins were dug up as a priority. Crimmins, dressed in a navy police jumpsuit and bucket hat, stood steadfastly beside the digger's bucket, his eyes fixed on every turn of soil. He was looking for anything, no matter how minuscule, that might indicate the presence of a body.

Gary Jubelin watched on, feeling blindsided. The unplanned, unwelcome hive of media activity that now surrounded the crime scene was frustrating for him and Craddock. They were both sleep-deprived and they could have done without the early exposure. The two detectives had been banking on another walk through the site with Michael Atkins; looking at the area during daylight hours could help jog his memory. But he was now unwilling to return under the spotlight of live television.

Instead, Jubelin had arrived with a handheld video camera. He recorded a narrated walk-through of the site before heading with Craddock to Sydney Airport, where Atkins was waiting for a flight back to Brisbane. A decision had been made to allow him to return home as the search took place. In a private room tucked away behind security, Atkins watched the footage. He said the site looked completely different to what he remembered. The trees he'd pointed out seemed a lot further back in the light of day – 80 metres from the road, Jubelin informed him. Atkins was shocked by this news, but there wasn't much more detail to be gleaned from him. He couldn't better describe the trees near the gravesite. He said the bush around him hadn't seemed overgrown, but provided just enough cover from the roadway. Again, he couldn't be sure if Matt was wearing shoes when Atkins had buried him.

After three days of digging, no body was found at Atkins' nominated spots. The police were disappointed but not defeated, and expanded the search parameters to a much larger area. The landscape, which posed plenty of challenges – strewn with trees and dense undergrowth, flat in some areas and sloping steeply in others – was scoured using a technique that involved digging trenches with 30 centimetres' distance between them. The method, which was based on past searches, gave police the greatest chance of finding Matt's grave.

For seven horrific days, Mark and Faye Leveson stood on the sidelines. I'll never forget the looks on their faces as they watched hour after hour with bated breath, yearning for the digger's next scoop to uncover their dead son.

As I sat next to the couple, their sons and Rachel Sanki in the SES-provided tent, behind the police tape, Faye despaired of their situation, while Mark remained chatty and upbeat. It took enormous effort on all our parts to find things to speak about, and to distract us from what we were doing there, for so long. Everything from beloved holiday destinations to favourite cocktails to the Levesons' dogs. Another distraction was the leeches. The slimy bloodsuckers were everywhere, slinking across the leaf-littered ground at lightning speed. Every so often a shriek would sound through the forest, followed by laughter, as a leech was discovered attached to our bodies. The police officers deep within the scrub copped it far worse, and no amount of insect repellent could save them.

But by the final day of the search, all jokes and smiles were put aside. Faye arrived that morning in a particularly distressed state.

'He's lying,' she said to me. 'Toying with us. Matty isn't here.'

By this point, the systematic excavation had covered 4000 square metres of bush. The whole area had been moonscaped. Only large trees remained as well as some large cabbage-tree palms, which the national park rangers had been careful to avoid. The riot squad had also been called in to perform a line search of the crime scene, plus an additional 20 metres either side of the boundary. They came up with nothing.

While the riot squad was there, Jubelin had an idea for an experiment. First he needed a mattock. I heard Jubelin, who knew that Mark and Faye usually carried one in their ute, ask if he could borrow their digging implement. Mark relayed the news that he didn't have one with him, to Jubelin's disappointment. I knew I shouldn't have been eavesdropping, but by the time Jubelin was asking Craddock to drive to Bunnings to buy a mattock, I had to interject.

'I'm sorry to interrupt,' I piped up from the side of the tent, 'but I actually have a mattock in the boot of my car . . . that you could use.' I quickly explained that the reason was innocent enough; I'd bought it months prior for our re-enactments on *60 Minutes*. The two cops and the Levesons burst out in laughter before Jubelin quite seriously asked me to fetch it.

The experiment saw two volunteers from the riot squad – one with the mattock and another with a shovel – dig two separate graves within a 30-minute timeframe. Unexpectedly, the officer with the mattock got further, but neither completed the graves to the dimensions provided by Atkins within the half-hour period.

Jubelin then provided the Levesons with the chance to enter the crime scene and mark with white flags some areas they'd like re-examined. It was a heartbreaking moment to watch as Mark, Faye and Pete traipsed into the bush, each holding a set of tiny white flags. Guided by their gut feelings, they pushed the flags into the soil. The backhoe returned and ripped apart the earth in each spot. But Matt was still nowhere to be found.

As the police packed down, Faye stared blankly as the digger was loaded onto the back of a truck and carted away.

News reporters gathered in a semicircle on the side of the road, in a bush-style press conference for the Levesons. With Mark clutching her trembling shoulders to keep her upright, Faye read from a card in her hands. It was a message she'd hoped to leave on her son's grave: 'Matt, our beautiful son and brother, we made a promise to you nine years, one month and 24 days ago to find you and bring you home,' she read through gasping breaths. 'Today we get to bring you home to where you belong . . .' Faye's body bowed over in pain. 'But I can't really say that now, can I?' she said to the cameras, as she wept. 'Because we didn't find him. And we haven't fulfilled our promise to him yet.' Her body rocked back and forth with every heaving sob. She concluded, 'But I promise you, Matty, we will bring you home.'

The search for Matt Leveson had failed. With the sun sinking beneath the horizon, Mark assisted his distraught wife into the car. They drove home empty-handed and in silence.

Driving myself home that night, I was overcome by grief for the parents. I cried in big, ugly sobs, wiping at the tears that ran down my cheeks and trying to catch my breath. My response caught me by surprise. As a journalist who'd told their story and was preparing to cover it again, I don't think I ever expected to get that emotional. But I'd spent so much time with the Levesons, and we had grown so close, that I keenly felt the importance of their mission. Finding Matt's body was everything.

39.

MANNEQUINS, HYPNOTISTS AND THE GAPS

December 2016

Gary Jubelin was questioning his instincts. He believed Atkins was telling the truth; he'd seemed so sure of the burial location. Yet there was still no body.

There was one point the detective kept coming back to. The commentary in his head went something like, *He's too fucking stupid to bullshit us.* Jubelin, and Scott Craddock for that matter, continued to believe Atkins was genuine in his efforts to lead them to Matt's body. There was no benefit for him to lie to police. He'd already made damning admissions about his involvement in Matt's disappearance, but without his boyfriend's remains Atkins still faced prosecution for perjury. If it was a simple case of forgetfulness or confusion, Jubelin was willing to give Atkins another chance.

For the second time in a month, two cops, Atkins and his two lawyers piled into a car as darkness fell. They set off to retrace Atkins' steps together, in a proposal put forward by Dr Sarah Yule, who was adamant that a walk-through would maximise his memory recall. Long-forgotten details could be triggered by all sorts of cues: a particular smell or sound in the bush, or the visual experience of tracking his movements.

Atkins sat in the front passenger seat, next to Jubelin. The detective did his best to make him feel at ease. But the more Jubelin interacted with Atkins, the more awkward he found him.

Usually the detective could build a rapport with most people, whether crooks or witnesses. But he found Atkins stunted with his emotions.

From the garage of his old unit in Cronulla, down the highway and into the depths of the Royal National Park, Atkins narrated his thoughts and recollections from the night he buried his dead boyfriend. He remembered, as he left home nine years earlier, feeling 'panicked' and under pressure to get to the bush quickly because 'time was getting on'. Mindful of keeping noise to a minimum, he'd manually pushed the car out of the garage and didn't start the ignition until it was in the driveway. The roads had been quiet that night. When he arrived at Waterfall Station, he'd remembered visiting the area as an 18-year-old with his mates. That night in 2007, there had been a group of cars and people gathered near the station's car park. Atkins had continued past them and had driven slowly down McKell Avenue, looking for 'a spot'.

Atkins' only memory of the parking bay he'd eventually pulled into was that it was 'little' and near a bend in the road. Jubelin pointed out a few areas on the opposite side of the road but Atkins agreed they were implausible because they were too steep and covered in thick, dense bushland.

Atkins revealed that when he'd first entered the bush, he'd become disorientated and lost. He'd heard a car but didn't see its headlights. The sound had helped to guide him back to the road and the boot of the car. The bush hadn't been overly thick where he'd stopped, and there was enough moonlight breaking through the trees for him to see. Atkins was unclear about whether he'd dragged Matt's body from the car or retrieved the mattock first. Either way, he had a memory of digging while the body lay on the high side of a tree. He thought he could remember still seeing the car from that location. Atkins told police that, while he straddled the grave, he'd pulled and rolled Matt's body inside. He'd flattened soil on top, and the pit was large enough that there was no distinguishable mound on the surface.

Jubelin interrogated Atkins on whether he'd ever returned to the burial site after that night. He claimed he hadn't, and Jubelin asked why. Atkins found the question hard to answer. He admitted that he was tempted to go back, but the trip never eventuated. He believed that if he'd gone earlier, he'd have found Matt's grave. But by now he had no new information to share.

With the first site ruled out, Scott Craddock was more determined than ever. Finding Matt Leveson became his personal odyssey. As the officer in charge of the case, under Jubelin's supervision, he spent a number of hours, many off-duty, circuiting the Royal National Park. The young detective possessed local knowledge, having lived in the Sutherland Shire all his life, but the bush was still a tangle of possibilities.

Much like his boss, Craddock believed Atkins was being authentic in his description of the site, and so he set out to find the most plausible alternative. The investigator was drawn towards a small pull-over bay 600 metres down the hill from the first site, on the opposite side of the road and on an uphill bend. One could hear vehicles on a nearby road without seeing their headlights. The site seemed to fit the bill. But when Craddock and Jubelin first took Atkins there during daylight hours, he was unsure. Atkins thought it was too open and too steep. He didn't remember a particular palm tree near the pull-over bay. But he asked to return at dark, just in case.

With hours until nightfall, the detectives took Atkins, Ramsden and Wasley to a nearby service station for dinner. They were an awkward bunch, but the detectives and lawyers did their best to remain civil by eating together. Atkins hovered in a world of his own, away from the table.

Once the sun had set, they plunged back into the Royal National Park. At the site, Craddock suggested, the police and lawyers waited on the edges of the bush while Atkins wandered alone. He admitted that the landscape looked completely different at night; the palm wasn't as noticeable, the hill didn't seem as steep and he felt concealed in the bush from the roadway.

Afterwards, Atkins made a comment that Jubelin will never forget: 'It's really scary down here,' he said. Coming from the man who'd buried a body somewhere in the surrounding bush, the comment didn't sit well with the cop who thought he'd heard it all.

But their night then took an even stranger turn. Still sceptical about Atkins' belief that he'd dug Matt's grave about 70 metres back from the road, Jubelin had held a brainstorming session with Dr Yule. They'd needed to come up with a new way to jog Atkins' clouded memory. In the end it was Jubelin who put forward a rather eccentric idea: what if they got Atkins to drag a mannequin? It wasn't exactly a conventional approach, but the circumstances were anything but ordinary. And Dr Yule was the one who kept telling the detectives to 'keep an open mind'. The police were also in a unique legal situation. It was highly unlikely there'd ever be another trial, which meant they weren't bound by the same risks associated with the contamination of evidence. They were free to try anything, and Dr Yule agreed that Jubelin's plan might just work.

The rendezvous in the forest with Michael Atkins and the mannequin was every bit as bizarre as expected. Jubelin flung open the boot of his car to reveal the life-sized dummy, borrowed from the police rescue squad, slumped inside. The re-enactment was deadly quiet, except for the sound of Atkins dragging a deadweight dummy across the forest floor. He grunted as he struggled. The mannequin, at 70 kilograms, was far heavier than he'd remembered Matt's body being. He conceded that he wouldn't have been able to carry Matt a distance of 70 metres into the bush, even when his adrenaline was heightened.

The re-enactment also triggered a new memory. Atkins remembered falling backwards while he carried Matt's body, which landed on the lower half of his legs.

When the activities finally came to an end, Jubelin drove his passengers back to the city and dropped them off before pulling over in a side alley where Craddock had left his vehicle. The detectives moved the mannequin from one police car to another as confused motorists passed them. It had been another strange night.

Atkins once again returned home to Brisbane's Fortitude Valley, to a life that no longer resembled what he'd known before. His creature comforts were in peril. Just days after the failed search for Matt's body, an online petition had been launched by a local gay man who was incensed by the injustice of Atkins' actions. He'd proposed that all gay clubs and bars around Australia ban Atkins, 'in light of the recent events surrounding Matthew Leveson and the search for his body in NSW bushland'. In a letter posted with the petition, he reasoned:

> This is affirmative action for the beautiful Leveson family and Matt's friends, who have been so brave in the face of adversity over the past nine years. Mr Atkins may have returned to his old life, and his pool parties, but banning him from gay venues such as The Beat [a club in Brisbane] and others around Australia will ensure it will never be quite the same for him again. All private venue entry rights are at the owner's discretion so the more support we can garner, the better chance we have of ensuring Michael Atkins won't be welcome in his favourite playgrounds.

The petition had already gathered hundreds of signatures, and resulted in Atkins being banned from his local gym. Even in his weekly outings to the grocery shop he was followed by photographers and television crews demanding he tell the Leveson family where their son's body was buried.

Monday 9 January – Wednesday 11 January 2017
Despite Atkins' lack of confidence in the second site proposed by police, there were similarities enough that Jubelin asked for

it to be searched. Over three days in January 2017, the bushland was torn apart by another backhoe. This time it was done in secret, away from the intense media spotlight. I went along to stand beside Mark and Faye, twice by myself and once with *60 Minutes* cameraman Mark Munro, who worked quickly and quietly, capturing a small amount of footage for what was now considered a long-term story. By that stage 14 months had passed since our first story about the Matt Leveson case had aired.

As the Levesons patrolled the outskirts of the search area, watching and waiting, they felt they were on another needle-in-a-haystack mission.

They were right. The search wrapped up and Matt remained missing.

The afternoon that search concluded, further up the road another search took place, this time without heavy machinery or police involvement. It was just two desperate parents looking for their son.

Mark clutched a mattock and Faye held a shovel, and the couple stumbled over fallen trees, splashed through a stream and fought their way through spider webs as they immersed themselves in a ferny valley. The location was diagonal to the first search site. They'd clocked it during one of their own countless expeditions up and down McKell Avenue. Since Atkins' induced statement two months prior, their obsession had hit a new high. This spot too was located on a bend in the road and had plenty of slopes and big trees around it, just as he'd described.

As I tagged along with them that Wednesday afternoon, it was a numbing experience to see them out there in the bush. Recently, they'd acquired a metal detector to try to pick up Matt's metal belt buckle under the earth. It pinged all sorts of things: old Coke cans, coins, bits of wire. The amount of rubbish buried in weird places throughout the bush was both startling and deflating. There were times the device beeped relentlessly over a spot and Mark would dig down a foot, sweat beading on his brow, before pausing. Their minds raced. There was always the minuscule chance they might find Matt. But after another round of digging the culprit would emerge: a metallic layer of soil, or a tiny ring from a soft drink can.

It wasn't the first or the last time I accompanied Mark and Faye on one of these harrowing expeditions. The most memorable dig occurred in late 2015 when we took a *60 Minutes* camera crew with us and picked a random spot in the bush. Mark was hacking into the soil when he suddenly froze in shock before pulling out a piece of cloth from the ground. He dug further, and to our horror a tiny grave emerged. Inside were bones wrapped within a blanket. Faye had cupped her hands over her mouth. 'Oh, God,' she'd cried, as Mark pulled out a long bone. Too small to be Matt's, but to the untrained eye it could have resembled a child's leg bone. We contacted Gary Jubelin, who sent out an officer to examine the grave. But the results came back negative for human remains. The skeleton had been that of a wombat. It seemed a motorist must have run it down and, feeling terrible, had wrapped the animal in a blanket before burying it deep within the forest.

But that bizarre and distressing experience paled in comparison to how Mark and Faye felt during our afternoon together in January 2017. Their feelings of despair were worse than ever. The agony they felt over the deal they signed with Atkins was profound. The 'lose-lose' deal, as Faye called it. By that stage she strongly believed Atkins was lying about where he had buried Matt. She thought he was playing games and relishing the opportunity to put her family through more hell.

'He's sitting up in Brisbane enjoying this,' she told me as we trudged through the bush. 'He should be made to come down here and search like us. Chain him to a tree until he tells us where Matt is.'

Her fury was understandable. I couldn't even begin to imagine how I'd feel in her shoes. But Mark felt differently. Like the police, he believed Atkins had nothing to gain by lying. If Atkins didn't come through with the goods, he'd go to jail.

Even so, after two failed police searches, he too was starting to doubt Atkins' sincerity.

Wednesday 8 February 2017

Lost and quickly running out of ideas, Jubelin and Craddock considered every avenue of opportunity. In their hour of need, the detectives turned to Australia's very own 'Queen of the Dead'. As a world expert in human decomposition, Professor Shari Forbes had recently opened the country's first 'body farm' at a top-secret location near the Blue Mountains, west of Sydney. Her facility, The Australian Facility for Taphonomic Experimental Research (AFTER), is essentially an outdoor lab where scientists can study the process of human decay. Donated bodies are placed in scenarios similar to what police might find at crime scenes: shallow graves, wrapped in plastic, locked in car boots, or left on the ground for flies and insects to devour.

Craddock reached out to Professor Forbes and asked her to provide an expert opinion on the state of Matt Leveson's decomposition, and what might remain of his grave. The straight-shooting forensic scientist advised that, after more than nine years, the only physical remnants of Matt Leveson would most likely be his bones. It would have taken three to five years for his body to fully decompose, but even in the early stages a passing bushwalker wouldn't have smelled a thing. The depth of the grave and the density of the clay in the soil meant odours would have struggled to rise to the surface. Unsurprisingly, the cadaver dogs that police had previously brought in detected nothing. The lack of smell would also have made the prospect of scavenger activity very unlikely. For that reason, Professor Forbes believed Matt's skeleton would remain fully intact. His clothing would be most likely degraded, except perhaps for some synthetic materials in the zippers, buttons and jewellery. As far as search methods were concerned, there was little else police could do. Professor Forbes didn't believe ground-penetrating radar or other techniques would assist them.

Their best chance remained Michael Atkins' memory recall.

March 2017

Michael Atkins was legally on thin ice but remained as hard as ever to read. While he was willing to assist when asked, he mostly seemed happy to wait for the next roll of the dice even though he faced being pursued for perjury, and with that came the possibility of going to jail.

Jubelin still had one last lifeline to throw to Atkins, but it was a hard sell.

'Hypnosis,' he put to Mark and Faye. Seeing their faces drop, he quickly added, 'But it's not the sort of hypnosis you'd be thinking.'

The official title was cognitive interview. Jubelin proposed the idea based on Dr Yule's advice on creating a 'non-judgemental' and 'relaxed' atmosphere for Atkins. Jubelin had used it once before, in a serial rape case in the late 1990s. A surfer walking to the beach had witnessed the rapist running past him, but he didn't realise it until minutes later when he stumbled across the victim. In an attempt to extract additional information about the rapist's description, the surfer underwent hypnosis. It worked, for all intents and purposes. But it wasn't exactly a common or well-accepted technique used by homicide detectives. Once again, there was nothing traditional about Jubelin's approach. But if Atkins was willing, it was worth a shot. The Levesons were sceptical, to say the least, but eventually they agreed to let it happen; whatever it took.

On the morning of the 'hypnosis' session, on 7 March, Atkins entered a private room and sat across from accredited clinical psychologist Dr Gary Banks. Their session wasn't taped and, for the record, didn't involve any swinging pocket watches or orders to cluck like a chicken. Instead, the process sought to minimise the chances of suggestibility, to heighten concentration and improve focus. Atkins was given an overview of how memory worked. Police didn't want him to fill in the blanks and take them from A to Z, but given his memory was likely to be incomplete, Dr Banks would seek to unlock pockets or islands of information.

Atkins was asked to get comfortable in the chair, close his eyes and focus on his breathing. He was taken through a relaxation session to minimise the distractions around him and in his mind. After going through several memories he had of Matt before his death, Atkins' attention was drawn to the night of the burial. He was asked to revisit it in detail. Rewind the video. Replay the video. Relive the moment in the present tense. Over two separate sessions, the night was painstakingly reconstructed.

But the strangest part of the entire strategy came afterwards. Knowing the Levesons had offered to help in whatever way they could, Jubelin approached them with an extraordinary request: would they consider lending Matt's car to police? It was the same car Atkins had used to dump their son's body almost ten years earlier. They'd kept the green Toyota Seca all that time, as a memento of Matt and a key piece of evidence in the case. Jubelin now wanted to give the car back to Atkins and send him off on an unnerving journey, alone at night, deep into the Royal National Park, to retrace the steps he took to bury Matt.

For three days, Atkins was given free rein. Round and round he went in his dead lover's car. The whole operation was done in secret, and not even local police knew Atkins was in the area. They couldn't risk word getting out and the media showing up.

At one stage Atkins parked and walked into the forest, meandering for a long time. As he wandered back towards the road, a passing motorist recognised him as the boyfriend of Matt Leveson. After the witness called triple zero, a local patrol car started making its way out. But Craddock found out just in time, and he shut the whole thing down before the police arrived and, more importantly, the press too. Atkins was none the wiser.

On Friday 10 March, the final day of the strange stint, the detectives and Atkins' defence team met him at the Royal National Park. After his three days of roaming, Atkins had a simple message for police: Matt was buried at the first site he'd chosen. The cognitive interview technique had only made him more resolute than ever. Dr Yule spoke with Atkins in person that afternoon. She recalls his lack of engagement with the entire process. While he was willing to help when required, he'd taken no initiative of his own, and didn't even know the name of the road they were on. He hadn't bothered to look at a map. But one thing was clear in his mind: the original site kept drawing him back. The railway station, the bend in the road, the gravel car park. This was it.

Jubelin and Craddock were reluctant at first to investigate the site further. The crime scene search had been extremely thorough, and police had used a proven excavation method that was intended to leave no stone unturned. But, Ramsden argued, there were still the gaps: the 30-centimetre spaces between each trench. She made no apologies as she warned Jubelin and Craddock they'd be ripped apart in the witness box if they tried to claim police had searched the site meticulously.

The heavy machinery returned to the first site for the second time.

40.
FINDING MATT

Wednesday 31 May 2017

It was the last day of the month, and the final day of autumn. The authorities had determined that at the close of 20 days, the search would be called off, as by then the area would have been thoroughly scoured. But with one hour remaining, as all hope seemed completely lost, Matt Leveson was found. The moment will forever remain with me. After everything that had happened, it simply didn't seem possible.

The day had started like any other during that latest search. At 7.30 am, I was standing beside Mark and Faye Leveson cocooned in five layers of clothing as each of us held lukewarm coffees. Deeper into the bush, Craddock was trudging through the crime scene; the sun poked its head through the trees. The young detective drew level with a bright orange excavator and said hello to the driver, Mitch Lombe. The senior employee from L. J. Williams, a private earthmoving contractor, was new at the crime scene. He'd joined the search only two days prior, when his boss received an SOS call from police. A backhoe, driven by a National Parks staffer, had become bogged on a muddy slope following an overnight downpour. They needed a bigger and better machine. Mitch's boss, a local, knew the Levesons and sent her worker on his way under strict orders to find Matt Leveson's body.

Mitch and Craddock scoured the previously searched area, but this time they left no small gaps. Every single square metre was dug down 60 to 90 centimetres, before the bucket's load, and the hole in the ground, were checked by police. It was a repetitive task. Every now and again Craddock would signal to Mitch to stop before bending down and inspecting something in the ground. A twig or a change in the soil. Never Matt. Still, the sound of the digger in idle made my heart skip a beat every time.

Mitch and Craddock made an unbeatable team. They'd set the ground rules early: if there was anything still left in the ground, they'd rip it out. From the sidelines I could tell that Mitch, with a cigarette dangling from his lips, didn't seem to share the environmental sensitivities of the National Parks staff.

On that final day, Faye especially was finding it hard to stay positive, out of anger but also fear. She was terrified of failing, of letting down her sons. She hadn't been sleeping. She'd barely eaten in days. Even finding the words to speak was draining.

2.30 pm
As the afternoon sun lowered in the sky, excavation efforts proceeded into the final stages. With the backhoe and Mitch's excavator now positioned in an area close to the road, I walked in silence with Faye and Mark through the completed sections of the now barren site. They were bracing themselves for more disappointment. As far as they could see, Michael Atkins would be charged with perjury and go to jail without them finding their Matt. As we stepped over pulverised roots and mounds of earth, we stopped and scanned the site, which was about the size of a soccer field. It looked like a wasteland.

When we returned to the gravel car park, Gary Jubelin was there waiting. He'd come down to be with the family and his officers as the search drew to a close. Sensing his apprehension, I left him alone for a moment with Mark and Faye and headed to my car for a drink of water. Standing on an embankment looking out over the search site, I got lost in my own thoughts.

The National Parks staffer and another police officer were to my right, deep within a ferny valley that fell outside the original site. Craddock and Mitch were closer to the road, right on the boundary of the area the previous search had covered. A large cabbage-tree palm hung above the machine. A smaller one growing next to it had just been hauled out of the ground; Mark had watched it happen and joked to his wife that the tree would look nice in their yard.

As I sipped water and watched, I saw Craddock suddenly raise his palm. 'Stop,' he said urgently. The digger came to a halt. Craddock edged closer, hunching over the dark soil. Using a long stick, he gently prodded at something in the ground. His body stiffened, a tiny movement but the most telling of signs.

'I think we've found him,' he quietly said to Mitch before making his way over to Jubelin, who excused himself from Mark and Faye and walked over. Craddock told him he thought they'd found Matt.

The grave was less than 15 metres from the car park. The boundary of the original search would have missed it by only centimetres. Jubelin stared down at the dense soil and saw a glimpse of creamy-coloured bone. He looked harder. Part of a pelvic bone. Leg bones. And the top of a skull. The remains were most definitely human.

The walk over to Mark and Faye felt like a lifetime for the detectives. It was a bittersweet experience. Craddock recalls, 'You're telling them that their son, their loved son is here, buried in the national park. Something they longed for. But that longing is something that is a horrible end as well.'

When they told the parents, Faye let out a sob. Her body and mind seized up in complete shock. She collapsed into Jubelin's chest. He draped an arm around her petite frame, pulling her in, before placing his other hand on Mark's stoic shoulder. As Faye wept, Craddock stepped in closer and hugged her to him as well. The four stood in silence and reflected on the heartache of the weekends spent searching; the trial, the acquittal, the inquest; the three separate excavations. The nine years, eight months and eight days since Matt had disappeared. And in the final hour of the police search, he was found.

I watched on from a distance, frozen to the spot. Beside me by this point was photojournalist Kate Geraghty, from the *Sydney Morning Herald*. 'You okay?' she asked me, before capturing the powerful moment that was playing out before our eyes. Geraghty and I had met a day earlier and bonded over the fact that we were the only two journalists down at the scene that week. The search for Matt's remains had been big news but, by day 20 of the dig, the interest of daily news bulletins had waned. Within the hour, all those other media contingents would return. But for now, it was still eerily quiet.

Nodding towards the bush grave, Jubelin made an unusual offer to Mark and Faye. He asked if they'd like to view their son. They said they would. It's difficult to imagine what they felt walking towards Matty's unmarked grave. Even now, Mark and Faye struggle themselves to describe it. 'Numb' is the only word they can ever come up with.

With their faces tilted towards the ground, they stared down at the bones. *Their Matty.* A howl pierced the air and shattered every heart within earshot. It came from the darkest depths of Faye Leveson. The nightmare she couldn't wake up from. A mother's terror. Mark held her tight, stroked her arm. There was nothing more he could do to ease her pain, or his.

Afterwards, when I walked towards the couple, I didn't know what to say. The circumstances were beyond devastating, but the find was also a victory. True to form, their faces told different stories: Faye's, paralysed with grief, and Mark's, smiling. They called their sons and Matt's best friend, Rachel. Pete was on a flight back from Townsville. He would land to a voicemail containing the news he'd waited so long to hear.

As we awaited the arrival of family and forensic teams, Mark asked if I'd like to walk down closer with him. 'To see Matt?' he offered.

For the second time that afternoon, words escaped me. 'Okay,' I managed.

The sun was beginning to slip out of sight altogether. I wasn't sure if I should look, if it was an intrusion. But Mark insisted. We crunched through the gravel car park, where Atkins had unloaded Matt's body from the boot. Down a slight slope where, dragging his lifeless boyfriend, he'd tripped and fallen. Past a formidable gum tree where he'd placed the body as he finished digging. And then there, under freshly turned soil, was Matt's grave.

From the distance we kept, I could see a tiny portion of exposed bone. The colouring looked more like that of a tree root than a skeleton. A shiver crept up my spine.

'Matt was lying directly underneath that palm,' Mark said.

I followed his pointed finger to a bowled-over cabbage-tree palm. It was a decent size, but was apparently less than ten years old. Its life had begun at the site of a young man's death. As my eyes strayed around the burial ground, it struck me that no matter how hard Mark and Faye had searched, they'd have never found Matt here. Under a palm.

Chaos descended quickly upon us. Within the hour, Crime Scene Officer Richard Crimmins returned with his team of specialists. Police tape was wrapped around a wide perimeter of trees. A plastic tarpaulin was angled along the roadside next to the grave, shielding Matt's skeleton from the gaze of the waiting press. Cameras clicked away and necks strained as an army of white suits worked to secure the scene.

Standing at the door of his truck, Mitch Lombe had packed down for the day and was preparing to go home. After one last cigarette, he approached the Levesons to say goodbye. He wasn't sure if he should interrupt them, as he didn't feel like it was his place. But, the fact was, he'd uncovered their son; he pushed himself to say something. Stepping forward to bid his farewell, he barely got the words out before, to his great surprise, he was pulled into a deep embrace.

'Thank you,' Faye said to him.

Mark shook his hand and echoed his wife's gratitude.

'Mitch and Scott are my heroes,' Faye often says of the digger driver and the detective. 'They found Matty for me. For us, for the boys. And they were so, so humble.'

As the sun dropped and the frost set in, the Levesons approached the media pack with Gary Jubelin by their sides.

'How are you feeling?' was one of the first questions to be asked of them.

'We're stunned, shocked, relieved – all sorts of emotions,' Mark said.

'We made a promise and we kept it, and now we can lay him to rest,' Faye said, weeping. 'Our boys won't have to go through their lives looking for their brother.'

'How do you feel about Michael Atkins' situation now that the remains have been found?'

'Don't mention that name,' Faye spat. 'He could have ended this . . . but he chose not to.' She made her disgust clear. 'He chose to stay in Queensland and not come down. He could have been down here helping but, no, he didn't.'

Mark took over. In his calm voice, he said, 'The accused has all the rights, we have none. That's the system.' It was certainly the system as the Leveson family had known it over the past decade.

'There's still more to do, so this is just one more step or one more battle in the war,' Mark concluded, referencing the long-awaited examination of his son's bones. Finally they would find out how Matt died.

Gary Jubelin stepped forward and told the media that the human remains hadn't been confirmed as Matthew Leveson's, but they were consistent with being his remains. Jubelin anticipated the exhumation of the bones to take a number of days, with a DNA confirmation soon afterwards.

With the site shrouded in darkness, a lone taxi arrived at the scene. Sharon Ramsden and Claire Wasley stepped out and traipsed into the bush. They'd come straight from the courtroom and were dressed accordingly in heels, blazers and knee-length skirts. Ramsden had called her client on the journey down. Atkins didn't seem surprised. He'd always been sure of the location of Matt's body. In hindsight, it's not hard to see that the mud map he originally drew matched the site where police had ultimately found the bush grave. Atkins had asked Ramsden what the discovery meant moving forward. She reiterated that he had full immunity from prosecution, and advised him that tests would be carried out on Matt's remains to consider the manner and cause of his death. Atkins did not appear concerned about what would be found.

At the search site, the two defence lawyers were joined by Deputy State Coroner Elaine Truscott, her Counsel Assisting Lester Fernandez and instructing solicitor Ian Lindwood. With the headlights of police vehicles beaming over the bush grave, men in white jumpsuits holding torches directed the group down to the site. They listened closely to the unsettling story of how the skeleton was found.

Over the following two days, Matt's remains were carefully exhumed from the grave. Each morning, Mark and Faye turned up to the crime scene at the crack of dawn and lay fresh flowers next to their son's grave.

Dressed head to toe in crisp white scrubs, forensic anthropologist Dr Denise Donlon conducted the entire excavation by hand. Down in the dirt, on her hands and knees, she brushed away until the entire skeleton was exposed. It was a slow and meticulous process, made harder by the two search efforts by police. The trenching process of the first search had possibly scraped the edges of the grave, which may have contributed to the scattering of bones. Then there was the removal of the cabbage-tree palm, unloading a further 50 centimetres of topsoil. Bones had been broken and gone missing.

Once the majority of the skeleton was removed, the earth surrounding the grave and within the digger's bucket was sieved, by hand and machine, to reveal any missing bones. The sieving method also uncovered tiny pieces of the clothing Matt had worn to ARQ on his final night: a label from his black Morgan-brand singlet; an iron-on print; a tag from his Industrie shorts; the sole of a degraded shoe. Tiny reminders of his last day alive.

Once the bones were packed up in large paper boxes, Gary Jubelin carefully placed Matt's remains in the boot of his car and transported him to the Glebe morgue. It was here, on a shiny stainless steel bench, where Matt's skeleton was pieced together like a jigsaw puzzle. But he would never be complete. No matter how hard forensic teams searched and sieved, a number of bones remained missing from Matt's feet, one ankle, his hands and the right ulna in his forearm. Also absent was the tiny xiphoid in the sternum and the hyoid bone in the neck. Shaped like a horseshoe, the hyoid is the only bone in the body not connected to any other. It hangs in the muscles of the neck and helps the tongue to move for speaking and swallowing. A fractured hyoid is generally associated with strangulation. But, in the opinion of the forensic anthropologist, even if the missing bone was recovered it may have suffered post-mortem damage. A number of other bones had, most likely, been caught by the digger.

During a post-mortem examination, Dr Donlon noted 'hinging' damage to Matt's skull and ribs, but she wasn't able to conclude whether the damage was done before or after death. She said the hinging effect that she found was more typical of peri-mortem damage, at or near the time of death, but it could also be caused post-mortem. Dr Donlon noted that aside from the excavator, the skull's damage may have been caused by mould and plant roots, and the hinging of the ribs may have resulted from soil pressure.

So far, there were no clues about how Matt Leveson died.

But if it was, as Atkins claimed, a drug overdose, perhaps there was a toxicological test that could confirm Matt's ingestion of the drug GHB. Professor Olaf Drummer, a forensic pharmacologist and toxicologist, advised that GHB is not only available 'on the street' as a liquid form of ecstasy, but is also a chemical produced in humans naturally. He wrote that GHB can be produced post-mortem 'and, within a day or more, significant formation can occur from bacterial action'. There was no way to make conclusive interpretations of post-mortem concentrations of the chemical. To complicate matters further, GHB is also chemically unstable and degrades with time. Professor Drummer confirmed that there was no toxicological test available to shed light on Matt's GHB use. The delay between death and discovery of his remains would have destroyed any GHB, even in overdose amounts.

Finally, during the examination, forensic pathologist Dr Istvan Szentmariay noted a lack of soft tissue, the missing bones and the overall condition of Matt's remains. He concluded that most of the injuries were post-mortem, and for a small number of injuries it was impossible to determine whether they had taken place before or after death. He recommended the cause of death be recorded as 'undetermined'.

Tuesday 13 June 2017

It was with heavy hearts that the Leveson family arrived at the Glebe morgue early one evening. Pete and Jason had come straight from work. Mark and Faye hadn't thought of anything else all day. It was an occasion they'd long prayed for and dreaded.

In the stark confines of the viewing room, the family peered down at their long-lost Matty. His soil-tarnished bones lay on the table. His hands and feet were missing. His skull was in pieces. This was the skeleton of a boy who lived only 20 years, and was on the cusp of what his parents had hoped would be a great life full of adventure, career success, happiness and perhaps even his own family.

If he'd lived, Matt Leveson would have been 30 years old that year. It was one of so many milestones missed and mourned since he'd disappeared. The family had pushed through them all, keeping themselves from drowning in sorrow by charging towards their ultimate goal. But now they were here, in the morgue, in the presence of the remains they'd fought so long and hard to find, they felt emptier than ever.

Bringing Matt's body home still didn't bring him back.

41.

A BITTER PILL

Tuesday 22 August 2017

It had been three months since the Royal National Park had given up its dark secret, but the searing pain written across the faces of Mark and Faye Leveson was still white hot. As I walked alongside the couple into the Coroner's Court that morning, I could sense their trepidation. Faye, in particular, was deathly quiet in the sea of chatter. Journalists had flocked to the inquest that morning in anticipation of Gary Jubelin taking the stand. It would be the first time, almost a year after Michael Atkins gave his induced statement to police, that Atkins' version of events would be revealed publicly.

In the foyer, Faye and Mark nodded politely and greeted the cohort of media, friends and supporters. But beneath their frozen smiles, I knew the couple was feeling both deceived and confused.

Mark and Faye were still grappling with the fresh revelation that Gary Jubelin now believed Michael Atkins' version of events: that he buried Matt in panic after finding him dead from a suspected drug overdose. The news had come as a shock for the Levesons. From where they stood, it felt like a personal betrayal. The opposing positions of the parents and the detective had come out during the embargoed filming, in late July, of our second *60 Minutes* story, which was scheduled to air following that week's court hearings, on Sunday 27 August.

During filming, reporter Tara Brown had probed Jubelin about what he thought of Atkins' account, and he'd revealed his opinion.

Jubelin's admission had instantly caused tension between him and the family. They'd spoken very little since an emotionally charged exchange in the Royal National Park on the final day of filming. Off camera, Faye had lashed out at Jubelin. She told him, 'The thorn's out of your side now,' referring to her dead son's case. She felt the detective's stance was 'convenient', allowing him to wrap up a 'neat little package'.

Jubelin strongly denied the insinuations. He insisted that he didn't gain anything by expressing his opinion under the circumstances. The detective had been anticipating the parents' backlash since he had interviewed Atkins for the induced statement and had come to believe his story. That belief was a bitter pill. As a homicide detective, he didn't often concede the bad guy probably wasn't a murderer after all, and he didn't expect Mark and Faye to believe him.

But just because Jubelin believes Atkins' version of events doesn't mean he has changed his view of the man, something he's at pains to convey to the Levesons. In his interview with Tara Brown for *60 Minutes*, Jubelin said:

> I have no sympathy for him whatsoever. I think it's despicable what he's put the family through. He can live with what he did. The person he claimed he loved he just dumped in the bush in an unmarked grave, and let his family go through this suffering. So he can deal with that.

But knowing how the Levesons felt, Brown had pushed: 'The family believes that he did more. The family believes that he is responsible for the death of Matt. Is there any way that, if he's lied again, somehow he's convinced you that his lie is the truth?'

Jubelin had stiffened in his chair, and his stare narrowed as he answered:

It's a matter for the Coroner to determine on the truthfulness of his account. But I'm not naïve. We interviewed this person. We've interviewed him with the view of catching him out with inconsistencies, and the information that he has provided isn't contradicted by any facts that we have available.

At the inquest, Jubelin wasn't allowed to voice his opinion. During his closing evidence before the Coroner, he was asked only to summarise Atkins' 21-page statement. Jubelin told the packed courtroom that the then 44-year-old Atkins alleged that he had found Matt dead in the bedroom and, after seeing a bottle of GHB in the kitchen, he assumed Matt had died of a drug overdose. Faye, in the row in front of me, sobbed into her hands as each painful detail emerged publicly. She held her breath as Jubelin told the court that Atkins' hand-drawn map of the location of Matt's grave was consistent with where the remains were eventually found. But the Counsel Assisting, who was now barrister Tim Game, avoided asking Jubelin's views of the truthfulness of Atkins' version of events. The detective only got as far as saying that there was no direct or circumstantial evidence in conflict with Atkins' version; neither was there any that supported his version of events.

But there was still cross-examination to come. Atkins' barrister suspected from her prolonged dealings with police that Jubelin did in fact believe her client to be telling the truth. It was a point Claire Wasley was determined to broadcast. But upon asking Jubelin whether he believed Atkins, she was stopped in her tracks.

'Objection!' the Counsel Assisting said as he sprang to his feet.

The Coroner agreed. She would not allow the question. An incredulous Wasley pressed the point; the inquest had heard the opinions of many witnesses by this stage of the proceedings, and the experienced homicide detective's expert opinion was relevant to the Coroner's findings, she submitted.

'Isn't my opinion the only relevant opinion?' the Coroner countered.

The courtroom fell silent, and Jubelin sat awkwardly in the witness box as it was determined that he was not allowed to answer the question. His opinion, expert or not, would not be considered in the findings.

Friday 25 August 2017

Two days later, Mark and Faye Leveson once again travelled the familiar route from Bonnet Bay to the Coroner's Court in Glebe. As they entered the building, they thought of their son downstairs in the morgue, now bones on a table. They'd come to court that day ready to attempt to put into words the pain they'd endured over the past ten years. Sitting side by side in the witness box, they each delivered their closing impact statements to the Coroner.

Mark Leveson positioned his spectacles and read from a speech he'd written from the heart:

> How was your day? How are things at work? How soon before your next holiday? These are some of the simple, everyday questions I will never again get to ask my son, Matthew. Matt is frozen in time to me, forever being a happy and gay 20-year-old man.

As he spoke, the back of my eyes stung with tears. It was a rare and poignant thing to hear him open up like this. Mark continued:

> We have reluctantly been forced to think like a criminal to assist in our search for Matt. Where can I hide a body?

How do I conceal a corpse? How hard is the ground? Can I dig a grave here? Would the smell of a decomposing corpse travel this far? What a great pity we are talking about our middle son.

He relayed how he and his family had continually fought a justice system that favoured the accused. They'd had to overcome incompetent police work early in the case, battle politicians for reward offers and witness firsthand the inequalities in the criminal court system. Mark said:

People remark to us how well we are coping. They only see the public Levesons and not the private ones who struggle every single day to be able to function, struggle to concentrate at work; the private heartache and strain placed on our relationships. The so-called friends we have lost because they just don't know what to say to us; they hide from us in supermarkets, they cross the road when they see us.

He straightened in his chair in preparation for his final line:

We had no idea of what an astute judge of character Matt was. In what would have been one of his final communications before his life ended, he described Atkins as a 'fucken cunt'. How right was Matt. God bless you, mate.

The lack of malice in Mark's words somehow made them even more powerful. But the man they were directed at, the one who put his son in the ground, wasn't there to hear Mark's message. Atkins had been discharged from his subpoena to testify when the Coroner ruled he held no credibility as a witness. Her Honour directed that it was not in the interests of justice to make Atkins give further evidence at the inquest because nothing he'd say would lead her to decide the manner and cause of Matt's death. While the family agreed he was a liar, they were still bitterly disappointed he wasn't forced to listen to their impact statements. 'He should hear firsthand what we have to say,' they'd told me only a day earlier. 'Why should he be allowed to go home?'

As Mark swapped seats with his wife, Faye positioned herself before the microphone and began, her hands shaking noticeably and her voice quivering:

> How do you put into words how the murder and the subsequent hiding of Matty's body has affected me? There are some things that can't be put into words. One can try, but the impact on myself and my immediate family will never be explained or justified by any amount of words. 'Devastating', 'heart-wrenching', 'broken', 'tormented', 'grief-stricken' are just a few, and nowhere near how I really feel. There are times I don't want to go on anymore; I just want to close my eyes and never wake up.

But the court heard that even when Faye slept she wasn't at rest:

> I replay images of Matty, but now instead of where he could be it is images of how he was found in the ground . . . I cannot and never will get those images out of my mind. They are burned into my mind for forever more.

Everyone seated in the public gallery was reduced to tears. In the front row, Rachel Sanki was distraught. The family's supporters passed around a tissue box. Mark, his hand on Faye's back in support, hung his head. Even the Coroner wiped a tear from underneath her eye.

From the witness box, Faye held up a photograph of her son's skeleton in the morgue. Calling out across the room, she directed her rage at Atkins' lawyers Ramsden and Wasley. She shook the photograph at them and said, 'I want you to look!'

Both women held her stare.

'This is what Atkins did to him!' she said in a trembling voice.

The tension was overwhelming. As she regained her composure, Faye continued:

I am starting to feel we were forced into this corner to do a deal so the police can just close another case and move on to the next. There is no evidence to support that Matt overdosed, no evidence at all. The only evidence is the word of a liar.

Outside, on the front steps of the Coroner's Court, the Levesons held an emotionally charged press conference.

'This is what Atkins did to him!' Faye cried out. In one swift movement she pulled out an A3 colour photograph for the cameras before her.

'You don't leave someone you love like that,' Mark said, as he pulled out another.

Journalists studied the confronting images held up by each parent. In one photograph was Matt Leveson frozen in time two weeks before he died in 2007. In the other was Mark and Faye's middle son weeks after his remains were pulled from the ground, his skeleton arranged on a cold hard surface. It was the same shocking image Faye had produced in court. The Levesons were adamant their audience should see the consequences of what Michael Atkins had done.

The whole nation certainly did that on the following Sunday night, when *60 Minutes* aired. In a three-part story titled 'Bitter pill', Tara Brown, myself and co-producer Sean Power depicted the family's heartbreaking search for their son, as well as the complicated immunity deals they'd grappled with offering Atkins. For the first time, the major revelation that Gary Jubelin now believed Atkins was telling the truth was exposed. Although difficult and delicate to report, our team felt it was vital to reveal his change of opinion due to the critical impact it could possibly have on the case down the track. Regardless of the impending Coroner's findings, the police opinion that Atkins was no longer lying added an extra layer of protection to him moving forward. But as the iconic ticking clock filled the screen, public support was firmly in the corner of the Levesons. Murderer or not, Atkins had put this family through hell.

42.

THE CORONER'S FINDINGS

Saturday 23 September 2017

Mark Leveson closed the door behind him and sat down at his desk. He had hours of work ahead of him, preparing his family's written submissions for the Coroner. He had no intention of watering down his and Faye's strong opinion that Matt had died at the hands of Michael Atkins.

It was ten years to the day since Matt had last been seen alive.

Earlier that afternoon, Mark and Faye had marked the sombre anniversary by journeying to the Royal National Park. Clutching bouquets of fresh purple flowers, the parents walked towards the spot where Matt's body was found. A large gum tree nearby had become something of a shrine to their son, a place to pay their respects. As they approached the familiar tree, their faces lit up. They'd been beaten to the chase. Ten purple balloons, tied around the trunk, billowed in the breeze. Rachel Sanki had already visited that morning to spend some quiet time with her long-lost best friend. And she wasn't the only one with Matt Leveson in her thoughts that day. An outpouring of grief was taking place on the 'Justice for Matthew Leveson' Facebook page, where dozens of friends and strangers alike posted photos of the candles they'd lit in memory of the 20-year-old.

Matt was far from forgotten.

Tuesday 3 October 2017

The words of the Counsel Assisting, Tim Game, came as a blow to the Levesons on the day they gathered in court for final submissions: There was 'no compelling evidence' to suggest Matt Leveson was killed by his boyfriend Michael Atkins.

That morning, Deputy State Coroner Elaine Truscott heard that she should deliver an open finding in the inquest due to lack of evidence. Game submitted that there was no independent, objective evidence about Matt's cause of death, and that Atkins' lies were not a sufficient basis on which to conclude he had been involved. But, equally, there was no evidence to suggest Matt died of an overdose, as Atkins had claimed.

The open-finding submission was a view shared by NSW Police and Atkins' defence team. Claire Wasley said that a finding on the manner and cause of Matt's death couldn't be made because Atkins' induced statement wasn't tendered as 'evidence of truth' in the inquest, and Atkins hadn't been subjected to an examination on oath about it.

Unsurprisingly, the Leveson family rejected the idea of an open finding. As Mark delivered his family's final submissions at the court's bar table, he laid out the points he'd so carefully composed. The family submitted that the Coroner needed to take into consideration the compelling circumstantial evidence heard by the inquest: Atkins' trail of lies; his cold, calculating, self-interested behaviour; the depth and breadth of his cover-up. His actions were not those of a person involved in an accidental death. Mark insisted that, when all these points were considered together, the Coroner could conclude that his son had died at the hands of Michael Atkins.

The courtroom tensed. The Coroner peered through her spectacles.

Mark said that his son's death was:

Most likely as a result of smothering or strangulation – as there were no forensically significant body fluids or blood located in the unit – after a short struggle, with Atkins gaining the upper hand due to his ninjutsu skills and/or Matt's possible drug-affected state.

As campaigners, the Leveson family had also taken the opportunity before the Coroner to make a powerful recommendation for the sake of other families of unsolved homicide cases. They wanted a line drawn in the sand following the issues they'd faced in obtaining a substantial reward for their son's case. It had been set at $1000 in 2007, before being bumped up to $100,000 in 2012. When no new information came forward, the Levesons had lobbied bureaucrats for an increase to $200,000, but their request was knocked back. It wasn't until their next attempt in 2017, by which point they'd become household names through the media, that the Levesons' application was granted within 16 hours. Even so, at $250,000, the reward was still not equal to some of the state's more high-profile cases. They strongly believed no victim was more or less important than another, and that all rewards for unsolved homicide cases should to be automatically set at $1 million.

For two more months, the Levesons waited anxiously for the Coroner's findings to be delivered. Her Honour's ruling would be final.

Tuesday 5 December 2017

It was two years to the week after the inquest into Matt Leveson's death had commenced. The Coroner's findings couldn't have come soon enough. Their release marked the conclusion of what had been a taxing and emotionally charged inquest for every party involved, from the lawyers on the bar table to the police team and the Coroner herself. But their experiences didn't compare to what the Leveson family had endured. They'd set out more than ten years earlier to find answers that they'd remained hopeful Australia's justice system would provide them with.

On that very last day, proceedings of the inquest commenced before an overflowing public gallery, a full bar table and a noticeably absent Michael Atkins.

Sitting directly behind Faye, I watched as her foot tapped nervously. Her hands were tightly clasped, and she rocked gently back and forth in her chair. I knew from our personal discussions in the lead up to this day that she and Mark were expecting the worst.

Deputy State Coroner Elaine Truscott prefaced her much-anticipated findings by saying:

Ever since Matt's death his family have been tireless in their search for his remains and answers about his death . . . The reason the inquest was held was because Matt's family wanted to know what happened to Matt, how he died, why he died and where he died . . . The evidence established that the only person who knew the answers to those questions was Michael Atkins.

The Coroner outlined how Atkins' account in his induced statement, that Matt died of a drug overdose, was given in circumstances where he didn't face the prospect of further criminal proceedings, knowing his statement would go untested under oath and cross-examination. But then came the first blow. Accordingly, the Coroner said she could not comment on the content of what Atkins told police, or make findings against him about the manner and cause of Matt's death.

'I do not accept Mr Atkins is a witness of truth,' the Coroner said, highlighting that he'd maintained a 'plethora of lies' since Matt's death. In her written findings, Her Honour further set out 72 references to Atkins' 'lies, contradictions, inconsistencies and nonsense' that dated back to when he first left ARQ that Saturday night in September 2007. She ruled:

I do not accept Mr Atkins' account of why he and Matt left the nightclub, and I do not accept Mr Atkins' account as to why he drove Matt home. The evidence leads to the only sensible conclusion that Mr Atkins wanted to take Matt home, because the evening was not going well, because Matt was angry with him and they were arguing . . . The evidence does not support Matt being asleep because he was drug-affected, waking up halfway home and then having a 'tiff'.

As to where Matt died, the Coroner made an open-ended finding. She couldn't narrow it down to Cronulla, specifically Atkins' unit, because forensics confirmed Matt was buried in the clothes he wore to ARQ. The Coroner proposed the place of death as Sydney, leaving open the possibility that Matt may have died in the car or elsewhere.

The Coroner said of the Leveson family's assertion that Matt had probably died by smothering or choking that it was inconsistent with the state of the forensic evidence. Further, she found that the circumstances in which the bones were uncovered, in addition to the likely damage caused during all the excavations, meant that she could reach no conclusive findings.

The Coroner ruled:

Ultimately, the lies that Mr Atkins told during the course of his evidence to the inquest, as with other lies he had told to a range of people, including the police . . . give rise to a considerable degree of suspicion that Mr Atkins had some connection with Matt's death, apart from the fact that he buried Matt's body.

However, that degree of suspicion still did not allow the Coroner to find that Atkins was involved in any acts which caused Matt's death. 'Accordingly, I have determined that in this inquest I cannot enter findings as to the manner and cause of Matt's death.'

Everyone gathered in the courtroom hung on the Coroner's every word. The only audible sounds were Faye's harrowing sobs and the Coroner's steady voice as she continued. 'Though the inquest has achieved, through the endeavours of the police, the recovery of Matt's remains, Matt's father Mark, Matt's mother Faye and Matt's brothers Peter and Jason would not think that this inquest has given them a sense of justice, and I regret that my findings cannot meet Matt's family's hopes and expectations.'

The Coroner thoroughly praised Mark and Faye Leveson for their undercover work on the case in January 2008. During a secret listening device recording, the parents had secured the only admission from Atkins that he lied to police about buying the mattock at Bunnings.

'It is shocking that the Levesons had to endure this experience,' the Coroner said. 'But I suspect that they would say it was just one example of what they, as Matt's parents, and what their sons, Peter and Jason, have had to endure due to Mr Atkins' actions.'

Furthermore, Atkins' claim in his induced statement that he awoke to find Matt dead, presumably from an overdose, was now in direct contradiction to his position back in 2008. In the recording, Atkins had told the Levesons that he didn't think Matt had overdosed because he was careful with his doses.

In her findings, the Coroner declined to make a recommendation on the reward system, but put forward one proposal, to the Commissioner of the NSW Police Force, that Mark and Faye Leveson receive an official commendation for their assistance to the police investigation into the death of their son.

Lastly, on behalf of the community, the Coroner thanked the police, commending Detective Senior Constable Scott Craddock as 'the unassuming detective whose dedication, hard and exact work under the direction of Chief Inspector Gary Jubelin should not go unnoticed'. She noted that Jubelin himself had been an instrumental advocate for the Levesons' plea to have the inquest.

'Can I once again express my condolences to Matt's family,' she said. 'It has truly been a privilege to be Matt's Coroner.'

In conclusion, she confirmed her findings that 'Matthew John Leveson died at Sydney, on 23 September 2007. As to the manner of his death and the cause of his death, I enter open findings.'

The Levesons had braced themselves for this outcome, but hearing the words was still a crippling blow. As the Coroner closed the inquest and stepped down, everyone in the court remained standing and silent for what felt like an eternity. It was a truly underwhelming finale to an overwhelming process. An anticlimax. The Levesons had reached the end of the tunnel, but instead of light they found only more darkness. More unknowns.

When the crowd in the court finally emptied out into the foyer, Gary Jubelin lingered. He wasn't sure how the family, particularly Faye, would react to his presence that day. Jubelin had worn a purple tie in memory of Matt, a small gesture of understanding for the victim and his family. Whatever they thought of him, he still admired how hard the parents had pushed the boundaries of the justice system. It simply blew him away how they'd fought as hard as they did, and for as long as they had, to find Matt's body. Jubelin knew Mark and Faye would be forever disappointed that they hadn't succeeded in their legal pursuit of Michael Atkins. But, in a way, Jubelin believed justice had still been served. While Atkins' life was now drastically diminished, the Levesons would go from strength to strength, as a team.

Standing shoulder to shoulder with his own team, he was also filled with pride for the dedication shown by Scott Craddock and Dr Sarah Yule in particular. The four-year case had tested their resolve, but they'd kept going above and beyond. In a way, their commitment reflected the sort of people Mark and Faye Leveson were. After meeting Matt's parents, you couldn't help but become invested in their mission. Still, Jubelin felt uneasy as the couple came towards him through the crowd. In spite of everything he and the Levesons had been through together, by this point they fiercely disagreed on the most monumental point of all.

But Jubelin needn't have worried. From across the court's foyer, I watched as Mark warmly shook his hand. Faye took a firm step towards him and stared up at his face before hugging him tight.

43.

THE FUNERAL

Friday 9 March 2018

At home in Bonnet Bay, Faye Leveson stood in front of the bathroom mirror and gazed at her reflection, just as her Matty had done all those years ago. More than ten years had passed since her son had left her life, and today she and Mark would finally say their goodbyes to him. Faye tidied her long blonde hair and straightened a carefully chosen purple floral dress. She'd dreamed of this day for so long, but now it was here she didn't know how to feel.

Faye's mind kept wandering to the events of the evening before. She and Mark had decided to visit Matty's memorial tree in the Royal National Park. They'd taken fresh sunflowers and colourful gerberas to lay at the base of the large gum tree. But their hearts sank the moment they arrived. Matty's memorial had been desecrated: photographs, handwritten cards, tributes, gifts and bouquets of flowers had all been ripped off and stolen. It was a low blow, an experience these parents could have done without on the eve of their son's funeral. Words had failed them. They'd simply looked at each other with steely resolve, their own secret way of saying, 'We'll fix it.'

Faye heard a car in the driveway and made her way downstairs. Matty was home. She was devastated at the sight of her middle son finally coming home in the back of a hearse, even more than she'd expected to be. Faye broke down in tears, then leaned over the polished timber coffin and said, 'I'm sorry, Matty.'

The service took place at Woronora Memorial Park. A sea of mourners clad in purple flooded through the gates, and the turnout took Faye and Mark by surprise. They hadn't known how many guests to expect, but had booked two chapels just in case – one for family and friends, and another with a video-link display. Faye had feared no one would come. Mark had anticipated about one hundred people. Instead, more than three times that number filtered past the stoic parents. The Levesons greeted as many as they could; there were familiar faces and complete strangers, each with their own reasons for being there. To Faye and Mark's delight, each guest had fulfilled their request to wear a splash of Matt's favourite colour, or something colourful. Today was a celebration of his life.

After the service began, Mark steadied himself at the lectern and said, 'Just look around among yourselves right now. How many of you had doubt over the last ten and a half years that we'd be where we are today?'

Looking out at the audience his son had drawn, Mark spotted Gary Jubelin and his team sitting close to the front. Behind the police was former Counsel Assisting, Lester Fernandez, and solicitor Ian Lindwood. Journalists from each of the major newspapers and television networks watched on keenly. The beaming face of digger operator Mitch Lombe shone through the crowd. Then there were Matt's school friends, his work colleagues from NRMA, his gay mates from ARQ and best friend Rachel Sanki. There were only two noticeable absentees: Pete and Jason Leveson had chosen to farewell their brother in their own quiet way.

Mark continued:

Today we can do what we set out to do. We can give our Matty the proper send-off he so justly deserves, in front of his family and his friends. Family and friends who have stood by us and Matty during this long journey. Today is about Matty, and yeah, wouldn't he love all of this attention too? We're here to give thanks to Matty for allowing us to have him in our lives for the twenty years that we had.

After Mark was finished, Faye stepped in closer and adjusted the height of the microphone. She said:

Matty was a happy baby, full of mischief. We just wish, now, that you didn't go through your camera-shy period of not letting us take your photo. You had the most cheeky glint in your eyes, with a huge smile and gorgeous dimples.

It was those dimples, and Matt's contagious smile, that had captured his soulmate's attention the first time they met as 12-year-olds. Through sobs, Rachel Sanki told the packed chapels:

I feel very privileged to have known Matty, to call him my best friend and my other half, to have spent as many wonderful years with him as I did. I know I wouldn't be the person I am today if it wasn't for Matty. He's given me so many happy moments and memories in life that I'll treasure forever.

In the final year of his life, Matt's favourite pastime was dancing up a storm with his mates at ARQ. Together, Luke Kiernan, John Burns and Brendan Arnold shared their memories of their dancing queen:

John first met Matty on the balcony at ARQ; he was bouncing around dancing like no one was watching. Luke introduced John, and they all had a boogie on the stage. They got along so well, and that was it! Matty's energy was so infectious and he always turned heads in the club, being the little hottie he was.

Like most gay boys back then, the shorts were short, the singlets were skin-tight, the tan and the bronzer was orange and our hair was straightened as flat as possible. We thought we were so classy . . . Everybody was drawn to Matty; he was young, charismatic, beautiful, and always had that huge smile on his face.

A slide of photographs played, accompanied by Matt's favourite songs: 'Breakaway' by Kelly Clarkson, ABBA's 'Dancing Queen', 'Raise Your Glass' by P!nk and 'Umbrella' by Rihanna. It was hard to watch the images of Matt's short life. The baby with the big blue eyes. The little boy with the white-blond hair and toothy grin. The chubby teenager who grew into a swan: gorgeous, proud and just starting to spread his wings. Tears streamed down the faces of Matt's most devoted support-ers. My eyes glistened.

An image of the Royal National Park flicked onto the screen. It was from May 2017, captured by Faye only days before Matt was found. She didn't know it at the time, but her son was under the cabbage-tree palm in the centre of frame. That same palm – Matty's palm – was now planted and tended to in the Levesons' garden.

The palm is one of many ways the parents commemorate Matt in their daily lives. It's hard to know how Mark and Faye will cope moving forward. For more than a decade they've fought an all-consuming battle, but the crusade to find Matt is finally over. In recent months, as they've reached the end of a long and painful chapter, they've been forced to readjust their lives. There are no weekend digs or court dates to map their routines around.

A few days after the funeral, I asked them what they'll channel their energy into next. Mark's answer came easily: 'The fight has begun,' he told me. 'We want to change the reward system – both the amount and the process. But we're also fighting to change the way in which victims are treated under the justice system.'

'We want Matt's legacy to mean something,' Faye added.

Together, the Levesons are fighters, a force to be reckoned with. And they're only just getting started.

ACKNOWLEDGEMENTS

I could never have foreseen the life-changing twists and turns that have transpired since I first met the Leveson family in 2014. Writing this book was perhaps, for my life at least, the most unexpected event of all. My decision to do so came both naturally and urgently in July 2017. I simply couldn't have done it without the unwavering support and input of the following people:

To my publishers at Penguin Random House, thank you for making what could have been a daunting and scary experience a thoroughly enjoyable one. My special thanks to the wonderful Alison Urquhart and my brilliant editor Tom Langshaw.

To Lyn Tranter at Australian Literary Management, thank you for your words of wisdom and for calming me down at every turn.

I am extremely grateful to my employers at the Nine Network, especially Darren Wick for his backing. Special thanks need to go to *60 Minutes* executive producer Kirsty Thomson, who insisted I write this book in the first place, and former chief of staff Steven Burling, who went out of his way to find me a publisher. To Tara Brown, thank you for inspiring me to always dig deeper and work harder to make a memorable story into an unforgettable one. To my co-producer Sean Power, thank you for your dedication to the Leveson family, and for your friendship and counsel. To Maureen O'Connor, thank you for your passion and guidance. And to my *60 Minutes* family, thank you for being the best bunch of journalists, cameramen, soundos, editors and mates I could ever hope to work alongside.

To Stephen Rice, my mentor and dear friend, the Scully to my Mulder, thank you for believing in me and my gut feeling that this was a story we needed to tell.

To the many people who were interviewed for this book about their memories and private experiences with Michael Atkins, thank you for your time and trust. Thanks also to Sharon Ramsden and Claire Wasley, for your honesty and professionalism.

Thank you to the NSW Police Force, including the former head of the NSW Homicide Squad and current Assistant Commissioner, Michael Willing, for your support and contribution to both *60 Minutes* stories. I am beyond grateful to Detective Chief Inspector Gary Jubelin for his invaluable insights, honesty and encouragement over the years. Special thanks also to Detective Senior Constable Scott Craddock, Dr Sarah Yule and Professor Shari Forbes from AFTER.

My deepest thanks to my first readers, my poppa, John Reese, and my parents, Narelle and Peter Tobin, for your constructive criticism, rigorous questions and undying support. I also need to acknowledge my late nana, Audrey Reese, who lived her life as a kind, compassionate and quietly strong woman. She inspires me to do the same every day.

To my loving partner, Daniel Andrews, another first reader and my 'co-pilot' through the many ups and downs of writing this book. Thank you for letting me tap away through countless early mornings, late evenings, weekends and two consecutive holidays with nothing but love and support for me.

Finally, to Mark and Faye Leveson, who have never received any payment for any media interviews or for this book, I cannot thank you enough for your trust in me. I'd barely even asked whether I could write this book before your words of encouragement rained down on me. It has truly been my greatest honour to tell Matty's story, perhaps only slightly overshadowed by the incredible privilege of being by your side during such a monumental fight. I'm so proud of what you've achieved. And perhaps more importantly, I'm so proud to count you as friends.

Discover a
new favourite

Visit **penguin.com.au/readmore**